GET WHAT'S YOURS
FOR MEDICARE

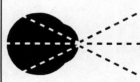

This Large Print Book carries the
Seal of Approval of N.A.V.H.

GET WHAT'S YOURS FOR MEDICARE

MAXIMIZE YOUR COVERAGE, MINIMIZE YOUR COSTS

PHILIP MOELLER

THORNDIKE PRESS
A part of Gale, Cengage Learning

Farmington Hills, Mich • San Francisco • New York • Waterville, Maine
Meriden, Conn • Mason, Ohio • Chicago

GALE
CENGAGE Learning®

LIBRARY OF CONGRESS CATALOGING-IN-PUBLICATION DATA

Names: Moeller, Philip, author.
Title: Get what's yours for medicare : maximize your coverage, minimize your costs / by Philip Moeller.
Other titles: Get what is yours for medicare
Description: Large Print edition. | Waterville, Maine : Thorndike Press, a part of Gale, Cengage Learning, [2016] | Series: Thorndike Press Large Print lifestyles | Includes bibliographical references.
Identifiers: LCCN 2016035685 | ISBN 9781410493224 (hardback) | ISBN 1410493229 (hardcover)
Subjects: LCSH: Medical care, Cost of—United States. | Health insurance—Economic aspects—United States. | BISAC: SOCIAL SCIENCE / General.
Classification: LCC RA410.53 .M63 2016a | DDC 368.38/200973—dc23
LC record available at https://lccn.loc.gov/2016035685

Published in 2016 by arrangement with Simon & Schuster, Inc.

Printed in Mexico
3 4 5 6 7 8 20 19 18 17 16

To the day when good health care
is a birthright

— PHILIP MOELLER

CONTENTS

1
No One Told Me

Glen didn't retire until he turned 70 in 2010. He and his wife, Margie, were covered until then by his employer's health plan. Glen read the annual *Medicare & You* guide put out by the Centers for Medicare & Medicaid Services (CMS). His clear understanding from the guide was that he had been automatically enrolled in Medicare since he turned 65.

This was not true. Glen made a big Medicare mistake by not asking anyone to confirm his understanding. In fact, Glen had no Medicare coverage as of 2010. Neither did Margie. But they didn't know this.

"No one told me" is a scary cautionary Medicare tale that could be the subtitle of this book. It is repeated in countless calls for help from people like Glen and Margie (not their real names) to Medicare consumer counselors and call-center staffers around the country. And it is voiced even by people who consider themselves otherwise smart and well informed.

As it turns out, there can be little about Medicare that is automatic or clear or, especially in the midst of a medical emergency, logical or perhaps even fair. Despite widespread contrary beliefs, people are free never to get Medicare and can simply pay their own health bills without insurance. However, if you forgo Medicare and later change your mind, there can be steep late-enrollment penalties and many months may pass before Medicare insurance takes effect.

Even for people who want health insurance, Medicare usually isn't even required at age 65 or, indeed, at any later age, so long as a person — or their spouse — is still working and has group health insurance coverage from a current employer. Social Security is supposed to send out Medicare cards to some people when they turn 65. Maybe it did send out a card to Glen. Maybe he thought this meant he was covered. But this doesn't always happen, especially when a person has not yet started taking their Social Security retirement benefit.

*There are three **really big deals** about getting Medicare right:*

1. **Enroll at the right time.** Medicare has a bewildering mix of enrollment periods. You need to use the right one.
2. **Choose the right mix of Medicare coverage.** There are only two main paths here. One is Original Medicare (Parts A and B), perhaps with a Medigap supplemental policy, plus a Part D prescription drug plan. The other is a Medicare Advantage plan, usually including a Part D plan.
3. **Understand what these various parts of Medicare cover and how to use them.**

For nearly four years, Glen and Margie had no health problems serious enough to have caused them to file a claim with Medicare and learn about their earlier mistake. But then, in 2014, Margie got sick and was diagnosed with terminal cancer. They then began trying to file claims for what eventually would be enormous medical expenses. That's when they found out that neither of them had Medicare coverage. Glen called the nonprofit Center for Medicare Advocacy seeking help.

Glen had missed his original window to

sign up for Medicare after he retired in 2010. Margie may have assumed she was automatically covered by Medicare as well. The details aren't clear, although it became clear in hindsight that they never really understood that there is no family coverage under Medicare, as is routinely the case with employer health insurance.

Glen and Margie needed to file individually for Medicare. When they realized their error in 2014, they had missed one of the many enrollment periods available during the year, and were told they had to wait until the beginning of 2015 to file for Medicare. Under its rules, their coverage would not become effective until July 2015.

Glen and Margie had to face her cancer with no insurance whatsoever. Instead of being able to focus on Margie's care and spending as much quality time with her as possible, Glen's life instead included the prospect of crushing medical bills and the need to worry about how he would pay for his wife's care. Medical expenses are, sadly, a leading cause of personal bankruptcy.

After the center said it had no immediate solution to their problem, Glen broke off contact. More than a year later, the center reached him again. "He is a defeated man," a staffer recalled. "Things had turned out terribly. He did, indeed, lose his wife."

And he still didn't know if he had Medicare.

CAROL

The Medicare rules say that private Medicare Advantage insurance plans must cover at least the same things that Original Medicare (Parts A and B) covers. Many people naturally assume this means the two approaches to Medicare are the same.

Big mistake.

Carol's husband, Ernesto, had a Medicare Advantage plan in Texas, when he was diagnosed in June 2014 with pancreatic cancer. Little more than six months later, Ernesto would be dead following complications from surgery. During this time, when Carol wanted to spend as much time as possible with her partner, she instead had to fight insurance company rules and respond to unexpected surprises about what his Medicare Advantage plan did not cover.

Her problems stemmed from the fact that Medicare Advantage plans restrict coverage to those doctors, hospitals, and other caregivers who are in the plan's provider network. Original Medicare, by contrast, insures covered medical services from any provider who accepts Medicare. When

Carol was forced to take over as the main caregiver for her husband, she didn't know about these restrictions. Even after she learned about some limitations, new ones kept cropping up.

"The gastroenterologist who diagnosed my husband met with us, explained the diagnosis, and called MD Anderson [the University of Texas MD Anderson Cancer Center] to refer him to a specialist. He was told that neither the doctor nor the facility accepted Medicare Advantage. Medicare, yes; Medicare Advantage no," she recalls. His insurer said it could not help her find a center with pancreatic cancer expertise, and that Carol would have to make these calls herself, which she did. "All the time I took to figure out how to track down information, and to do it, took time away from being with my husband.

"We even found that the local oncologist we chose told us that he would accept the plan and was 'in-network,' " she adds, "but for the entire six months he saw my husband for chemotherapy and related studies," the benefit statements from the insurer showed he was not. Inaccurate billing statements flew back and forth, making it impossible for Carol to keep up with expenses and payment schedules.

"In the meantime we paid bills, got refunds, and completely lost track — if there really was a track — of where we were on the maximum out-of-pocket payments," she says. "Incidentally, this was not how I wanted to spend my time, and was not what either my husband or I needed in order for him to continue to live well and enjoy life as long as he possibly could."

Carol, not surprisingly, thinks that no one should ever get a Medicare Advantage plan. But millions of people do and find no problems with their coverage and service. However, if a serious medical issue arose, they may be no more equipped to deal with possible shortcomings in their plan's provider network than was she. "It can be difficult in the midst of a crisis to figure out what you can control and what you cannot," she cautions.

"My husband and I shared a great life," Carol now says. "He lived well up until the moment he died, and even his manner of dying was a gift to me. Mostly what I relive are warm and appreciative memories. Occasionally, of course, the bad stuff surfaces. . . ."

PHYLLIS

Let this story be your cautionary guide for the more practical road-blocks that Medicare may erect. Phyllis is pretty much always the sharpest tack in the box. While she loved being a partner in a big corporate law firm, she finally retired from the firm when she turned 75. Like many sharp tacks, however, Phyllis was no match for Medicare. And when she explained her problems to me, she repeatedly used the phrase "No one told me."

Fortunately, Phyllis's efforts to properly enroll in and use Medicare have not had disastrous consequences — no financial or health care catastrophes. She got covered in time, seems to have avoided late-enrollment

16

penalties, and more or less got the coverage she wanted. But as she makes clear, these results are due primarily to her remaining healthy and needing to take a grand total of one prescription medication — an inexpensive blood pressure pill.

Phyllis's employer did provide her notice of the impending end of her employer health coverage. But its statement did not explain the specifics of her existing coverage and the things she would need to replace with Medicare.

Phyllis never would assume what a legal client needed or how opposing lawyers might behave. But she, like too many other Medicare newcomers, did assume that Medicare was a relatively straightforward process.

"I absolutely did" make that assumption, she recalls. "My assumption was that thirty days or so before I needed Medicare, I could go and apply" and everything would be taken care of.

At the outset, she didn't know she needed to contact Social Security and not Medicare to enroll in Medicare. She didn't know about prescription drug coverage or that it was called Part D of Medicare. She didn't even know that Medicare Advantage plans existed. And she didn't know that her cell phone needed to have a full charge before calling Medicare for help, because her wait times often would be so long that her phone would run out of juice while she was still on hold!

No one told her. "I had Part A," because she already was receiving Social Security retirement benefits. "I thought all I needed was Part A. I thought I could get Part B automatically. I didn't know I needed to apply to Social Security for Part B."

Phyllis's first phone call with the Social Security Administration (SSA) began to make her see that thirty days was a laughably short time frame, even for someone as skilled as she in figuring out how things worked. Social Security, it turns out, does a lot of Medicare enrollment work and is the official Medicare traffic cop when it comes to determining if people have enrolled for various parts of Medicare on a timely basis.

Adding Part B, which covers doctors, outpatient and medical equipment expenses, along with Part A hospital insurance, would provide her with what's called Original Medicare coverage. It also would qualify her to purchase other types of Medicare insurance, including a Part D drug plan and either a Medigap policy or a Medicare Advantage plan.

After waiting on hold for more than an hour, Phyllis was told by the SSA representative that she could apply for Part B online. She was uncomfortable with that, so the rep provided her detailed instructions about how to download and complete a Part B application form. This guidance included how she should address and mark the envelope to make sure it went to the right place. She did this weeks in advance of her employer coverage ending. After waiting and waiting for a response, she finally called the local office again, waited on hold for more than an hour a second time, and was told no one at that office had ever seen her application form.

During the first of what became three trips to a Social Security office, Phyllis tried to sign up for Medicare. The office was located in a congested area, with street parking whose meters permitted no more than two hours of parking time. So, Phyllis thought it would be prudent if she scheduled an appointment. The Social Security website provides information on how to do this, but she was told by someone in the local office that it did not do visits by appointment.

Being a walk-in, as she later learned, guaranteed long delays. And when she wanted to go refill her parking meter and avoid a possible parking ticket, she was told she would lose her place in line if she left the office. Phyllis found another Social Security office farther away, where parking was not a problem.

While she was signing up for Part B, no one told Phyllis about the need for Part D prescription drug coverage or even about the existence of Medicare Advantage plans, which are formally designated as Part C of Medicare. They have become an increasingly popular alternative to Original Medicare, and now are the choice of more than 30 percent of Medicare users. More than 40 million people have Part D drug plans. But the first that Phyllis learned about signing up for a Part D plan was shortly before being dinged with a late-enrollment penalty. Four months after signing up, she had still not seen any evidence that she actually had a Part D plan, and acknowledged that penalties might still be possible.

Phyllis wound up with Original Medicare, the hoped-for Part D plan, and a Medigap policy. **This is one of two classic paths into Medicare.** The other involves a Medicare Advantage plan, usually bundled with Part D drug coverage. She later admitted she chose her Medigap insurer because it was the only company that answered the phone when she called.

"All my assumptions were wrong," she says. Although her coverage didn't begin until August 2015, Phyllis quickly realized she might have made key mistakes, and began a new round of research to get ready for Medicare's annual open enrollment period, which runs each year from October 15 to December 7.

Open enrollment is the annual equivalent of a Medicare do-over. It permits people to choose new plans, usually with no adverse coverage or pricing consequences. It's a great deal, but like much else about Medicare, people often don't understand how it works.

No one told them.

Read on, and consider yourself told.

2
LIVING LONGER IS GREAT; PAYING FOR IT ISN'T

As the nation becomes older and grayer, the idea of a golden age for America's senior citizens has become the stuff of dreams. Instead, we have two major retirement crises. One is the financial crisis. It gets daily attention. Most workers have saved far too little to afford even modestly enjoyable retirements. Record numbers of people in their late 60s and 70s are continuing to work — some because they like to but most because they can't afford to stop. Our second crisis, and it fully merits this label, is the retirement health care crisis. Despite vibrant images of aging from companies who peddle financial, health, and lifestyle products to seniors, the health profile of a typical aging America is less glamorous. Aging in America is a tough contact sport.

The health needs of rising numbers of baby boomers will be an increasingly expensive personal and national burden, not only driving many families into bankruptcy but also threatening the finances of our national government. We face bruising entitlement wars. Can we put a lid, even a porous one, on the funds we spend to take care of the people we know and love — our parents and grandparents, our uncles and aunts? Then there are the people we don't know — an enormous number of impoverished Americans who live largely unseen, often by themselves, in decaying housing and nursing homes that far too often cope with infirm seniors by drugging them into docility.

Standing in the breach to protect these people, as well as the interests of taxpayers, is an enormous bureaucracy called the Centers for Medicare & Medicaid Services (CMS). Since Medicare and Medicaid were created in 1965, they have led to a degree of centralized control over the nation's health care system that on a bad day (and there are many of them) rivals the worst excesses of any five-year plan in the former Soviet Union. While CMS oversees the health needs of only older, poor, and disabled Americans, these groups represent such a large share of the nation's health care consumers that what CMS does or does not do sets the tone for all of American health care.

Even a benevolent despot is still a despot, and critics think CMS is far from benevolent. At the same time, Medicare and Medicaid operate in a world filled with big and powerful health insurers, pharmaceutical companies, and makers of medical equipment. Managing key aspects of a sixth of the national economy is a no-win job from the get-go. Some medical experts, of which there are no shortage, think the United States should join other industrialized nations and nationalize health care. Others point to those nations and argue just as passionately that a private health care system is the only hope we have for providing quality care at a price tag the nation can afford.

We all may have our hopes and dreams for the future of health care in America. But this debate will still be alive and kicking after you've finished this book and, I hope, after you have learned what you need to get what's yours from Medicare. This is no easy task. Navigating Medicare is challenging even to health care professionals who must deal with it every day. It is often unfathomable to the older and disabled people it is supposed to serve.

WANT TO LIVE FOREVER? IT WILL COST YOU

Once you reach 65, the traditional sign-up age for Medicare, you will have an average of nearly 18 years of remaining life if you're a man and 20.5 years if you're a woman. These are averages, of course. If you attend to your diet, exercise, and practice healthy lifestyle behaviors, the odds are good that you will live longer than these averages — well into your 90s or even beyond.[1] (The endnotes in this book — the first of which was just provided to you — include website addresses and other reference sources. I urge you to use them. They will, in many cases, lead you to the detailed information you need to address crucial questions about Medicare. For example, I say later in the book that you might need to get in touch with the contractors who administer Original Medicare. The endnote to that statement includes information to locate the identities of these firms and how to contact them.)

Futurists say the first human to live to 150 years of age is already alive. It could be me! There already are days when I feel like 150. Maybe you do, too. So, while it certainly is more years that we're after, that's not the ultimate endgame. It's more *healthy* years, with a quality of life that is good enough to make our remaining time worthwhile. Ideally, we'd like to remain healthy and active until the very end — a phrase the experts call "compressed morbidity." That would be more than fine with me.

IT'S ALWAYS ABOUT THE MONEY

The longer we live, the more likely we are to run up larger, not smaller, medical bills. Likewise, people who take better care of themselves spend more money on health care, not less.[2] No wonder that opinion surveys regularly find that many people fear running out of money more than they do death itself.[3]

Ruinous health expenses are a major if not the major cause of personal bankruptcies in the United States. They can destroy the financial futures of entire families, not just the person incurring the expenses. Let me give you just one example of how this can happen, even for people who have Medicare.

About 70 percent of all Medicare beneficiaries — more than 35 million people — use what is called "Original" Medicare. This includes Part A for hospital expenses and Part B for doctors, medical equipment, and outpatient medical costs. The other 30 percent get private Medicare Advantage plans. Original Medicare is also called "basic" Medicare or "traditional" Medicare.

Now, Original Medicare can be great. But it requires beneficiaries to fork over a 20 percent copay for most covered Part B services. Forever. There is no ceiling on this copay. Other Medicare insurance, called Medigap or Medicare supplement insurance, is available to close this gap. But this fact does you no good if you don't know it. Or if you don't buy such a policy before encountering that catastrophic health event that you were sure would never happen, but which does happen over and over again each and every year to many, many Medicare users.

Among all Original Medicare beneficiaries, fewer than 25 percent get Medigap policies.[4] Retirees fortunate enough still to have employer health coverage or high-quality union health coverage may have coverage that replicates what Medigap does. But many others are simply taking a big gamble. Perhaps they don't have enough money to afford Medigap premiums. But perhaps they just don't know about that huge hole in Original Medicare.

Medicare Advantage policies provide annual out-of-pocket caps to protect people and families from catastrophic expenses. These will be explained here in plenty of detail to help you make an informed Medicare purchase decision. But to millions of seniors on Medicare, catastrophe is not thousands of dollars in big health care bills. It's $20 a month for the copay on a prescription that a senior simply can't afford.

These seemingly modest health care expenses turn out not to be modest at all. They pit health care use against food on the table, heat in the radiators, and rent money. These are the small money "killers" that cause people on Medicare to stop taking their prescribed medications, or perhaps to cut their pills in half and hope that half an apple a day will keep the doctor away as well as a whole apple. Medication "non-adherence" is the phrase used in pharmacy circles to describe this kind of problem. Making smart choices about Medicare policies can reduce the financial pressures that contribute to non-adherence.

So, good health is about the money, too, but then, isn't just about everything?

WHAT WE DON'T KNOW ABOUT MEDICARE CAN COST US DEARLY

I've been writing about Medicare for decades. Two years ago, I began writing about it full-time for the *PBS NewsHour* website and *Money* magazine. And for more than a year, I've spent nearly all of my time researching this book and talking with leading experts.

Even so, there have been more days than I care to admit that I ended up convinced not only that I knew little about Medicare but that I actually knew less than I had when the day began. I kid you not. This stuff is complicated. So, don't feel bad if you know little about Medicare, that some or even most of what you think you know is wrong, that you are uncertain even about the things that you do know, and that the good people who man the enormous machine we collectively call Medicare may well be among the last people you should turn to for advice or information you actually can understand.

Don't get me wrong. Medicare is a terrific program. It has improved the health of millions of Americans since its creation in 1965. But it has grown as complicated and opaque as the increasingly sophisticated medical services it helps deliver.

THE BATTLE OF BIG VERSUS BIG

CMS tells health care providers what they must do and in most cases what they can charge you for what they do. This includes deciding what's covered and, in concert with private vendors, building and managing the unbelievably detailed and extensive medical billing and procedural coding systems that fund that blob of Jell-O on your hospital plate. If you want to get a nasty response from your doctor's office, ask folks there how they like the new "ICD-10" codes that were implemented in 2015. It was hard enough to understand the 14,000 codes in the old system. The new one has 70,000!

The fact that such a massive and crucial

public benefit is so complex and impenetrable to the very people it is supposed to serve is a national tragedy. How complex? Thanks for asking. CMS has an online glossary that lists its initial-crazed acronyms — more than 4,400 sets of often incomprehensible initials the last time I looked! Every citizen deserves better, particularly those Medicare beneficiaries who are among the nation's most vulnerable souls. Making Medicare accessible and clear, or as clear as this mortal can make it, is the rallying cry for *Get What's Yours for Medicare.*

It's the same rallying cry that emerged from the 2015 book I coauthored called *Get What's Yours: The Secrets to Maxing Out Your Social Security.* My partners for that book were Boston University economist Laurence Kotlikoff and PBS economics correspondent Paul Solman.

Now, all three of us think we are pretty well informed. Just ask us! But as we discovered during years of research into Social Security, we often were not smart and well informed about the nation's dominant retirement benefit program — a program on which *most* older Americans depend for *most* of their income. The more we looked into this seemingly straightforward and plain-vanilla retirement program, the more we realized that it was incredibly complex, not even well understood by many of the people in the Social Security Administration itself, and was costing retirees billions of dollars in lost or poorly claimed benefits.

Many people who bought that book later reached out to us and we received thousands and thousands of questions. Their problems navigating the system even after carefully reading our book have led us to many, many additional discoveries about how Social Security hurts rather than helps some retirees. One of the common laments of people who reviewed our book was how sad it was that such a book was even necessary. Social Security is more than eighty years old and provides nearly $900 billion a year in benefits. If there is one program that should be transparently clear and comprehensible to Americans, this is it. But this is not the case. And while there are almost daily demands from some group or another to "reform" Social Security, there are nearly no demands to turn it into a program that Americans can actually understand and make better use of.

Unfortunately, the same truths apply to Medicare, perhaps to an even greater degree.

LIKE GAUL, MEDICARE DECISIONS ARE DIVIDED INTO THREE PARTS

If you want to simplify Medicare, and who wouldn't, a good place to begin is with the three big deals from the last chapter. Here they are again:

1. Sign up at the right time and avoid penalties and the loss of coverage.
2. Choose from one of two Medicare paths: Original Medicare (with or without Medigap supplemental insurance) and a Part D drug plan, **or**, Medicare Advantage, which usually comes with a Part D plan bundled in.
3. Understand what Medicare covers and how to get the most from whichever coverage path you choose.

Okay, I know that third one is really more than one decision. The point is that by breaking down Medicare into smaller decisions, it's easier to make sense of this sprawling program.

The *first* big deal is about the confusing rules for signing up for Medicare in the first place. If you get this one wrong — well, how to say this delicately? You will be shafted. I hope the damage won't be as tragic as it was for Glen. But his extreme case does illustrate a broader point. One of the greatest shocks that many people have when leaving their employer-provided health insurance is how complicated it is even to sign up for Medicare.

Medicare lets people choose a new plan every year should they wish, but few people do, and many of them wind up with plans that cost too much and cover too little. There are lots of other possible paths to make the transition into Medicare, including retiree health plans, temporary coverage after a job loss, and, increasingly, moving into Medicare from one of the state insurance exchanges created by the Affordable Care Act. Growing numbers of people who continue working past age 65 face their own transition into Medicare.

Each of these pathways has its own process and rules that need to be understood. They're not hard, mind you, but most people, even ones as smart as Phyllis, don't even know about them. How can you comply with rules, even simple ones, if you don't know they exist, or where to find them?

There is, not so coincidentally, no coordinated government communications program to let people know about their

Medicare options and responsibilities. People approaching their 65th birthdays get flooded with well-wishing notes and Medicare touts from private insurance companies. They often receive nothing from their own government, or, at best, a note for those taking Social Security that they also can sign up for Medicare.

Second, what are the different types of Medicare coverage out there and how can you choose the best plan to meet your needs? The major fork in your health care road is, as noted earlier, the decision whether to buy just Original Medicare or to buy one of the increasingly popular Medicare Advantage (MA) programs. Original Medicare customers also often buy a Medigap policy. Separate chapters on these choices await.

Increasingly, many MA plans also offer dental, hearing, and vision insurance, which are not offered by Original Medicare. They can afford to offer more features while still staying competitive on price because they offer their services through proprietary provider networks of participating doctors, hospitals, other care providers, pharmacies, and even medical equipment companies.

These networks can be cheaper for insurers to operate than the costs paid for medical services in Original Medicare. Original Medicare is a fee-for-service program that allows people to choose whatever caregivers they wish (provided the caregiver accepts Medicare, which not all caregivers do). However, even if MA plans can be cheaper and cover more health needs than Original Medicare, there is no free lunch here, meaning there can be some big downsides to MA plans.

More than 40 million Medicare beneficiaries using both Original Medicare and Medicare Advantage plans also buy a Part D prescription drug coverage. Of all the things that Medicare is authorized to regulate, it is expressly forbidden to negotiate drug prices with pharmaceutical companies. This prohibition is one reason Americans pay the world's highest prices for drugs. There is a separate chapter here for Medicare prescription drug plans, and perhaps also a special spot reserved in you-know-where for the pharmaceutical companies who have so effectively shaped and then gamed the Medicare drug pricing rules.

Once you've figured out how to sign up for Medicare and which mix of coverage you want, I'll also help you with the *third* and final step of the process — how you should actually use the insurance you have.

This will include a step-by-step tour of what's covered and what's not, plus a walk-through of Medicare's annual open enroll-ment period, during which anyone with a Medicare policy can get just about any other kind of Medicare policy they wish.

HOW YOU CAN RULE MEDICARE INSTEAD OF IT RULING YOU

As noted earlier, money plays a big role in Medicare, and there is a separate money chapter here. Part of making your dollars go as far as possible is understanding the extensive government subsidy programs that can defray Medicare costs for lower-income seniors, helping to pay insurance premiums, deductibles, and even copays as well as helping offset the price of prescription drugs. These programs provide assistance based on not only your income but also your other financial resources. But how does CMS define these things? And how can unintentional changes in income affect your eligibility for these programs?

Are there mistakes made by Medicare? Do your Medicare claims get rejected for the wrong reasons? Do your doctors and other health care providers make mistakes when they file their insurance claims on your behalf? Of course, all of these things happen. A lot. Because they do, there is an enormous and enormously complex Medicare appeals process, which is explained in its own chapter, along with details on your extensive rights under Medicare. Now, I hope you'll never need to use this chapter, but it is here for you (and odds are you *will* need to use it).

Part of choosing the right Medicare policy or policies is understanding which health care providers you want to use and why. Having access to your preferred doctors continues to be the most important variable that people cite in explaining their Medicare insurance purchases. But there is a big wide world of health care providers out there. Whether it's a doctor or a hospital or some other provider, how do you choose them? Or, as likely as not, if you're an adult child of a parent using Medicare, how do *you* choose the best health providers for *your* mom or dad? Help is on the way later in the book.

This is not stuff you want to grapple with while a family health crisis is unfolding. In the "old" world of health care, we relied on doctors to tell us what to do. We probably didn't even know what hospital we'd go to if we became ill. Or what specialists we would see. That's what the doctor was for, right?

Not so in the new "you're on your own" world of health care. The good news is that you can call on a growing armada of powerful health care ratings services and tools to help you make informed choices. The bad news is that, as elsewhere in health care, it is hard to know how to use all this information. There are just so many of these tools, and new "big data" about health care are being released all the time.

I have read so much about retirement planning in the past thirty years that my body has involuntary convulsions when the subject is raised. I have read nearly nothing about health care planning. We have a pretty good idea of the health issues people will face in their later years, up to and including the very end of their lives. This is when a lot of Medicare spending occurs, often with little appreciable benefit. We don't like to discuss these things with family members or, perhaps, admit them to ourselves. This is understandable. But it's also wrong. So, there is a separate chapter here devoted to helping you build a personal plan for your later-life health decisions. Getting ready to leave life's stage is important stuff.

There also are oodles of examples and

answers to real Medicare beneficiary questions to help explain the often confusing rules and forms that are a plague on so many Medicare beneficiaries. You'll find a glossary of terms that will help you understand Medicare-ese spoken by the bureaucrats.

You can read the book cover to cover or cherry-pick topics. There is repetition and then emphasis on the repetition because you need to know this stuff to make the best possible use of Medicare.

3
LEAVING THE HEALTH INSURANCE HERD
YOU'RE ON YOUR OWN NOW

Is Medicare complicated and often opaque and impenetrable? You bet. But the larger story here is that *all* health insurance is complicated and often opaque and impenetrable. Many of us have been shielded from this unpleasant reality by our employer group health plans. They had to navigate this complexity, not us. We just had to pay a premium, usually reduced by an employer subsidy (so we didn't really know what health insurance cost). Usually, we got plain-vanilla health coverage and that's all we expected. Maybe, if we worked for forward-thinking employers or had gilt-edged union benefits, we would get a little choice — Neapolitan ice cream health insurance. But that was it. The complexity was there all the time. Ask anyone without employer health insurance who has had to navigate this system. It can be a nightmare. But we were spared.

This false sense of simplicity began disappearing sometime ago. Employers, burdened by rising health care costs and often facing new and lower-cost global competition, started loading more health care costs onto their employees. Borrowing a page from their 401(k) retirement playbooks, they began shifting more and more health care decisions onto us. No wonder that surveys by benefits insurer Aflac found that employees do not understand their health benefits, spend little time trying to do so, and, according to one report, would rather clean their toilets or complete a tax return than grapple with this topic.[1]

The trend has accelerated since passage of the Affordable Care Act. The ACA, of course, has created state health exchanges and, as it turns out, navigating them is a lot like shopping for Medicare coverage. Believe me, this is no compliment to the exchanges! But it does mean that more and more Americans will be making the transition to Medicare from a health insurance product that is similar to it.

WHY DOES ORIGINAL MEDICARE FEEL LIKE ORIGINAL SIN?

It also means, however, that more and more of us, used to the false simplicity of employer health care, will be on our own. Based on the record to date, it is not a pleasant experience and we have been struggling with it. We are, thank goodness, getting better at it, and so are the private health insurers who sell Medicare Advantage (MA) plans, Medicare Part D drug plans, and private Medicare supplement policies, also known as Medigap. But most people just use Original Medicare.

There are no private insurers or big marketing and communications staffs helping you make sense of Original Medicare. This job is done largely by CMS, directly and through contractors it hires. The result is often a communications vacuum. Social Security handles a major administrative load for Medicare, and its level of clarity also leaves a lot to be desired. But at least Social Security does this through its own employees, not cadres of hired outside contractors.

As mentioned, Original Medicare includes Part A for hospital insurance and Part B for doctors, outpatient expenses, and medical equipment. Both parts cover lots of other things as well, which will be explained in Chapter 5. For now, just keep in mind that Part A is free for people who have enough Social Security earnings (40 quarters) to qualify to receive Social Security retirement benefits. Even if they don't, they qualify for free Part A if their spouse or even ex-spouse qualifies. (It's not well known, but people who do not qualify for free Part A are entitled to buy an ACA exchange plan instead of Medicare when they turn 65.) Part A is a terrific benefit but it also has some holes, which I'll get to in due course.

Part B is not free, but requires a monthly premium that is set each year by CMS. For people receiving Social Security, Part B premiums are deducted from their monthly Social Security payments. This has led to some serious problems in recent years that are explained in Chapter 9.

This is as good a place as any to point out something that everyone knows if they stop to think about it, only many folks don't stop to think about it. These Part B premiums are what an individual must pay each month. If someone is married and both spouses are signed up for Medicare, there is no family plan. Each spouse must pay the premium. Ditto with other Part B charges. People are so used to getting family or couple's health insurance at work that they may overlook this simple yet fundamental difference in Medicare. Yet it can throw some households for a loop, particularly if they have kids who are still covered on an employer health plan when their parents retire and begin taking Medicare.

CMS cares about Part B premiums but, as with many other aspects of Original Medicare, does not do a good job of reaching out to beneficiaries to let them know about the kinds of unforeseen changes that occur with these premiums and other crucial aspects of Original Medicare. You can, in theory, find out nearly everything you need to know by going to Medicare.gov and spending endless hours hunting for information that you didn't know you needed to know. Finding a needle in a haystack is tough enough, but at least you know what the needle looks like. What if you don't? Or if no one tells you to look for the needle in the first place? Or how to find it?

MEDICARE ADVANTAGE COULD BECOME OUR PREFERRED CHOICE

MA plans already look a lot like ACA exchange plans, and the two will morph in ways that make them increasingly alike. The insurance industry wants this, of course, because it sells and manages MA plans as well as exchange plans. It would like to move people from exchanges onto Medicare as easily and seamlessly as possible. So, while Original Medicare now has more than two-thirds of the Medicare market, this ratio might be flipped in the next 10 to 15 years.

The freedom of choice provided by fee-for-service Original Medicare to beneficiaries comes at a financial cost. The reason is as obvious as the phrase. Fee-for-service means that health care providers get paid for the surgeries, care, and other health care services they provide. It says nothing about whether all this health care is needed or even in the best interest of the patient.

Medicare Advantage health networks, by contrast, can be cheaper providers of care than can fee-for-service Medicare. Insurers can control costs more effectively by assembling their own groups of doctors, hospitals, and other service providers. Cheaper health care, not surprisingly, has its own downsides. Provider networks are so important to the present and future prospects of Medicare beneficiaries that they merit their own chapter (12) later in this book.

ARE YOU READY TO LEAVE THE MEDICARE HERD?

If networks are favored on cost grounds, they also are increasingly preferred as mechanisms that are better structured than Original Medicare to provide coordinated care programs to Medicare patients. The ACA and Medicare are both moving aggressively to tie insurer and provider reimbursements to overall beneficiary health and satisfaction. Providing and — of equal importance in the bureaucratic world of health care — measuring the quality of medical care is something that Medicare Advantage provider networks are built to do. This could be a good thing but not if less expensive and more targeted health care translates into inferior care.

But leaving the health care herd is not all bad news. It doesn't just mean we're on our own. It also means the health care system is changing so that we can and should expect care that is tailored to our personal needs. This will be more and more possible and, eventually, individualized health care will be the standard of care we expect. But it's not the default standard today, not by a long shot. To demand what's theirs and get it, Medicare beneficiaries need to know how to operate in today's world of health care.

Today, managed care is where it's at. And while managed care and health maintenance organizations (remember them?) were rightly criticized in years past, they not only deserve a second look but deserve your most serious consideration as a potentially superior (with the emphasis on *potentially*) way to provide you better health care at lower prices.

OF JAMS AND MEDICARE HEALTH PLAN CHOICES

Sheena Iyengar[2] is a leading expert in how people make choices. One of her most famous experiments involved a food store where shoppers were asked to taste a new line of 30 jams on a display table and told they would get a dollar off on any of the new jams they later chose to buy. A few days later, the store repeated the promotion, but instead of displaying 30 flavors of jam, only 6 were on the table. Because all *Get What's Yours for Medicare* readers are above average, you probably already know the answer to this story. People tended only to look at jams when there were 30 on display but the level of actual jam sales was *10* times higher at the table where only 6 were offered. Too much choice, it seems, is a bad thing. People's minds are overloaded, and they often respond by shutting down and doing nothing.

So it is with Medicare or, more precisely, the various Medicare insurance products offered by private insurers. More than 2,000 Medicare Advantage plans were offered in different markets across the country in 2016, with the average consumer having a choice of 19 plans — 21 for those in urban markets and 11 for people living in nonmetropolitan counties. Most of these plans included coverage for Part D.

The choice among Part D drug plans was even more extensive, which of course means worse in terms of consumer confusion. More than 40 million Medicare beneficiaries purchase such plans. Part D plans are voluntary per Medicare rules, which strikes me as a really bad idea. Who except the 1 percenters can afford to pay for their own meds? Yet while Medicare is telling people they are not legally required to have Part D plans, it will sock them with potentially enormous penalties should they fail to enroll in the plans when they first take Medicare.

Medicare slices up the country into 34 regions for stand-alone drug plans. I don't even want to try to reconstruct how the bureaucrats came up with this number or agreed on the boundaries. Nearly 900 such plans were offered across the country in 2016, and while the number has been declining, it still amounted to 26 stand-alone Part D plans in each region. About 40 percent of people get their Part D plans bundled in with their MA plans, so if you have an MA plan, your choices will differ.

Whatever the exact number of plans you can choose from, it's clear there is too much jam on the Medicare table for people to make good choices. Behavioral psychologist Barry Schwartz teaches at Swarthmore College and is the author of *The Paradox of Choice: Why More Is Less.*[3] "People make worse decisions when there are lots of options," he told a meeting about Medicare policy choices convened by the Kaiser Family Foundation, which tracks all flavors of health care. "This is especially true when the things people are deciding about are multi-dimensional and complicated, as for example, choice of a prescription drug plan or a health insurance plan." Lots of research has been done that supports the conclusion that people make poor Medicare Advantage and Plan D choices because they are presented with too much of what might otherwise be considered a good thing.

The other thing that happens when we have the option of choosing among lots of things, Schwartz said, is that we think we should make the best choice because there are so many good options. Instead of empowering us to move forward, we tend to become paralyzed because we have little confidence that we have what it takes to choose the best option.

I am convinced this confusion is the dominant reason why so many people do not venture beyond Original Medicare. It also is the reason that they are so reluctant to switch Medicare coverage in later years.[4]

MEDICARE POLICIES CHANGE; SO SHOULD YOUR CHOICES

MA and Part D drug plans can change a great deal from year to year. This year's cheapest plan may not be the cheapest next year. The prices of drugs in what are called plan formularies can change a lot. (This just in from Glossaryland: Formulary is a key concept in health coverage. It describes a health plan's list of covered drugs.) A drug covered one year by a plan may not even be in its formulary the next year. Or it may have shifted to a different pricing category, or "tier," in the plan.

Medicare users generally don't pay a lot of attention to such detailed shifts. As a result, many pay more money for coverage that may be inferior to what's available at a lower cost. Later chapters will tell you exactly how to become comfortable with Medicare insurance policies, including the key aspects of coverage and how to understand and compare them. By spending at most a few hours a *year* looking at new Medicare options during each fall's open enrollment period, you can become a savvy shopper for better Medicare coverage.

HEALTH INSURANCE 101

Justin Sydnor, an economist at the University of Wisconsin, had an unusual real-world opportunity to learn how consumers actually choose health insurance.[5] A big company with more than 50,000 employees was trying a different approach to employee benefits that included having people sign up for health insurance from an extensive menu of some 50 insurance policies. These weren't Medicare policies but findings apply to insurance choices made in the Medicare space.

The company is not identified, and I'm sure would be mortified should its identity be known. The reason is that it created an abysmal set of health insurance plan choices. By mistake, for example, the company offered a number of plan choices where the level of insurance (that is, how well the policy covered a person's health needs) was the same but the prices for the policies differed, often by a lot. So, all that employees had to do to make a smart choice was to pick the cheapest policy. They did not need to go into the details of what was covered or under what circumstances.

Still, faced with this unintended set of easy

53

choices, employees overwhelmingly made the wrong choice. In other words, they did not understand the policies' pricing variables well enough to figure out the cheapest policy. In so doing, they revealed a lack of insurance literacy that was alarming. So, let's go over this topic to make sure you know these important basics.

Premium. This is what you plunk down, usually every month, to buy a health insurance policy. It is hardly the only or even best gauge of policy costs. Yet it is often the only number that consumers look at when making a purchase decision. Not surprisingly, Medicare plans with the lowest premiums tend to sell the best.

Deductible. This is the amount of covered expenses that you must first pay, usually each year, before your insurance begins helping you pay your medical bills. Consumers are attracted by low deductibles because they think this will hold down their out-of-pocket expenses. Choosing low-deductible plans with high premiums, however, could boost spending without providing any more coverage.

Coinsurance. After you've paid the deductible and your health insurance kicks in, what percentage of medical expenses does it pay? Many Medicare plans pay 80 percent of covered expenses, usually based on the maximum prices Medicare will pay for doctors, medical equipment, and other provider expenses. Original Part B has no ceiling on expenses subject to coinsurance, but other plans do. For extra credit: What kind of ceiling does your Medicare plan place on your 20 percent cost sharing? Do you even know whether your plan has a ceiling? How is that low premium or low deductible looking now?

Copayment. This is usually a set amount, but sometimes a percentage, that you must pay for a medical service, again after you've paid your deductible. You might, for example, have a $20 copay for a doctor's office visit. Insurance plans have different copay policies.

Out-of-pocket maximum. Part B of Original Medicare has no ceiling on beneficiaries' exposure to their 20 percent copays, as mentioned. You could owe 20 percent of a very large number. Medigap policies, to be covered in Chapter 6, can protect people from this copay risk. Medicare Advantage health plans offer out-of-pocket ceilings to avoid exposure to catastrophic health expenses. Drug plans, whether separate Part D plans or those packaged with Medicare Advantage plans, also offer catastrophic coverage. This reduces but does not eliminate your risk. Should you need one or more of those superexpensive drugs, you are still responsible for 5 percent of the costs. People with low incomes can get help paying for their prescriptions and Medicare premiums.

Sydnor's research found that people did not understand these different health insurance policy features or how they could be used to help them determine the best policy for them and their families. When researchers tried to tell this to people, they met with limited success. Most people did not understand insurance well enough to process the advice and act on it. As Sydnor, his fellow researchers, and a growing array of experts agree, we need clearer and simpler health insurance choices, including for Medicare.

In addition — and this is a big, big problem — it never occurred to the employees that their employer would make a mistake and offer them a menu of bad insurance choices. Applying this lesson to Medicare, *you* need to learn enough to buy the right policies and then, of equal if not greater importance, how to best use them to get the best medical care you can at the lowest price.

Do not expect Medicare or your insurers to

do this for you!

Chapter 4 provides key lessons about when you need to sign up for Medicare. Why, you might say, it's when I turn 65, isn't it? Ha, ha. How quaint. No, Dorothy. We're not in Kansas anymore.

4
GET IT RIGHT THE FIRST TIME

Signing up for Medicare should be a snap, right? You turn 65, you retire from your job, and you sign up for Parts A and B of Medicare with the Social Security Administration (SSA). You then decide if you want other coverage. Beginning and end of story. And, for the most part, this is how things used to work.

The linkage between Medicare and Social Security is hardly accidental. The SSA is legally responsible for a lot of Medicare work, including alerting people when they're eligible, signing them up, sending out their Medicare cards, and withholding Medicare premiums from monthly Social Security payments.

Until 2008, 65 was the full retirement age for Social Security as well as the primary enrollment age for Medicare, so signing up for the two programs at the same time was common. Well, *no más*.

Today, signing up for Medicare can cause a major brain freeze, as was the case in our opening chapter with Phyllis. Based on questions I get to the "Ask Phil" column on the *PBS NewsHour*'s Making Sen$e website, people often are confused by getting just this piece right.

SOCIAL SECURITY AND MEDICARE GO THEIR SEPARATE WAYS

Based on changes to Social Security rules included in the program's major 1983 reforms, Full Retirement Age has been steadily rising. Full Retirement Age, by the way, is the age when benefits are not reduced by early claiming reductions or hit with earnings test reductions. It moved in two-month increments from 65 in 2002, for people born in 1937 or earlier, to 66 in 2009, for those born from 1943 to 1954. It will stay there until 2020 and then begin moving again in two-month stages, for people born from 1955 to 1959, settling at 67 by 2027, for anyone born in 1960 or later. This shift is not only a big deal for Social Security but also a big deal for Medicare, because it further reduces the linkage between the two programs in terms of claiming dates.

This bond also has been weakened if not

blown up by the historic rise in the percentages of people who keep working well past their 65th birthdays. Roughly a third of people aged 65 to 69 are still in the labor force, and about 20 percent of those aged 70 to 74 are also still included. For sure, retirement is not what it used to be.

For good measure, the Great Recession erased trillions in retirement assets. And, while these losses have been recovered for the economy as a whole, they certainly haven't been recovered by many of the individuals who took the hits. Some were forced to defer retirements; others took their Social Security benefits early.

The big picture here is that we no longer have two programs where people elect benefits at the same time. We have two programs with an enormous range of different claiming patterns. This is a big deal for Medicare because it means you can't simply assume you will need Medicare as soon as you turn 65.

Some people will and others won't. But the circumstances under which we do or don't need Medicare at age 65 are often unclear. And neither Medicare nor Social Security has done a particularly good job of explaining what all of this means to the mere mortals who have to figure out when and how to claim their Medicare benefits.

Adding injury to insult, if you will, the government has also created a set of potentially harsh financial penalties for people who get this decision wrong and miss one of Medicare's many enrollment deadlines.

OKAY, MAYBE ROCKET SCIENCE IS EASIER THAN UNDERSTANDING MEDICARE ENROLLMENT PERIODS

Later in this chapter, I'll review details of all the rules about who needs to sign up for Medicare and when they need to do so. But first, here's a primer on Medicare's sign-up periods, the situations where they apply, and the lifetime financial penalties that must be paid by people who don't get Medicare right the first time around.[1] To repeat, the clock doesn't necessarily start ticking on these periods when you turn 65. It starts when one of several possible enrollment windows opens.

First, there is not one but several enrollment periods. Second, they apply — differently in some cases — not only to Original Medicare (Parts A and B) but also to Medicare Advantage (MA) plans (Part C) and to prescription drug plans (Part D). Oh, just for fun, there also are separate enrollment rules for Medigap policies —

the policies that plug many of the payment holes in Original Medicare.

For starters, for people who need to have Medicare when they turn 65, there is a seven-month *initial enrollment period,* which includes three months before you turn 65, your birthday month, and three months afterward. This window applies to Parts A through D. Keep in mind that usually you need to have Parts A and B before signing up for other types of Medicare insurance.

Don't assume that jumping through this initial enrollment hoop will meet your needs. If your birthday is in September, for example, you can sign up for Medicare anytime from June through December. But, and it's a big one, your Medicare coverage will begin at different times within this window.

For example, if you sign up from June through August, your coverage will begin September 1. If you sign up in September, it will begin October 1. But if you sign up later, there may be coverage gaps. The coverage date is December 1 for October sign-ups, January 1 for signing up in November, and February 1 for those who signed up in December. Let's look at this as a table:

SIGN-UP MONTH	MEDICARE COVERAGE BEGINS
June	September 1
July	September 1
August	September 1
September	October 1
October	December 1
November	January 1
December	February 1

Make sure your current health coverage does not end before *your Medicare coverage begins. This warning applies to all enrollment situations.*

If you do sign up for MA during initial enrollment and then find you don't want it, you can drop your MA plan anytime within the following 12 months and just use Original Medicare.

There is a *separate six-month open enrollment period for Medigap* (also called Medicare supplement insurance), which begins when you've enrolled in Part B. During this period, insurers usually must sell you any Medigap policy they offer, and they can't charge you more because of your health condition. Folks younger than 65 who are on Medicare because of disabilities may not be so lucky, as explained in Chapter 6.

This guaranteed access may be crucial

because if you miss this window and try to buy a Medigap policy later, insurers may not be obligated to sell you a policy and may be able to charge you a lot more money. Medigap policies and MA plans both plug holes in Original Medicare, so you don't need both. In fact, Medicare rules prohibit this.

If for any reason you missed enrolling in Part A or B during the Initial Enrollment Period, there is also a *general enrollment period* from January 1 through March 31 each year. Waiting until this period could, however, trigger lifetime premium surcharges for late Part B and Part D enrollment. The Part B penalty is 10 percent for each full year you are late; the Part D penalty is 1 percent a month.

These are cumulative penalties, folks. For example, if you have failed to get Part D drug coverage for five years, your penalty will be 60 percent of the average Part D monthly premium. It has been running a bit more than $33 a month for stand-alone Part D plans that aren't part of a Medicare Advantage plan. You could be paying a $20 monthly penalty (60 percent of $33), or $240 a year, for as long as you have a Part D plan.

Worse, perhaps, than the penalties is that

late sign-ups might leave you with no primary health insurance at all for an extended period.

If you enroll in Part B during the general enrollment period, there is *another enrollment period* from April through June 30 during which you can sign up for an MA plan with or without Part D drug coverage. In most cases, coverage will not take effect until July 1.

There are lots of special conditions that can expand your penalty-free options for when you sign up for Medicare. And there also are what's called *special enrollment periods* for people who have moved, lost their employer group coverage, or face numerous other special circumstances. These special periods may have enrollment windows that differ in length from the standard ones.

Finally, if you already have Medicare, there is an *open enrollment period* every year during which you can select new MA and drug plans, including moving back and forth between Original Medicare (Parts A and B) and MA. It runs from October 15 through December 7.

And if you have a MA plan, there is also a special MA *disenrollment period* from January 1 through February 14 to move back to Original Medicare and also get a Part D plan if you need one (most MA plans include Part D). However, this is a one-way street — you can't switch MA plans during this period or switch from Original Medicare to an MA plan.

Medicare.gov has additional details on all this smorgasbord of enrollment periods. Just search by the *italicized names* listed above.

Last but hardly least in the Medicare enrollment maze, there is yet another set of enrollment rules for Medicare Advantage and Part D drug plans that have received Medicare's highest 5-star quality ratings. To encourage these plans to pursue the 5-star rating, and to make it easier for Medicare users to purchase the plans judged tops, Medicare allows people to sign up for these plans during an enrollment period that runs from December 8 to November 30. You read that right. This is literally a 51-week enrollment period.

Don't feel bad if you can't keep track of so many different enrollment periods,[2] let alone the A, B, C, and Ds of Medicare. You can always check back here.

How do you avoid these penalties, yet at the same time avoid paying Medicare premiums that may be unnecessary? *Step one is not to take anything for granted as you approach your 65th birthday.*

WHAT REALLY HAPPENS WHEN YOU TURN 65?

It is tempting here to do a riff on the dubious joys of aging and decrepitude that seem to visit us with increasing regularity when we turn 65. But let's stick to Medicare eligibility.

At any age, if you are disabled and approved to receive Social Security disability income payments, you should be automatically enrolled *after two years and a month* in Parts A and B of Medicare. There is normally a five-month lag in disability processing, so it will take most disabled persons 30 months to get Medicare.

Reminder for all readers: You usually must

have Part A (primarily coverage for hospitals, skilled nursing facilities, other inpatient treatment facilities, home health care, and hospice) and Part B (primarily coverage for doctor, outpatient, and medical equipment expenses) *before* you can purchase other Medicare policies, including MA plans (Part C), Medicare prescription drug plans (Part D), and Medicare supplement insurance, also known as Medigap.

At 65, if you're a U.S. citizen, or if not, you have been a permanent resident of the United States for at least five consecutive years, you are eligible to begin Medicare. Being eligible does not mean you *must* sign up right then. This is a big distinction that clearly trips up lots of people. And one of the big reasons it does so, of course, is that it's been pounded into our heads for years that Medicare is required when people turn 65.

If you already have started receiving Social Security benefits when you turn 65, you should be automatically enrolled by Social Security in Parts A and B, and receive a Medicare card. Don't panic! This does not mean you have to actually accept Part B and pay its monthly premium. It does mean you have free Part A coverage. This is usually a good thing but, as we'll see in a bit, not always.

However, the key determinant of whether you must sign up for Medicare Part B is not whether you're receiving Social Security. At 65 or older, if you have — yourself or through your spouse or even ex-spouse — an active employer group health insurance policy, you usually *do not have to sign up for Medicare Part B* or the rest of the alphabet soup. You do need to take Part A if you receive Social Security and are 65 or older.

Even if you don't have to get Medicare, you might prefer it in favor of your employer plan. Perhaps Medicare coverage is more comprehensive, cheaper, or both. If so, it is your right to enroll in Medicare at 65 and drop your employer plan. Be warned, however, that if you do this and later change your mind, you might not be able to rejoin your employer plan.

Before doing anything that might be irreversible, talk with your employer benefits folks and make sure you know all the possible consequences of dropping your employer plan. In most cases, you're probably better off not signing up for Medicare in this situation. This is especially true if you have family members on your employer plan who are not eligible for their own Medicare coverage.

You still might wish to get free Part A, and can do so by getting in touch with Social Security, either online or via phone (1-800-MEDICARE or 1-800-633-4227). If you do this, don't be surprised if you also get signed up for Part B and get a Medicare card. But you should be able to send back the card and reject Part B for the time being.

Based on the many sad tales tied to our Social Security book, I am leery of telling people to rely on any Social Security process without personally contacting a representative and making sure your wishes are being carried out. This should not be a confrontational process but more of a courtesy. Unfortunately, Social Security is short-staffed and is trying to restrict — not encourage — face-to-face meetings.

The major exception to this "don't need it" rule is for people who are covered by an active employer group plan and who work for an employer with fewer than 20 employees (the exclusion size is 100 employees for Medicare coverage for the disabled). And for members of the fine-print club, if this employer is part of a multi-employer group plan, then there must be fewer than 20 people in the entire group to render it a small-employer plan.

Employees at such places have to get Medicare when they turn 65. This is because at age 65, their group plan will stop being what's called the "primary" payer of their insurance claims. Medicare will assume that role. Their employer insurance moves to the backseat as the "secondary" payer of claims. In this role, it can help to pay expenses not fully covered by Medicare, including Medicare deductibles, copays, and coinsurance.

But if you work for a small employer, don't know this rule, and don't get Medicare, you might unknowingly find yourself with *no* primary insurance coverage! What you think of as your primary coverage — your employer group plan — is not permitted to fill that role when you turn 65. You will be on the hook for nearly all your health care expenses. And, in many cases, you won't even know this until you get the bill for medical expenses. Pray that they are minor.

To recap, you can't be forced to get Medicare if you are actively covered at a plan offered by an employer with more than 20 employees. This employment ceiling goes up to 100 if you're disabled. At larger employers and multi-employer plans, Medicare is usually the secondary payer for those situations where employees have both coverages. This can still be worth a lot. Even the primary payer of claims under Medicare may not pay everything, and so the secondary insurer may be able to fill some important coverage gaps.

HERE'S A POP QUIZ BUT IT HAS ONLY ONE QUESTION

As a prize for taking this quiz, I promise to send you a Web link to a picture of *someone else's* trip to Disney World. Ready? Here's your snarky one-question pop quiz.

Without looking up what I just wrote, did you notice that my reference to employer group insurance was preceded by the word "active"? Be honest!

I bet you didn't. Neither did I when I began fielding reader questions about Medicare. But it turns out that "active" is an important modifier. Why? Well, because people who receive a retiree health plan from the same employer that insured them when they worked no longer have an *active* employer group health insurance plan. Usually, neither do people who get health insurance under the COBRA law. (The acronym stands for the Consolidated Omnibus Budget Reconciliation Act, which contained the provision allowing people to get 18 to 36 months of continued health insurance

72

should they lose their employer group coverage.)

Down the road, COBRA use will diminish because people will have guaranteed access to health insurance from a state insurance exchange under the Affordable Care Act. But it will continue to be very helpful in some circumstances. However, while the insurance coverage people receive may be nearly identical to that from their employer group health insurance plan, it's not considered active employer insurance.

If you are 65 or older when you get COBRA, the clock may start ticking on your Medicare enrollment obligations. Check with your former employer or your COBRA insurer, or both. Otherwise, you could face late-enrollment penalties or worse. COBRA insurance benefits always pay secondary to Medicare.[3] If you have COBRA and don't know this, and don't know that you might be required to get Medicare, it's possible you might have no primary health insurance at all! So, if you are on COBRA, it's vital that you find out your Medicare obligations and the possible adverse consequences of failing to enroll in Medicare.

COBRA may seem like a landmine for Medicare users but there are some strong benefits as well. First, while COBRA is not considered active coverage for Medicare Part B, that's not necessarily the case with Part D drug coverage. According to the Center for Medicare Advocacy, if your COBRA drug coverage is creditable, meaning it's at least as good as a Medicare Part D plan, you will not need to get a Part D plan until your COBRA coverage ends. And when you do, you will have a special enrollment period to do so and will not face a late-enrollment penalty.

More importantly, COBRA can be a godsend to an employee who turns 65 and loses his or her active employee coverage. When this happens, the employee can get a COBRA policy and continue protecting any insured family members for as long as 36 months. If this applies to you, just make sure you sign up for Part B right away and also check whether you need Part D or if your COBRA drug coverage is creditable.

WHY "ACTIVE" IS A KEY WORD IN RETIREE PLANS

Dennia from Missouri asks:

I retired from an employer who partially paid my medical coverage as part of my retirement compensation in 2013. I did not take Medicare B at 65 because I worked for another company until two weeks ago. I am 66 now and am at Full Retirement Age for Social Security. I discovered that although I have retirement medical coverage partially paid by my ex-employer, I have to pay a penalty for Medicare Part B coverage because I refused it when I turned 65 thinking that since I had retirement coverage and paid more than $675 a month for medical benefits, that I did not need to take Medicare B and pay another $208 a month on top of the $675 I already was paying. To add salt to the wound, I found out that I have to wait months before Medicare Part B becomes effective. Can you help me understand how they can make me wait before I can use Medicare Part B and also have to pay a penalty on top of the $208 each month? The bills I am getting already have reached more than $5,000.

You are correct that the requirement to get Medicare at age 65 is waived if you have group health coverage from an employer (unless the employer has fewer than 20 employees). But the fine print here (which, honestly, I had never stopped to think about) is that this group health coverage has to be provided by an employer where you actively work. In your case, you were working for an employer, but your health insurance was not from that employer but from a previous employer.

Medicare has a special enrollment period that allows 65-year-olds with group health coverage from a current employer to defer enrolling in Medicare until they leave their job or cease getting health coverage from this employer. Because this was not your situation, you fall under the program's general enrollment provisions. And because you missed the time frame for applying under these general rules, you face premium penalties and the related coverage hassles you describe.

It will not come as a surprise that I am not on the list of people that Medicare consults about its rules. But it seems to me that paying a premium penalty is bad enough without also having to go without coverage for months because of what is nearly always an unintentional failure to sign up for Medicare. The purpose of the program is to insure people and encourage healthy behaviors. That's not happening here.

THE BASIC RETIREE
HEALTH PLAN RULE

There is one simple rule to keep in mind if you are fortunate enough to have a private retiree health plan: such plans *always* pay secondary to Medicare.

Jo from Maryland says she

retired in 2012 but will turn 65 this June. I am a retired county employee and am covered under its retirement insurance. Do I need to sign up for Medicare? Is there any reason why it would be good for me to continue my retiree plan and to also get Medicare?

Well, because you have to. Retiree plans become what are called "secondary payers" to Medicare once their members reach age 65, so you must sign up for Original Medicare (Parts A and B). Jo will need to enroll no later than this fall or she may face a premium penalty for late enrollment. Another set of decisions Jo needs to make is how the total costs for her retiree coverage plus Original Medicare compare with a Medicare-only solution that could include a Part D drug plan and a Medigap policy or an MA plan that includes Part D drug coverage. This can be a complex decision and one that your employer's retirement benefits department can help you make, preferably well before you turn 65.

Jo also doesn't say if her plan includes only her or also covers other family members. If your spouse and children are covered on your plan, you probably should keep your retiree coverage. At the very least, check with the administrator of your retiree health plan and make sure you understand how its coverage of your family members would be affected by your decision.

Some employers sponsor MA plans for retirees who are eligible for Medicare. If you worked for such an employer, you can get both your Medicare benefits and your retiree health benefits by signing up for an MA plan that has a contract with your former employer. You can always choose not to take your employer's coverage and sign up for other Medicare plans. But if you do this, you may not be able to rejoin the retiree plan later.

AND FOR THOSE 10 MILLION OF YOU WITH MILITARY SERVICE

I receive a steady drumbeat of questions from military families about TRICARE, which covers nearly 10 million active and retired service members and their families.

With the help of folks at TRICARE, here is a basic description of how it works and where to find additional information.

First off, TRICARE morphs into TRICARE for Life for retirees. At this point, people need to have Medicare Parts A and B. TRICARE's rules require it to send out alert postcards before TRICARE members turn 65, but of course these things do get lost in the mail. TRICARE members can get Medicare enrollment details and help at milConnect.[4] TRICARE members also need to be registered with the Defense Enrollment Eligibility Reporting System (DEERS).[5]

Getting Medicare and switching to TRICARE for Life means that Medicare then becomes the primary payer and TRICARE is secondary. Military folks often have second careers after leaving the service and may have another retiree health program besides TRICARE for Life. In this case, TRICARE for Life usually moves into the third-payer slot. Claims first would flow to Medicare, with unpaid amounts then claimed against the secondary insurer. If any part of a claim still remains unpaid, TRICARE for Life then would be asked for payment. You can file a claim with the company that processes TRICARE for Life payments: Wisconsin Physicians Service–Military and Veterans Health (1-866-773-0404).[6]

TRICARE for Life tends to have comparable, and usually cheaper, drug coverage than a Medicare Part D drug plan. As a secondary payer, it also usually provides coverage that is comparable to a Medigap policy. If anyone says a TRICARE for Life beneficiary needs either of these additional policies, I'd be skeptical. Look at the coverage terms of your policy, or get help from TRICARE or Wisconsin Physicians Service. However, TRICARE for Life users on very limited incomes might do better on a Part D plan because they could qualify for financial assistance from Medicare in paying for their Part D drugs and even for plan premiums and other expenses. Chapter 9 has details on such assistance, which goes by the name of Extra Help.

WHAT'S YOUR RETIREE HEALTH PLAN CHECKLIST?

Retiree health plans are diverse. If you retired from XYZ Corp. and are on its retiree health plan, it may take more time than it's worth for you to compare it with other retiree plans. The good news is that this would for the most part be a waste of time anyway. You don't qualify for those other plans, so your job really is to learn how XYZ Corp.'s plan works, and whether there is anything you should do to improve its coverage.

To me, the most pressing concern would be if I had family members on my retiree health plan that were not covered by or even eligible for Medicare. When Medicare becomes the primary payer of my health claims, what if anything might happen to the health coverage and claims of my spouse and children? Will they still be covered or will they have to find their own health insurance, possibly from a state exchange? Find out from your plan's benefits experts.

Because the plan pays secondary to Medicare, another concern is how well your plan plugs any holes in Medicare. Keep in mind that if Medicare does not cover an expense, odds are other plans won't, either. This is an important distinction you need to explore: does your plan cover things that Medicare doesn't, or just help you pay expenses for things that Medicare does cover but for which it does not pay all expenses?

For Medicare-covered items, does it pay any uncovered copays, coinsurance, and other remaining expenses, which is what a

Medigap plan with Original Medicare does? If you have an MA retiree plan, does it provide additional coverage of things like dental, hearing, and vision needs? If such protection seems unacceptably skimpy, what would it cost you to get better stand-alone plans from other insurers?

Likewise, drug coverage traditionally has been a strength of many retiree health plans (keeping in mind that Original Medicare does not provide drug coverage). How does your retiree plan's drug coverage compare with what you could get from a stand-alone Part D drug plan?

More and more retiree plans are reducing benefits due to competitive cost pressures on their parent businesses. Increasingly, retiree plans are using health reimbursement accounts (HRAs), which are funded by employers and may be used to pay qualifying health care expenses, including Medicare premiums. If you have such a plan, learn how it works *before* you access such funds.

WITH ONE BIG ASTERISK

There is one exception to the rule that people on retiree health plans need Medicare to be their primary insurance payer. If you have health insurance from a health maintenance organization (HMO) under the Federal Employees Health Benefits Program (FEHBP), your coverage may be comprehensive enough that you will not need to sign up for Medicare Part B coverage. Note, though, that if you wish to sign up for Medicare later you may still face a penalty and will be able to enroll only during certain times of the year.

UNDERSTANDING THE COBRA MEDICARE SLITHER

Gerry from Oregon says:

I had agreed to take an early separation package from my company and this summer signed up for Medicare Parts A and B. My separation package includes 12 months of paid COBRA coverage, which also provides dental and vision insurance. Otherwise the COBRA-funded coverage is secondary to Medicare and is sort of superfluous. So that's the set up. Here's the question (or questions):

I'm not sure at this time if I will go with traditional Medicare or an Advantage plan. I've read that when my paid COBRA ends, I should be able to sign up for a Medigap policy, and that I'll be guaranteed coverage because going off COBRA counts as a life change event. I'm dreading getting to next summer and learning that everything I heard was wrong, so I wonder if I should make a decision now and sign up for something sooner during one of Medicare's open enrollment periods. I would essentially be double-paying for another health insurance policy for half a year but I'd rather be safe than sorry. Can you help me figure this out?

Gerry has done a really good job of understanding her health insurance. So, it's a sad tribute to Medicare's complexity that she is still considering double-paying for health insurance rather than risk running afoul of some arcane sign-up rule that requires top-secret clearance and a Hippocratic handshake.

The good news here is that Gerry needn't worry about getting guaranteed access to a Medigap policy (also called Medicare supplement insurance). She has the right to buy such a policy *if* she has Original Medicare or an employer group health plan (including retiree or COBRA coverage) or union coverage that pays after Medicare pays, *and* that plan coverage ends. She will have 63 days (my kingdom if someone can tell me why this number is so widely used in Medi-

84

care late-enrollment rules) after the formal end of her COBRA coverage to preserve her guaranteed access to Medigap. The clock will start ticking on the *latest* of these three events:

- The date the COBRA coverage ends.
- The date on the notice you get telling you that coverage is ending (if you receive one).
- The date on a claim denial, if this is the only way you know that the coverage ended.

However, if Gerry decides to sign up for a Medicare Advantage plan, she may be out of luck, at least for a while. That's because COBRA is not considered to be an extension of her active group health insurance plan. This means she will not be afforded a special enrollment period when her COBRA ends, and that her enrollment clock really began when the active coverage ended.

Had she already had the COBRA when she became eligible for Medicare, it should have ended when she signed up for Medicare. To avoid paying premiums on two policies in this situation, people should work out the transition details with their COBRA benefits manager or the insurance company providing COBRA coverage.

Diamonds May Be Forever, but Not Medicare

Alongside the notion that we all have to get Medicare the day we turn 65 is the idea that once we have Medicare, we will need to keep it the rest of our lives. Not true. And especially not true in today's economy, where people regularly move into and out of the labor force after they turn 65.

Elizabeth from Washington, D.C., says:

My husband and I married in July. I am 58 and have health insurance through my employer. He is 67 and has Medicare (A, B, and D). Is it possible for us to drop his Medicare coverage and enroll him as my spouse through my plan? Once one has signed up for Medicare, is it possible for him to go off it and then resume it after I retire? Or is signing up for Medicare a "once and for all" type decision? My employer coverage is very good so it would definitely be cheaper to sign him up on my plan, but I don't know if it's possible to do so at this point.

What a great question! It seems like most of us are going to need to work years if not decades beyond 65. Depressing as this may be, employer-provided health insurance usually costs less than Medicare and is worth hanging on to.

Of course, the Affordable Care Act could end up driving lots of employees onto state insurance exchanges if their employers find that a better option than continuing to provide health insurance. And employer health coverage would be threatened if Congress ever removes or materially reduces the tax benefits of employer-provided health insurance.

If you are actively employed and your spouse can be covered on your employer group health insurance, he can drop Medicare Parts B and D without facing a penalty when he signs up again later for this coverage when you retire and no longer are covered by an active plan. Always check these things out with your plan *before* you act. Ask for written confirmation of these things. Your husband should contact Medicare to make sure the agency is aware of his altered insurance status. Even when the rules are clear, it's possible for mistakes to be made. If someone incorrectly slapped a penalty surcharge down the road on his Part B and Part D premiums, who knows what a hassle it might be to deal with it? An ounce of prevention here might be worth *two* pounds of cure!

There is no reason for him to drop Part A. If he is already receiving Social Security benefits, he gets Part A for free, and can't drop it anyway without withdrawing from Social Security. I'll have lots more to say about Part A when I explain how Original Medicare works.

One footnote, which is nearly always the case with Medicare: the ability here to drop Part D prescription drug coverage hinges on the drug coverage included in your employer plan being what's called "creditable." That's an important code word in Medicare, meaning that the coverage provided is as good as or better than typical Medicare drug coverage. Your employer also should provide this information, but if the plan is as good as you say, this shouldn't be an issue.

And, with apologies, another footnote: to drop Medicare coverages, Social Security will require two documents to be signed and sent in showing the person has obtained employer coverage (forms CMS — 40B, and CMS — L564). Social Security also says it may require a face-to-face meeting before letting someone drop Part B coverage.

FAMILY ISSUES AND THE TRANSITION TO MEDICARE

In the classic transition to Medicare, as already explained, a person turns 65 and gets the coverage. But life is often not so neat. As I've emphasized, a third of all 65-year-olds are still in the labor force. And they often have spouses and kids who need health insurance. Making sure you *and* your family have needed health insurance can entail a lot of planning and care. Read about Elizabeth from Maryland to get some idea of the variables you might need to consider:

I am turning 65 soon and have signed up for and have been accepted into Medicare Parts A and B. My husband will turn 65 this spring and plans to sign up for Medicare A and B soon. Our 24-year-old son is now on our plan. It's an excellent plan with virtually no deductible unless you go out of network and then the deductible is maxed out at $600 for the whole family. Everything is about a $10 copay and we get to choose our own doctors. The family premium is $265 per month.

Here's my quandary. I am working and can get insurance for myself and my family through my company. That insurance would be a little less expensive on premiums but the deductibles are quite high. My retiree plan requires us to be secondary and Medicare primary for me and for my husband when he becomes Medicare eligible in April. The plan premiums are not reduced even though my husband and I are on Medicare and are Medicare eligible because we are on the family plan. Our son's insurance is primary, through the county. Medicare has sent me several notices stating that because of my income, my monthly premiums are not $104, as they first billed me, but $272 per month because of our joint income; Medicare will likely also charge my husband $272 per month starting in April.

So, our premiums have just jumped from $265 per month (our retiree health insurance through the county) by an additional $544 per month to $809, with zero additional services provided. AAAGHHH! :-) Do you see any options for us?

Wow, what a great deal! Seriously, I'm sorry these costs are higher but you deserve to be congratulated for finding these things out when you still have time to do something about them. I'd suggest you look further into your own employee group plan.

Congratulations on planning ahead. Like

almost all retiree plans, yours requires Medicare Parts A and B for the retiree and eligible spouse at age 65. That is typical. If you stay on this plan, you will need to pay the freight, I'm afraid. Looking ahead, however, will your Part B premiums always be this high? Chapter 9 will explain the provisions of the Social Security program known as IRMAA, which stands for income-related monthly adjustment amounts. IRMAA sets forth the monthly premium surcharges for Parts B and D of Medicare for those with relatively high incomes. In retirement, your income may well drop, and your IRMAA surcharge could disappear. The point here is not to make a decision with long-term consequences based on short-term conditions.

Alternatively, you say you're eligible for an employer group health plan through your current employment. How long will you continue to be employed and potentially have that coverage? How much would it cost to cover you, your husband, and your son? Also, under terms of the Affordable Care Act, I assume he will need to roll off your plan when he turns 26 and find his own coverage. This may affect your short-range solution. If you like the employer plan and it would pay primary to Medicare, then you and your husband could consider terminating your Medicare Part B and saving the cost of the premium. After your current employment ends, you would then have an eight-month special enrollment period to reenroll in Medicare without a penalty.

Of course, this advice depends on your family's health and pattern of health care use. Can you afford to pay the copayment out of pocket, and how would these expenses compare with your savings from terminating Medicare?

WHEN PART A IS NOT A GOOD DEAL

I said earlier that accepting free Part A hospital coverage is usually a good thing, even if you continue to be covered by an active employer group health plan after turning 65. This is because your employer plan might not cover all of your hospital expenses and Part A can become a secondary payer and help with some of these expenses.

There is one situation, however, where accepting "free" Part A insurance is anything but free. I learned of this *gotcha* from Jim in Connecticut:

Does it make sense for this 70-year-old to

postpone filing for Social Security to avoid Medicare Part A so that he can contribute to a health savings account (HSA)?

This is a deceptively complex question. And Jim, like many readers, is a lot smarter than I am. He was way ahead of me with this question. I had never considered that filing for Social Security could force someone to take Medicare even if they were still employed and had employer-provided health insurance. And I certainly never thought it would make it illegal for them to continue making pretax contributions to their HSA.

Silly me.

I was wrong and Jim is correct. So, be warned. If you are 65 or older and file for Social Security, the government will require you to take Part A, which triggers your official filing for Medicare. And if you have an HSA and are on Medicare, you will no longer be able to make pretax contributions to it. In fact, the rules say you need to stop contributions six months *before* Social Security benefits begin!

HSAs are available to most people whose employers offer them high-deductible health plans. The plans generally have lower premiums than standard coverage but higher deductibles.

Uncle Sam made these deductibles more palatable to consumers by pairing them with tax-exempt HSAs. Only individuals can have HSAs, not couples. But these individual accounts may be in either a family or individual plan. In a family plan, the total of allowable tax-deductible contributions is higher.

Contributions can be up to $6,650 for a family plan and $3,350 for a single person (plus up to $1,000 per person in catch-up contributions for people 55 and older) in pretax earnings. The funds can be placed in 401(k)-type investment accounts. Many employers sweeten the deal a bit more by making their own contributions to an employee's HSA. Their contributions are counted in the allowable annual ceilings. Like all IRS regulations, the details matter.[7]

Neither the contributions nor investment gains on the accounts will ever be subject to federal income taxes so long as account distributions are spent on qualifying medical expenses. Better still, any unused balances in the accounts will not be lost but will roll over to the next year and beyond.

HSAs can be a terrific retirement savings vehicle for people who don't rack up large out-of-pocket medical expenses. Alternatively, people with the financial means to pay such expenses without tapping their HSAs can allow their HSA account values to rise over time, and then tap them in their later years, when they almost certainly will have less income but more medical expenses.

Jim likes his HSA. He also is one of fewer than 2 percent of all Social Security participants who has elected to defer taking retirement benefits until he turns 70. By electing to defer benefits, Jim's monthly Social Security payment will be 32 percent higher (plus inflation adjustments) than if he began taking benefits at 66, and 76 percent higher than if he took them early at 62.

But Social Security benefits reach their maximum values at age 70, so there is no longer any reason for Jim to delay taking them. He still plans to work, mind you, and his employer presumably is still willing to provide him with health insurance.

However, as confirmed by spokespersons for both Social Security and Medicare, Jim's filing for Social Security will force him to also sign up for Part A of Medicare. And signing up for Part A, whether he wants to or not, qualifies as being on Medicare. And once Jim, or anyone else, is on Medicare, they can no longer contribute to an HSA.

Here's what Medicare said:

When he applies for Social Security and Medicare coverage, his Social Security entitlement and Part A coverage will be retroactive for 6 months, as outlined in law. He can't apply just for Social Security benefits and not also get Medicare Part A as he is over age 65. IRS rules for the HSA state that someone can't contribute to an HSA when they have Medicare, so the individual will need to stop contributing 6 months in advance of applying for Social Security benefits and Medicare. If he contributes to the HSA after Medicare coverage begins (not when he applies for Social Security/Medicare), he may be subject to IRS penalties.

Jim must lose his HSA or pass up his Social Security until he leaves his job. I think losing the HSA is far and away the less painful path for him. Average Social Security retirement benefits are more than $1,300 a month, and I'm betting Jim's benefit would be higher.

While Jim is out of luck, the fallout could be minor if his wife and not Jim were the covered employee and had a family HSA. Assuming she was not on Medicare, she could still participate in the HSA. And all of the allowable annual family contributions to the plan could still be allowed, save for Jim's $1,000 catch-up contributions.

Even so, there should be a better and less confusing way forward here. The last time I looked, every new user of Medicare cost Uncle Sam money (and that's us taxpayers, folks). So, I am thinking that the government should be happy to keep people on employer-provided insurance as long as possible. Forcing them out of HSAs hardly seems a wise move in that respect.

What it does do is force Jim into a bad and costly decision. This policy should be changed, if not for Jim then for the millions of older workers who are staying in their jobs and will face the same set of two bad choices that Jim faces.

Lastly, we should be encouraging Jim and others to defer Social Security and improve their retirement finances. Millions and millions of baby boomers have saved so little for their retirements that they will have a hard time even affording Medicare. They will need government assistance to pay for it and also may need Medicaid in their later years. So, we can pay a little bit more now in the form of HSA tax benefits, or we can pay a whole lot more later via government safety-net payments.

But I have wandered yet again from this chapter's theme, which is the importance of signing up for Medicare at the right time and for the right reasons. Once you understand these basics, which I hope you now do, you can move on to the next event: understanding what Medicare covers and what it doesn't.

5

WHAT MEDICARE COVERS AND WHAT IT DOESN'T

Every interaction between a consumer and their insurance company is a problem waiting to happen. When people have had a car accident, or house fire or been injured or sick, they're not in the mood to be reminded of the limits on their insurance coverage or of the things it *doesn't* cover. Consumers want to be made whole and, in many cases, anything less feels like a rip-off.

At the same time, the only way insurers could offer the kinds of coverage that consumers often expect is if they charged premiums that few people could afford. Wait! I think I've just described how long-term care insurance works! We'll save that rant for another day. The point here is that in the real world, as my late father used to say before docking my allowance, things don't work the way you wish they did. They work the way they have to for companies to make a buck and consumers to emerge more or less intact, although rarely happy.

So, by definition, consumers are inclined to dislike if not actively despise their insurance companies when they actually file a claim for insurance coverage. Take this feeling and amplify it for health insurers, who often appear to reduce our coverage in order to increase their profits.

In the case of Medicare, of course, most of the things it doesn't cover were decided by the government. But there's no doubt that the insurance industry has influence over these Medicare rules, just as the regulators have leverage on insurers and other health providers. In theory, consumers should benefit from competition and government oversight. In reality? I think my dad's rule still applies.

Before you even begin looking for a particular kind of Medicare policy, you need to know what is covered and what's not. This journey begins with Original Medicare — Parts A and B. Part A covers certain inpatient care at hospitals, skilled nursing facilities, home health agencies, and hospice. Part B deals with covered services involving doctors, durable medical equipment, and other outpatient expenses.

Everybody usually needs to have Parts A and B, before they can buy any additional

Medicare coverage, including a Medicare Advantage (MA) plan, Part D prescription drug insurance (often included in Medicare Advantage), or a Medigap policy that supplements Original Medicare. Medigap and Medicare Advantage plans don't play well with one another, meaning that you can't get both of them at the same time.

MA plans have to offer coverage that includes all Part A and Part B covered services (except for hospice, which is provided to MA customers outside of their plan through Part A under Original Medicare). However, the costs you pay for these services may not be the same as they are under Original Medicare. MA plans also are free to offer additional coverage, and most do. These details will be covered in a later chapter dealing with MA. There also is a separate chapter dealing with Part D drug plans, which may be the most crucial part of the book for most of us most of the time.

SORRY, CHARLIE:
THAT'S NOT COVERED

Let's start with some of the major shocks to people when they learn what's *not* covered in Parts A and B. And if you think some of these things are unsettling in theory, imagine how you would feel if you learned this

101

after the fact — after you had had some expensive procedure or lengthy illness only to discover that what you thought was covered was, in fact, not covered at all, or only partially covered.

These things happen all the time, according to people who work closely with beneficiaries. The topics for this book were influenced by extensive discussions with these folks, including consumer information experts at nonprofit Medicare counseling organizations, people who process Medicare claims and appeals, and call-center staffers. The details about who these people and organizations are may be found in the Acknowledgments at the back of this book.

From a high elevation, here's the short list of things Medicare does *not* cover:

Long-term care in nursing homes. Medicare does cover short-term stays in a skilled nursing facility (SNF) if doctors say such care is medically necessary. It does not cover custodial care in any setting, either in a nursing home or assisted living facility or your own home. Custodial care is defined as help with everyday activities — eating, bathing, dressing, and the like. Only medically necessary care is covered by Medicare and, even then, only up to defined limits.

Drug prices. People often are amazed

when they ask me why Medicare "lets" drug companies charge such high prices for prescription medicines, or why prices are not the same in different insurance plans. But when Congress created Part D of Medicare in 2003, it expressly forbade Medicare from negotiating drug prices with pharmaceutical companies.

This omission is costing us dearly. First, of course, it means that Medicare beneficiaries pay more and sometimes much more for their meds. This situation was made worse because Part D plans originally made consumers pay all of the cost of their medications once they hit, and while they remained in, what is called "the coverage gap" during the year. Once people emerge from the gap, they enter the catastrophic zone of Part D coverage, in which they usually pay small amounts for their prescriptions, or 5 percent of the cost, whichever is greater.

The coverage gap is also known as the donut hole, although this analogy has never made sense to me. I'd call it the donut pyramid, with a big hole in the center rising up to that small catastrophic peak at the top.

MEDICARE   **HEALTH INSURANCE**

1-800-MEDICARE (1-800-633-4227)

NO ONE TOLD ME

Medicare Advantage plans may not insure you at all if you use doctors or hospitals outside a plan's provider network.

SIGN
HERE ➡ _____

The Affordable Care Act is gradually eliminating the coverage gap. This is great for Medicare beneficiaries but turns out to be a lousy deal for taxpayers (a group that of course includes lots of Medicare beneficiaries). As noted, consumers pay only 5 percent of the cost of their drugs in the catastrophic zone of Part D plans. Insurers pay 15 percent. How much does this leave, class? Correct! Eighty percent. And who pays it? Why, Uncle Sam, of course.[1] The government is left footing the bill for all these outlandish prices for new miracle drugs. Something will have to change here, regardless of which party wins the White House. You might be able to tell that I am only warming up here about Part D drug plans. You will find a whole lot more on this subject in Chapter 8.

Dental, vision, and hearing coverage. Broadly speaking, nope, nope, and nope, although there are some exceptions.[2] Even though these issues are of rising importance to an aging population, Medicare tends to cover only procedures that are medically necessary. So, for example, Medicare will cover cataract surgery and a single pair of eyeglasses, but then you're on your own. If you are injured and require certain dental surgeries, you're covered. But Medicare would not cover subsequent dental care this surgery may require, and of course it won't pay for the regular maintenance of your teeth (which might have made the surgery unnecessary in the first place). As Chapter 7 explains, one of the reasons people like Medicare Advantage plans is that many of them do cover these items.

Other Items:

Acupuncture, no.
General foot care, no. (Medically necessary podiatrist services, yes.)
White canes for the vision-impaired, no. (General canes, yes.)

Gym memberships and fitness programs, no.

Home-based twenty-four-hour-a-day care at home, no.

Meals delivered to your home, homemaker services, and personal care, no, no, and no.

Room humidifiers, room heaters, dehumidifiers, or electric air cleaners. All no.

Incontinence supplies or adult diapers, no.

Massage therapy, no.

Common medical supplies, such as bandages and gauze, no.

GOOD SOURCES OF CONSUMER HELP WITH ORIGINAL MEDICARE

Medicare.gov has a wealth of online information about Original Medicare's covered benefits. You may have to poke around to find what you need but a little patience usually will be rewarded. In particular, I'd recommend Medicare's online tool that will tell you if a specific procedure or piece of medical equipment is covered.[3] I also am a fan of the Medicare Rights Center (MRC), a nonprofit providing free consumer Medicare information and counseling. Its Medicare Interactive online service[4] lets you pose specific questions or subject areas that will lead you to helpful information. And you can always pick up the phone and call its national helpline at 800-333-4114 if you have questions. The State Health Insurance Assistance Program (SHIP) is another strong source. SHIP is funded by the federal government and has thousands of trained volunteers in locations[5] around the country who can help you with Medicare questions and problems.

Lastly, in addition to understanding what Medicare does and does not cover, you also may encounter situations where Medicare normally covers something but may not be the primary payer for health care expenses you incur in certain situations. This often happens in auto accidents, where auto insurance's medical coverage may have the primary payment responsibility. Or in workplace injuries. Or home accidents. Anything possibly covered by another form of insurance might entail different Medicare payment responsibilities. Fortunately, but not surprisingly, Medicare has a publication for this![6]

These are called "coordination of benefit" issues and can be a big deal, given how many health components there are in commercial insurance policies. Medicare does not want to be responsible for payments it feels your other insurers should make. Its efforts to be "made whole" in these situations may involve major payment hassles, usually in terms of timing issues over when health care providers get paid. You may even have to pay some of these expenses yourself, but you should eventually get repaid for insured expenses.

AND NOW, LET'S LOOK AT ALL THAT *IS* COVERED BY MEDICARE

Premium-free Part A insurance is available to those who have qualified for Social Security, meaning they've worked for at least 40 quarters at jobs where Social Security payroll taxes were deducted from their wages. If you haven't worked enough hours, free Part A insurance is still yours if your spouse has qualified for Social Security. Also, lots of government workers are not in Social Security but have paid the hospital insurance (HI) component of the payroll tax, which is 1.45 percent of all wages. They qualify for free Part A if they have the requisite 40 quarters of paying HI taxes.

Lots of people think they are ineligible for Medicare if they don't qualify for free Part A. That's not true. To qualify for Medicare, you need only be 65 and either a U.S. citizen or a legal resident of the United

States for five consecutive years. But if you don't qualify for free Part A, the premiums are steep — $411 a month in 2016 for people with fewer than 30 quarters of covered work and $226 a month for those with 30 to 40 quarters.[7]

If you must pay for Part A, you might be qualified to get insurance from a state exchange set up under the Affordable Care Act. In nearly all cases, people eligible for Medicare can't get health insurance from a state exchange. However, there is an exception for people who do not qualify for free Part A insurance.[8] Call Medicare or a SHIP counselor for details.

Part A of Medicare doesn't cover everything and the omissions can be real shockers to people. You need to know this stuff ahead of time.

For starters, having hospital insurance under Part A of Medicare doesn't mean that your hospital expenses are covered.

Here are the basic terms of Part A coverage. These numbers are for 2016 and change every year. When future numbers have been released, you will find them here[9] on the Medicare website.

PART A INPATIENT STAYS

You must pay a $1,288 deductible before Part A kicks in. This is not an annual deductible, as is the case for most insurance situations. It is a deductible for each benefit period, which begins when you're first admitted to the hospital and ends when you have not received inpatient care for 60 consecutive days. It is possible to have multiple benefit periods in a year and multiple deductibles.

During each benefit period, you pay $0 coinsurance for the first 60 days you're hospitalized, $322 a day for days 61 through 90, and $644 a day for days 91–150, assuming you have not used any of what Medicare calls your "lifetime reserve days." You get 60 of these your entire life. After 150 days, or after 90 days if you've already used up your lifetime reserve days, you're responsible for all hospital costs.

Also, Medicare does not cover private-duty nursing, a television or a phone in your room, or a private room, unless it's medically necessary.

Mental health stays are covered identically except there's a lifetime limit of 190 covered days.

Skilled nursing facility (SNF) stays charge you $0 for the first 20 days in a benefit period and charge you $161 coinsurance for each day from day 21 to 100. After that, you pay all costs. Once again, keep in mind that SNF stays must be medically necessary and require a doctor's approval.

In most inpatient care situations, keep in mind that you also will face 20 percent co-pay requirements for fees from doctors and other Part B expenses.

Hospice care has no per diem charges but may charge you a $5 copay for drugs and may also charge you a 5 percent copay for the cost of so-called respite care, which provides temporary care so that people caring for you can take a breather. Keep in mind that Medicare does not cover room and board charges when care is provided in your own home or in a nursing home (here providing custodial care, as opposed to the medical care provided in an SNF).

WHY HOME-BASED CARE IS LIKE GOLDILOCKS AND THE THREE BEARS

People prefer to stay in their homes and outcomes often are better (and cheaper) for home-based versus institutionalized care. Nearly all hospice care is provided where the patient resides — at home or in an institutional setting such as a nursing home or assisted living facility. Medicare also covers certain types of home health needs.[10] Keep in mind that when you're receiving home health care — not hospice care — you may still face 20 percent coinsurance for some items unless you have a Medigap or Medicare Advantage policy that will pay some or all of the coinsurance.

A person needs to have considerable health issues to qualify for Medicare's home health care coverage. As in the story of Goldilocks, you can't be either too healthy or too sick. Medicare does *not,* as I've said before and will say again, cover nonmedical care at home. If you need a home health aide to help you (or a parent) with what's called custodial home care, Medicare will not cover such expenses. At the same time, if you require full-time skilled nursing care, you won't qualify for home health care, either.

What is the "right" amount of frailty or illness? You must be homebound or nearly so. You must be under a doctor's plan of care and need intermittent skilled nursing care or various types of physical, occupational, or speech therapies. Your care must be provided by a Medicare-certified provider. Intermittent is defined by Medicare as being "fewer than 7 days each week or less than 8 hours each day over a period of

21 days (or less) with some exceptions in special circumstances." Perfectly unambiguous, right? Which is why you should clear such care with Original Medicare or your MA insurer *before* making home health care plans.

For qualified care situations, Medicare makes a single payment to a Medicare-certified home health agency that covers a 60-day "episode of care." Additional episodes can be approved should care still be required. Certified agencies have already agreed to this arrangement, including accepting Medicare's payment schedule. Odds are, you will face additional expenses that are not covered by Medicare, so it's important to discuss your needs with someone from the home health agency you select. Chapter 11 provides further details about the Medicare rating system and an online locator tool for these agencies.[11]

WHEN YOU'RE IN THE HOSPITAL, BUT NOT REALLY

Before leaving Part A coverage rules, I have to note a particularly nasty hospital *gotcha* that Medicare helped to create and which it has been trying ever since to resolve. It occurs when people enter the hospital but instead of being admitted to the hospital, they are treated there as outpatients. It may sound like a benign regulatory difference but it is hardly that.

For reasons I'll get to shortly, hospitals have compelling reasons to "observe" people as outpatients instead of admitting them as in-patients. The distinction is important because Medicare may pay different amounts for observational hospital stays versus admissions. By the way, this is true even if the actual care a person receives in both situations is identical — same doctors, same procedures, same medications, same supplies, same everything.

When Medicare pays less, Medicare beneficiaries usually pay more, and occasionally a lot more. This is an "it depends" consequence that hinges on the differential costs of whether the visit is covered by Medicare Part B (as an outpatient) or Medicare Part A (as an inpatient). Being responsible for steeper out-of-pocket expenses would be something nice for patients to know before they undergo treatment. But until recently there has been no national requirement for hospitals or doctors to tell patients whether their stay is considered observational or an admission. And in their defense, of course, caregivers may not know which it is at the time the patient enters the hospital for evaluation.

Further, and potentially more serious, in order for Medicare to insure subsequent stays in skilled nursing facilities, patients are required to have had at least three days of hospital care as admitted patients. When they are treated as observational patients, Medicare won't cover skilled nursing care.[12]

A related factor here is that Medicare also has stepped up its efforts to reduce hospital readmissions, which cost it a pretty penny. Its thinking is that hospitals' efforts to discharge Medicare patients prematurely have contributed to this trend, and that socking offenders with financial penalties for high readmission rates will improve care and save money.

One way to avoid readmissions is never to admit the patient in the first place, but classify the visit as observational. Is this a cynical explanation for why some Medicare beneficiaries are not admitted to the hospital? You bet. The *New England Journal of Medicine* reported this was not the case. But I remain skeptical.

Efforts to get rid of excessive observational stays, including proposed legislation and legal action, have not yet succeeded. However, a new law that took effect in August

2016 requires care facilities to tell patients when they are being classified for observational stays and not admission. Additional consumer safeguards may be needed, but until we see how well the new law is followed, vigilance is the word of the day. Ask about your admission status or authorize a family member or friend to do so on your behalf.[13]

NOW, ON TO THE BIG, BIG WORLD OF PART B

Part B covers doctors, outpatient expenses, and medical equipment. It is used more frequently by Medicare beneficiaries than Part A. Providing all the details of Part B would require a separate book, and a thick one at that.[14] As a general rule, don't assume something is covered by Part B. The corollary to this rule is, as clever readers will already have surmised, that neither should you assume something is not covered! Part B is an enormously broad and changing benefit that reaches into not only all corners of health care but most of its nooks and crannies as well. This includes drugs administered in outpatient settings.

The issue of what part of Medicare pays is also important for people with end stage renal disease (ESRD). Only about 1 percent of Medicare beneficiaries have to deal with kidney dialysis or transplants, and it's not a focus of *Get What's Yours for Medicare.* But patients and their families do have access to extensive Medicare benefits here, including drug coverage that can be confusing. ESRD Medicare treatments can be covered by different parts of Medicare depending on the nature of treatment and where it is provided. Call Medicare or the free counselors at SHIP or the MRC for help.[15]

Your best bet is to verify, verify, verify that something is covered *before* committing yourself to a health care spending decision. If you have Original Medicare, you would ask your doctor or other health care provider to find out if something is covered. They know the situation better than you do. And trying to see into the world of Original Medicare claims management is, frankly, just about impossible to you, even though you are the ultimate consumer of Medicare services. If you have an MA plan, your health care provider will need to contact your private insurer for such questions, although you can do this as well.

This assumes, of course, that you're not in the midst of a medical emergency that can rob you of both time and options. The good news here, if you want to call it that, is that Medicare's many, many rules usually have emergency provisions that will cover you in such a pinch, even if you've not gone about things in the proper way.

We're often confronted with medical emergencies, and rarely know ahead of time whom to call or what exactly to do. When you call an ambulance company or 911 because your partner of forty years is having trouble breathing, you're not likely to pay attention to whether the driver takes you to a hospital in your insurance plan's network. Truth be told, I'm not sure I'd want the driver to take even an extra second quizzing me about my health coverage or looking for an in-network hospital. This is an enormously important real-life topic, and I will return to it in Chapter 10, which is about Medicare consumer rights and appeals.

Part B charges a monthly premium that in 2016 is $104.90 for most beneficiaries. However, about 5 percent of Part B subscribers earned enough money to push them into higher premium brackets. This set of surcharges is known as the income-related monthly adjustment amount, or IRMAA.[16] Social Security makes this call and bases premiums on federal tax returns two years prior to the program year in question.

So, the agency used 2014 returns to determine any 2016 Part B premium surcharges. For the detail-minded, the agency uses a measure of taxable income called "modified adjusted gross income."[17] Chapter 9 includes details of Part B premiums and surcharges.

AND THEN ON TO PART B DEDUCTIBLES

Harking back to our primer on different insurance charges, you also will face an annual deductible that Part B enrollees must pay before their Part B insurance coverage kicks in. The Part B deductible is $166 in 2016. If you decide to also buy MA, your plan may impose a different deductible.

AND THEN ON TO PART B COINSURANCE

Medicare Part B usually covers only 80 percent of medically necessary procedures and related expenses. This means you are responsible for 20 percent of these costs. There is no ceiling on your exposure here, which in my less-than-humble opinion is why no one should settle just for Original Medicare if they can afford additional coverage.

And Then on to Part B Copays

Original Medicare also generally requires a copay for outpatient services. Keep in mind here that if you've been hospitalized and need a follow-up appointment, the charges in a hospital outpatient setting may be higher than for the same care provided in your doctor's office.

An Ounce of Prevention May Not Be Worth a Pound of Cure, but It May at Least Be Free!

The Affordable Care Act (ACA) was not directly about Medicare but it contains some big Medicare provisions. One of them is that by the year 2020, the ACA will fully close the so-called coverage gap in Part D prescription drug plans. I'll be taking a deep dive into the coverage gap in Chapter 8.

Another big impact on Medicare from the ACA is that it greatly expanded the menu of preventive screenings and wellness care available to Medicare beneficiaries, often for free or reduced rates. Medicare maintains an online list of such services, which numbered about two dozen at last count.[18]

Items include a free wellness visit with your doctor each year. This is a wonderful habit to get into. Doctors may not be as excited about this benefit as I am, but you should take full advantage of it by using this appointment to review your health during the past 12 months, make sure your doctor is up to date on your health condition and needs, and talk about what the coming 12 months might look like.

For what I hope, for your sake, are longer-range issues, Medicare began in 2016 also to cover discussions with your doctor about health care planning involving the end of your life. Check Chapter 14 for this and other end-of-life Medicare matters.

Whether you call your list of health needs a checklist or a fancy personal health care plan is not so important. Paying attention to your health issues and understanding how to deal with them is important. These visits can be a great way to take better care of yourself. There is no reason why the tires on your car should have a better maintenance plan than your body!

Do be careful, however, that your covered wellness visit doesn't unintentionally include other medical procedures that may not be free. Innocent or not, taking medical tests or even questioning your doctor can cost you.

There are cancer screenings and other preventive services dealing with some of our greatest health concerns — hypertension, diabetes, obesity, glaucoma, depression, and tobacco use. You can get free flu, hepatitis B, and pneumonia shots.

There also is a free "welcome to Medicare" appointment with your doctor to make sure you get off on the right foot when you begin Medicare.

Remember, you are entitled to these services. Many of them are woefully underused. Even though most are free, you may face coinsurance should the visits and screenings lead to additional tests and medical services.

The Secret to Medicare Wisdom? Control "F"

No book can answer everyone's Medicare questions. The topic is too broad, the rules too extensive, and our attention spans are too — wait, did a pretty bird just fly by the window? But if you don't find answers here to your specific questions, you can find ways to get your own answers.

I repeatedly recommend the free counseling services of the State Health Insurance Assistance Program (https://www

---

.shiptacenter.org/) and the Medicare Rights Center (http://www.medicarerights .org/). While they have lots of knowledge-able people, the ultimate sources of Medicare information usually are the Centers for Medicare & Medicaid Services (CMS), the Social Security Administration (SSA), and other federal agencies that make, enforce, and explain Medicare rules.

So, how do these experts get answers to Medicare questions? I sought out a CMS official (the agency prefers he not be identified) who is an expert presenter at the agency's annual "train the trainer" workshops. These sessions are held around the country every year to train Medicare counselors at SHIP and other organizations. While this official clearly knows more about Medicare than I ever will, his most impressive skill was not encyclopedic knowledge but an under-standing of *how* to find that knowledge.

When he trains people who provide Medicare counseling to consumers, here are his six "go-to" websites:

- Medicare.gov, the Medicare website

- CMS.gov, the CMS website
- Regulations.gov, the federal regulations website
- eCFR.gov, the electronic Code of Federal Regulations website
- SSA.gov, the Social Security Administration's website, and
- HealthCare.gov, the federally facilitated medical marketplace website

Each of these sites is enormous in its own right. Rather than zeroing in on a specific page or even section of one of these sites, the CMS official says, he begins by opening up the search window in his Internet browser (hence the "control f" advice above) and asking the site what he wants to know.

Here are some commonly asked Medicare questions, and how this expert would go about finding answers to them.

I'm being told I missed my Part B enrollment period and can't get insurance until next July. What's going on here?

The "secret" here is that Social Security

handles Medicare enrollments. Its official rules are in the Program Operating Manual System (POMS). It has a Health Insurance section abbreviated as "HI." Search for "enrollment period" and you'll find several pertinent pages. (One clue: the formal name of Medicare Part B is Supplementary Medical Insurance or SMI.)

I never worked enough to qualify for Social Security. Now, I'm being told that Part A of Medicare will cost me a small fortune. A friend told me that if I have to pay for Part A I might instead be able to forgo Medicare and get insurance from the Affordable Care Act marketplace in my state. How does this work?

The questioner's friend is correct. Go to Medicare.gov and search for "Medicare." Scroll through the results until you come to "Can I choose Marketplace coverage instead of Medicare?" *Voilà.*

My husband is in a nursing home and they're telling me they will no

**longer cover his care. I don't under-
stand these rules.**

The key here is not to look for information about nursing homes but about
"skilled nursing facilities" or "SNFs." These
are the places that provide medically
necessary care that is covered by Medicare. If a patient gets better and needs
only custodial care, Medicare does not
cover this and the skilled nursing facility
(SNF) will discharge the patient. The
source here is CMS.gov. Scroll down its
home page and find "Manuals" among its
most popular resources. The IOMs
(Internet-Only Manuals) are the CMS
equivalent of POMS. The Medicare Benefit Policy Manual (100-02) explains coverage provisions. Chapter 8 deals with
"Extended Care (SNF) Services."

**If I have COBRA when I turn 65, do I
need to sign up for Medicare?**

Named after the law that created it —
the Consolidated Omnibus Budget Reconciliation Act — COBRA provides continued

health insurance to people who've lost their employer group policies. Go to Medicare.gov and search on COBRA. You will see a list of files, including "Should I get Part B?" This file explains that COBRA does not delay your need to sign up for Medicare.

CARE IS COVERED EVEN IF IT DOESN'T MAKE YOU BETTER

Medicare will cover skilled care in skilled nursing, home health, and outpatient settings even if you are not expected to get any better. So long as the care is medically necessary, it's covered. After a number of Medicare contractors denied claims for patients whose care could not be expected to improve their health, the nonprofit Center for Medicare Advocacy sued CMS and in 2013 won what has come to be known as the Jimmo settlement.[19] CMS has since clarified that Medicare covers medically needed skilled care, regardless of the expectation for the results of such care.

MEDICAL NECESSITY — A PHRASE YOU MUST REMEMBER

Tucker from Washington asks:

Why does Medicare only consider reimbursement for a wheelchair used in the home? Do they want us to be shut-ins?

You're correct that Medicare's standard[20] for wheelchair use is your doctor's assessment that you have a medical need for a wheelchair inside your home. But you are then free to use it wherever you wish. I don't see this as meaning that Medicare wants you to be a shut-in. However, if you can putter around your home without needing a chair, but you can't walk very far outside the home, I can see where you'd feel this standard is unfair. In practice, basing Medicare coverage on your mobility outside the home would create a very slippery slope. How far would you need to walk unaided before you didn't need a wheelchair? A mile? Less? More? How would this distance be tested? The medical need requirement is consistent with other Medicare coverage determinations. And the in-home standard, while certainly murky in some circumstances, is easier to consistently interpret.

If You Travel Abroad,
Don't Get Sick

I cannot leave the subject of what Medicare covers without stressing — and stressing out about — the failure of Original Medicare to cover beneficiaries outside the United States. There are limited exceptions, mostly involving Canadian hospital care for Americans who cannot get timely care at a U.S. hospital. With foreign medical care often better and cheaper than care in the United States, this prohibition is increasingly outdated.

Readers ask me about this restriction all the time. I must have lots of successful readers, because they often seem to be spending their retirements on cruise ships, the Orient Express, grape-crushing sessions near Châteauneuf-du-Pape, and other similarly idyllic locations. They don't understand these restrictions. Neither do I. And neither, in a different way, does Medicare.

I can see a philosophical objection to allowing Americans to fork over U.S. dollars to foreign health care providers. I also can see that there may have been substantial concerns when Medicare was enacted in 1965 that the quality of foreign medical care was just not up to Marcus Welby standards.

But that's hardly the case these days.

Check out international health care rankings. Look at the surge in medical tourism, driven not only by lower costs but also by the high quality of foreign surgical centers. A friend of mine born in the Middle East periodically faces expensive medical treatments. They are so costly in the United States that she has them done in her former homeland at a wonderful facility. The cost is less than in the States, *including* the travel and temporary living expenses in the Middle East for her *and* her entire family!

Unlike Medicare, people can get their Social Security benefits sent to them anywhere. Presumably, these folks spend their dollars on foreign goods and services. Somehow, our nation has survived this outpouring of dollars. Why not Medicare? Here's how a reader named Steven put it. I can't improve on his logic:

Why should there be such resistance to using American benefits abroad? I understand that American insurance companies and the federal government say that they have designed their service to use networks of doctors and hospitals with whom they have agreements, to reduce costs. But my experience over the past 30 years, in the UK and France, has been that health care costs are far lower in these countries that have adopted national health services than they are in the U.S., with our fee-for-service philosophy. As I look to retirement, I am not anxious about using medical services here in France, and I expect that the costs that I will pay will be far less than what providers in the U.S. will charge. And if I were able to have Medicare pay me what they customarily pay providers in the U.S. for the same services, I might not see any cost at all. If that is the case, why wouldn't both the government and private Medicare supplemental insurance companies welcome expatriate customers? The more Americans drew on less costly services abroad, the greater the reductions would be for U.S. payments for retiree health care.

Medicare does pay for medical care provided outside the United States in a few limited circumstances. These include when a beneficiary is traveling between the contiguous states to Alaska by the most direct route, and when a beneficiary requires emergency care while near the U.S.–Canada border and the nearest emergency care is located on the Canadian side.

If you're aboard a ship and get sick,

Medicare will want to know whether the ship was registered to a U.S. or foreign flagship line. And it will want to know where you were in relation to a U.S. port when the medical care was administered. For example, you may be covered if you're on a cruise ship but only if your medical care was provided within six hours of either arrival at or departure from a U.S. port. Further, a Medicare spokesman told me, you will not be covered if the ship is of foreign registry and within 40 miles of a U.S. port. This makes no sense to me whatsoever, except if the law is trying to distinguish a foreign ship from a U.S.-flagged ship that is also within 40 miles of a U.S. port. Now, you might ask, how does one equate 40 miles with six hours? Does this mean the U.S. vessel must be traveling at least 7 miles an hour? Do I need to know that in knots? Or maybe I am just tied up in knots?

Social Security does far more than simply send payments to beneficiaries outside the United States. Through bilateral agreements with many nations, the earnings of Americans who work in foreign countries can be credited to the earnings records on which their Social Security retirement benefits are based. Would it really be so hard to make Medicare similarly responsive to those beneficiaries who live and travel overseas? They are still American citizens, right? Providers of health care services in the States might not be so happy. But if the customer is the Medicare beneficiary, is there any doubt that he or she would be better off? Or that in the process, federal spending would be reduced?

I'm laughing even as I write these words because the prospect of Congress doing anything so helpful and logical these days is such a nonstarter. And this reality, of course, is no laughing matter at all.

Not so coincidentally, the federal government has lots of employees around the world. The Federal Employee Health Benefits Program (FEHBP) that insures them does not require people to come back to the United States for their health care needs. How silly would that be, right? FEHBP does operate an extensive program of overseas health insurance[21] that somehow has managed to include things like networks of foreign health care providers, mail order pharmacies for drugs, and the like. In the meantime, readers have asked about other private insurance help for foreign health care needs. Dan, from Pennsylvania, says:

I will turn 65 this year and will enroll in

Medicare as well as take out a Medicare supplement plan. I intend to keep working for the foreseeable future. My work involves a fair amount of international travel, and I have an emergency medical evacuation service. However, I wonder what I will need to do to be insured for any urgent or emergency medical expenses while I am outside the U.S. Are there supplement plans that cover medical expenses outside the U.S.? If not, what other options are there (short of traditional medical insurance)?

Several Medigap "letter" plans, also called Medicare supplement insurance, offer emergency coverage for foreign travel, as do some MA plans. Check with insurers if you plan to travel abroad. Beyond this, you may need to seek non-Medicare insurance. If you spend lots of time in a single foreign country, you should explore health coverage issued by an insurer in that nation. You might investigate health care options in travel insurance policies for shorter trips.

WHEN ORIGINAL MEDICARE IS NOT ENOUGH

Original Medicare is, despite all its covered services, not enough health coverage. Most consumers realize this, and seek ways to eliminate or reduce the 20 percent copayment gap in Original Medicare. Medigap has been the preferred way of doing this but MA plans also are a popular way to limit out-of-pocket insured health expenses.

"Most people on Medicare have some source of coverage that supplements Medicare," the Kaiser Family Foundation said in a 2015 report,[22] "including Medigap policies (23 percent), employer or union-sponsored health plans (35 percent), and Medicaid for individuals with low incomes (19 percent)." MA plans now account for more than 30 percent of the total Medicare market, and they also provide annual caps on health expenditures.

And, of course, Original Medicare does not include prescription drug coverage, except in limited circumstances usually related to hospital stays.

Part D prescription drug insurance can be complicated and, in some cases, expensive. But I think you absolutely must have a Part D plan. Even though it is not legally required, it should be. People without drug coverage are at risk for all or nearly all of their medication costs. These expenses can bankrupt even affluent households.

But what worries me the most is that

people without Part D coverage tend not to fill their doctors' prescriptions for drugs, assuming they even see a doctor regularly. People of modest means usually can qualify for Medicare subsidies. But these, too, are underutilized. People who avoid the health care system are not likely to learn about or use Medicare subsidies.

This is truly sad, but it also can inflict longer-term costs on the rest of us. Subsidizing Medicare expenses and providing a broad range of free health screenings and wellness services is hardly cheap. But it is cheaper than the medical bills that people are likely to incur later in life to deal with the chronic conditions and severe health issues caused or worsened by the failure earlier in life to get the kind of health care that Medicare can provide, often with extensive payment support.

For readers who do have sufficient financial means, getting Original Medicare is the first step on a longer health care journey.

That journey should include, as I've just stressed, getting a Part D drug plan. But there is a major fork in the road that requires careful consideration well before you get there.

After you've signed up for Original Medicare (Parts A and B), should you get a Medigap policy (also known as Medicare supplement insurance) and a stand-alone Part D drug plan? Or should you get an MA plan (which is technically called Part C of Medicare), which usually will include Part D coverage?

Chapter 6 will, at a more forgiving length, discuss what you need to know about Medigap policies. Subsequent chapters will then explain MA and Part D plans.

6

MEDIGAP

THE GLUE THAT HOLDS ORIGINAL MEDICARE TOGETHER

Medigap policies, also known as Medicare supplement plans, are private insurance plans that fill a lot of the gaps that expose Original Medicare beneficiaries to enormous medical expenses. Part B generally pays only 80 percent of the cost of covered services and medical equipment. You pay the other 20 percent — forever. Part A has fewer gaps, as explained in the last chapter, but you are still responsible for any deductibles. And the costs of long hospital stays not covered by Part A can bankrupt all but the wealthiest households.

Medicare Advantage (MA) policies, also sold by private insurers, likewise shield people from catastrophic costs. And if it weren't for Medigap policies, I would just tell you to buy an MA policy. Fortunately, there is Medigap. It's not for everyone but when it meshes with your needs and, especially, your lifestyle, it can be your best choice.

Not to get too far ahead of myself, but sometimes dessert is so good it deserves to be eaten at the beginning of the meal. The dessert part of Medigap is that some policies cover emergency medical needs during foreign travel, which Original Medicare does not do (but some Medicare Advantage plans do). Also, because you can retain fee-for-service Original Medicare with a Medigap plan, snowbirds who live in more than one place in the United States during the year can take their coverage with them. This may not be possible with an MA plan that is tied to a local network of providers. Some Medigap policies can close all the major payment gaps in Original Medicare — a benefit that does not come free, of course, but may require paying relatively high premiums.

WHY GUARANTEED ACCESS IS SUCH A BIG DEAL

Once you have secured Part A and Part B coverage, the clock normally starts to tick on your Medigap enrollment period. The "cost" of missing this first enrollment window for Medigap is not a financial penalty but something that may be even greater. You might lose valuable health insurance guarantees.

People aged 65 and older have guaranteed

access rights to Medigap within the enrollment window — insurers must sell you the plan you want (assuming they offer it), can't refuse to insure you because of preexisting conditions, and can't nail you with higher premiums because of these conditions. Also, the policy is guaranteed to be renewable on these terms so long as you keep up with your premiums. These guarantees may go poof if you miss your enrollment window.[1]

If you think guaranteed issue rights are a huge deal with Medigap, you are correct. By all means, don't lose these rights. Medigap plans are regulated primarily by the states, unlike other Medicare policies, so there may be consumer protections and other Medigap benefits in your state. Fortunately, there is an extensive network of Medicare volunteers in every state in the State Health Insurance Assistance Program (SHIP).[2] The nonprofit Medicare Rights Center is another good source of help.[3] And your state insurance department also may be able to help.[4]

MEDIGAP MAY NOT BE FRIENDLY TO THE DISABLED

Guaranteed issue rights may not be available to disabled Medicare beneficiaries younger than 65. In fact, insurers in more than 20 states do not even have to sell Medigap policies to people younger than 65. Insurers in these states are required to do so: California, Colorado, Connecticut, Delaware, Florida, Georgia, Hawaii, Illinois, Kansas, Louisiana, Maine, Maryland, Massachusetts, Michigan, Minnesota, Mississippi, Missouri, New Hampshire, New Jersey, New York, North Carolina, Oklahoma, Oregon, Pennsylvania, South Dakota, Tennessee, Texas, Vermont, and Wisconsin.

If you are disabled, younger than 65, and do have a Medigap policy, you can suspend that policy should you gain access to an employer group health plan, either through yourself or your spouse. This suspension period has no time limit and, if you later want your old Medigap coverage back, your insurer must provide the same benefits for the same premium as before, and cannot ding you for any old or recent preexisting conditions.

Wherever you live, call your state insurance department to find out your rights, including whether insurers can charge higher Medigap rates for disabled people younger than 65 than for policies sold to older beneficiaries.

BACK TO OUR REGULARLY
SCHEDULED PROGRAMMING

To avoid confusion, keep in mind that the premiums you pay for Medigap are on top of the premiums for Original Medicare. Further, neither Original Medicare nor Medigap cover what I consider must-have components of a solid old-age insurance plan: long-term care and the troika of needs that will grow for nearly all of us as we get older — dental, vision, and hearing.

Also, Medigap doesn't work with Medicare Advantage plans. Nor with Medicaid, Department of Veterans Affairs benefits, or TRICARE, the insurance program for military members and their families. If you have a retiree program from a former employer or a union, check with a benefits manager to see whether the program is compatible with Medigap. Remember that Medicare is the primary insurer in most retiree health programs, and the retirement plan is the secondary payer. But in this role, a retiree plan might cover a lot of the things covered by Medigap, reducing or even eliminating your need for a Medigap policy.

Combining Original Medicare with Medigap is one major fork in the road in terms of the decisions you need to make about the kind of Medicare insurance you will purchase. Buying an MA plan is the other fork in the Medicare road. And, as I've also already noted, a Part D Medicare prescription drug plan should be part of both Medicare paths.

There are 10 different types of Medigap policies that can be sold by insurers. They are designated by different letters and — surprise! — known as letter plans. Due to the creation of new letter plans and the retirement of old ones, the array of Medigap plans is *not* lettered A through J but currently consists of A, B, C, D, F, G, K, L, M, and N. There are two types of letter F plans, so if someone says there are 11, I'm fine with that, too.

MEDICARE   HEALTH INSURANCE

1-800-MEDICARE (1-800-633-4227)

NO ONE TOLD ME

You must be formally admitted to a hospital for at least two midnights before you're eligible for certain key Medicare benefits.

SIGN
HERE ➡

Part A coinsurance and hospital costs up to an additional 365 days after Medicare benefits are used

Part B coinsurance or copayment*

Blood (first 3 pints)

Part A hospice care coinsurance or copayment

Skilled nursing facility care coinsurance

Part A deductible

Part B deductible

Part B excess charges

Foreign travel exchange (up to plan limits)

Out-of-pocket limit**

* Plan N pays 100 percent of the Part B coinsurance, except for a copayment of up to $20 for some office visits and up to a $50 copayment for emergency room visits that don't result in inpatient admission.

** After you meet your out-of-pocket yearly limit and your yearly Part B deductible, the Medigap plan pays 100 percent of covered services for the rest of the calendar year.

PLUS ÇA CHANGE, PLUS C'EST LA MÊME CHOSE

An insurer does not have to offer all 10 plans. But the Medigap policies it offers must cover exactly the same things as the same-letter plans sold by other insurers. In other words, every Medigap A policy must cover the same things, regardless of which insurer sells it.

Different Medigap insurers are free, however, to charge differing prices for the same letter policies. And they do, so comparing prices when you shop for Medigap is essential.

The chart here is reproduced from Medi-

MEDIGAP PLANS									
A	B	C	D	F*	G	K	L	M	N
100%	100%	100%	100%	100%	100%	100%	100%	100%	100%
100%	100%	100%	100%	100%	100%	50%	75%	100%	100%
100%	100%	100%	100%	100%	100%	50%	75%	100%	100%
100%	100%	100%	100%	100%	100%	50%	75%	100%	100%
No	No	100%	100%	100%	100%	50%	75%	100%	100%
No	100%	100%	100%	100%	100%	50%	75%	50%	100%
No	No	100%	No	100%	No	No	No	No	No
No	No	No	No	100%	100%	No	No	No	No
No	No	80%	80%	80%	80%	No	No	80%	80%
N/A	N/A	N/A	N/A	N/A	N/A	$4,940	$2,470	N/A	N/A

* Plan F also offers a high-deductible plan. If you choose this option, this means you must pay for Medicare-covered costs up to the deductible amount of $2,140 in 2014 ($2,180 in 2015) before your Medigap plan pays anything.

care's annual guide to Medigap.[5] There is a version of this grid in virtually every explanation of Medigap. I'm going to spend some time carefully explaining it. Remember: *every* Medigap insurer must offer these features in its letter plans.

Part A coinsurance and hospital costs up to an additional 365 days after Medicare benefits are used up. All Medigap policies cover these items. This single feature can easily be worth the annual Medigap premium for many, many years. Further, Original Medicare covers only 150 days of hospitalization your entire life. Having an additional 365 days would save just about everyone from the poorhouse. It is true that few people would ever need that much time in a hospital. But remember: this is insurance for something you hope will never happen.

Part B coinsurance or copayment. Blood (first 3 pints). Part A hospice care coinsurance or copayment. All Medigap plans except K and L must cover all of these gaps in Original Medicare. The Part B 20 percent coinsurance in particular could be a steep cost.

Skilled nursing facility care coinsurance. Remember from the last chapter that this coinsurance costs $161 from days 21 to 100. Letter plans A and B do not offer this coverage and plans K and L cover only parts of it.

Part A deductible. The 2016 hospital deductible is $1,288. Most but not all plans cover this.

Part B deductible. The 2016 Part B deductible is $166. Only two Medigap plans — C and F — will pay the deductible for you. But they are far and away the most popular plans, with 56 percent of all Medigap policyholders choosing Part F plans as of the end of 2014, and another 10 percent picking Plan C.

Newly sold C and F plans will be able to

offer this so-called "first dollar" coverage only through the year 2019. Under terms of the Medicare Access and CHIP Reauthorization Act of 2015 (MACRA), C and F plans sold to newly eligible Medicare beneficiaries will not cover the Part B deductible beginning in 2020. However, if you already have one of these plans, you will be allowed to keep it and renew it each year. This restriction may cause large numbers of Medicare newcomers to no longer buy these now-popular plans, so premiums may rise for remaining plan members. You will need to pay attention to these market trends when considering buying or keeping one of these plans.

Part B excess charges. Some doctors and other health care providers may charge you more than the Medicare-approved rate for their services. These excess charges are covered by only two Medigap plans — F and G. Your doctors might accept the lower payment but not always. And with these two plans, you will not be faced with paying the excess charges yourself or perhaps looking for another doctor. Further details on how doctors charge for Medicare are in Chapter 9.

Foreign travel exchange (up to plan limits). This coverage is for emergencies, not medical tourism or a cleansing ritual at a five-star spa. If you travel outside the United States frequently, you should compare the details of Medigap travel coverage against other trip insurance and decide if Medigap will meet your needs or if you need more coverage.

Out-of-pocket limit. Letter plans K and L are the only two Medigap policies that provide this protection. However, based on your likely health needs, you might face lower out-of-pocket costs with some of the other letter plans. So, you need to see how these limits would affect the premium comparison with other Medigap letter plans.

Medicare provides an online policy search and price comparison shopping tool.[6] You can enter your ZIP code to see which plans are available where you live. Unfortunately, the tool does not tell you what each plan costs, but it does give you a price range for what each type of letter plan costs where you live. You will still need to contact individual insurers to find their costs.

MEDICARE SELECT PLANS

Medicare Select is a lower-cost type of Medigap plan that must adhere to the coverages provided by the letter plans but does so using a limited care network of hospitals and doctors that the insurance company has selected. If you go outside of this network, except for emergencies, you will pay more and perhaps a lot more of what Original Medicare does not pay. Medicare Select policies are not widely available so you should check with your state insurance department to see if they are offered in your state. If they are, compare network restrictions among the available plans.

DIFFERENT STATES, DIFFERENT RULES

Massachusetts, Minnesota, and Wisconsin don't allow the sale of Medigap letter plans but do authorize Medigap policies with many features found in letter plans. You can find details of these plans through Medicare or your state insurance department. There may be other Medigap safeguards in your home state, so please check before you buy a Medigap policy.

If you move to a different state, you should be able to keep your Medigap policy. If you run into transition snags, call the state insurance department in your new home state and ask for help. Or call SHIP or the Medicare Rights Center.

MEDIGAP PLANS WITH ADDITIONAL COVERAGE FEATURES

A number of states have approved what are called "innovative" Medigap plans. These plans may cover some of the things that Original Medicare does not cover, including dental, vision, and hearing needs. They are not big sellers and tend to be offered by smaller insurers. Check with your state insurance department if you want to know more.

DIFFERENT INSURERS, DIFFERENT RATING APPROACHES

Medigap insurers may use one of the three different rating systems explained below for how they set premiums. The rating approach used by the insurer you choose can affect your access to coverage, your premium, and how it may change in the future. This can be a big deal.

If you have guaranteed issue rights to a Medigap plan, you surely will recall (gosh, I hope you do) that an insurer can't refuse to sell to you because of any preexisting health conditions you might have.

However, this doesn't mean that your insurer won't raise your premiums in the future. And, in doing so, the type of rating approach it uses can come into play:

1. **Community-rated (also called "no-age-rated").** Everyone insured in the same-letter plan in the same state by this insurer will pay the same premium. Premiums can increase over time but not selectively.

2. **Issue-age-rated (also called "entry-age-rated").** Your premium is set for the age when you first buy the policy. A person who buys a Medigap policy at age 65 will pay less than someone who buys one at age 70. Once purchased, an entry-age-rated policy premium cannot be increased in later years solely due to your age.

3. **Attained-age-rated.** While premiums are also based on your age at the time you first bought the Medigap policy, premium increases pegged to your age in later years can occur.

State laws are important here, so check to see how your state regulates these rating approaches, and whether it offers additional consumer safeguards.

As with other forms of insurance, don't be wowed by an initial premium that is very low. Pay attention to the insurer's rating approach. Ask about its pattern of past rate increases. Call your state insurance department and see what you can find out about the rating approaches used by insurers in the state and premium trends (also check out consumer complaints by insurer). The Kaiser Family Foundation did a report that included the types of Medigap insurer rating systems used in each state.[7] It was done in 2013, so make sure the entry for your state is still accurate before buying.

If you have Original Medicare and a Medigap policy, you are not able to buy an MA plan. But as the next chapter spells out, MA plans have become the hottest Medicare insurance product. They are steadily taking market share from Original Medicare because they often are easier to use than Original Medicare, provide better customer service, and in many cases cover things that Original Medicare does not. They usually don't cost any more than Original Medicare, either, and may cost less. Read on to find out how MA plans work their magic.

7

THE HORSE INSURERS WANT YOU TO RIDE

MEDICARE ADVANTAGE PLANS

Bob, a friend of mine, turned 65 several years ago. As the arguably blessed date approached, Bob was inundated with birthday greetings from people he didn't know. Clearly, however, these folks knew him. And they were so persistently happy at the prospect of his coming birthday that Bob decided to save all their happy tidings. He is a research scientist by trade, and he wanted to document this phenomenon. To say that his birthday missives filed an entire grocery bag would not be an exaggeration. By now, of course, you surely know who these people were. And if your 65th birthday is in your own real-view mirror, you've probably shared Bob's experience.

No one, it seems, is happier about our coming 65th birthdays than the private insurers who want to sell us policies to cover either Medigap (our last chapter), Part D drug plans (the next one), or Medicare

Advantage (MA) plans, which are also known as Part C of Medicare. And among these, MA plans possess the most boisterous and persistent well-wishers.

Medicare is a government-run health insurance program. As such, it is often criticized by conservatives who volunteer to lie down on the tracks to block this train they claim is carrying socialized medicine. But some of America's largest and savviest Medicare champions are the private insurers who have figured out ways to make excellent livings selling and servicing the Medicare needs of 45 million of us who are at least 65 and another 9 million disabled persons of all ages.

That MA exists at all is in itself a surprise, if not a miracle. It is built upon the ashes of earlier Medicare managed care programs that gave health maintenance organizations such a bad name that the initials HMO may still evoke cringes when uttered at meetings of insurance marketers. But managed care, like the phoenix, started rising with the 2003 passage of the Medicare Modernization Act. This law is better known for creating Part D drug plans, but it also created a new playing field for managed care. To help its reincarnation, Medicare also handed out hefty subsidies to insurance companies to encourage them to offer these new MA plans.

There is a fascinating business and regulatory story behind the rise of MA plans. As a citizen and a voter, you should know this, so I've placed it on the book website. But as a consumer of Medicare, it offers little help in deciding whether to buy a specific MA plan or, indeed, whether to buy any MA plan at all.[1]

MEDICARE   HEALTH INSURANCE

1-800-MEDICARE (1-800-633-4227)

NO ONE TOLD ME

Millions of people fail to sign up for Medicare's payment assistance programs for drugs and other costs.

SIGN HERE ➡ _____

BACK TO OUR REGULARLY SCHEDULED MEDICINE

During the past decade, MA has flourished, in no little part because insurance companies have learned what not to repeat from their earlier HMO fiascoes. Today, these plans have become a financial sweet spot of American health care insurance. In fact, MA and the Affordable Care Act were major forces behind last year's gigantic-piranha-eats-huge-piranha health insurance mergers. Assuming these deals ultimately are approved, we will have only three massive private MA health insurance companies — Aetna (which would buy Humana), Anthem (it will take over Cigna), and UnitedHealthcare. Together they now cover more than half of all MA enrollees in the country. They also have worrisomely high market shares in many states and counties. Critics warn these insurers will use their market power to raise prices, reduce beneficiary services, and keep more and more money for themselves.

Of at least equal note, these plans dominate a high-growth business. As mentioned earlier, the ranks of the 65-and-older population are growing faster than the general population. And within this growing market, MA has been taking more and more business away from Original Medicare.

From a nonexistent base, MA plans now have captured nearly a third of the Medicare business. The other two-thirds of Medicare beneficiaries use Original fee-for-service Medicare (Parts A and B), usually with a stand-alone Part D drug plan, and often with a Medigap policy added to the mix as well. The executives who lead these enormous MA businesses see no serious obstacles to reversing these percentages in the next 15 or 20 years. Read on to find out why, and what you need to know to look out for you and yours. When swimming with piranhas, it helps to have sharp teeth of your own.

TRY IT, YOU'LL LIKE IT

MA plans are usually sold with a Part D plan bundled in (I'll save the Part D details for Chapter 8). They are simpler to buy and use than Original Medicare. They usually cost less. Many also include dental, hearing, and vision coverage, filling in one of the major holes in Original Medicare. And whereas Original Medicare has no cap on annual out-of-pocket expenses (unless one buys a Medigap policy), MA plans do limit your maximum exposure. What's not to like?

This apparent simplicity and thrift, however, may mask potential concerns that will be addressed in due course. For certain Medicare beneficiaries, some plans are clearly superior to Original Medicare. You'll learn in these pages how to make that call for yourself. But in terms of why MA popularity is soaring, let's return to my friend Bob and his birthday notices.

MA plans are marketed and sold aggressively. That's what insurance companies do. It's not in the playbook of the people who lead Medicare. The folks at the Centers for Medicare & Medicaid Services (CMS) have their hands full administering the program, devising and testing new Medicare programs to try to improve care and reduce costs, and wrestling with an enormous and enormously influential group of doctors, hospitals, other care providers, medical equipment companies, pharmacies, and pharmaceutical companies, plus the raft of trade groups, lobbyists, and others who represent these interests.

MA insurers get roughly $10,000 from Uncle Sam for each and every beneficiary who buys a policy. As you'll see, this is such an attractive incentive that some plans can make money by selling policies that effectively pay people to buy them! Beyond these supports, which are comparable to the subsidies provided to Original Medicare users, Medicare began several years ago to pay bonuses to MA plans with high-quality ratings of 4 or 5 stars. These ratings will be explained in a bit. The takeaway here is that MA plans with high ratings are receiving several billion dollars each year in additional payments from Washington.

Where are the financial incentives for anyone to hawk just Parts A and B? These plans are overseen by Medicare Administrative Contractors,[2] or MACs, largely faceless firms under contract to Medicare. No one in the MACs is out there shilling for or marketing Original Medicare. Their job is administrative — processing claims for the most part plus some other duties. I couldn't get some of these MACs even to return my calls and emails, let alone actually talk to me about what they do.

As Bob learned from private Medicare insurers, their plans are peddled as an elixir that can be your key to a long and prosperous life. And as I earlier noted, MA plans can look a lot like plans sold on the ACA's insurance exchanges by these same private insurers. Talk about another growth market! As ACA exchange users get comfortable with their coverage plans and choices, just imagine how many birthday greetings they will get when they turn 65!

SO, WHAT'S THE SECRET SAUCE?
Original Medicare, as noted, is fee-for-service Medicare. Its members can use any care provider they wish so long as the doc-

tor or health facility they choose has registered with Medicare and agrees to treat Medicare beneficiaries. The program is so big and influential that few care providers can afford to opt out. Still, their complaints about the low rates Medicare pays for services are the rule, not the exception. On the bright side, users of Original Medicare have great freedom in selecting their caregivers, and can travel freely within the United States and know they will still be covered.

MA plans, by contrast — and it's a major contrast at that — usually require members to use only the care providers within a plan's network. The plan picks the doctors, hospitals, and other key health care providers that you can see. If your doctors and preferred hospitals are in the network, terrific. If not, you sometimes can't use them at all or, if you do, you will pay higher out-of-network fees.

You don't see how the plans "make sausage" when they put together these networks. This is where the great size and reach of the big health insurers really comes into play. I am not suggesting these insurers are doing bad things, although there are regular reports of them doing so. They are just big. Very big. And they use this size as powerful leverage to get doctors and hospitals to join their networks and accept payment terms that are favorable to the plans. Also, in case you haven't noticed, hospitals are bulking up as well, and so are doctors' group practices, many of which have been bought by hospitals. In some local markets, these big care providers are a match, and then some, for the big health insurers.

There are lots of ways that MA plans make money, but none is more important than their ability to build efficient provider networks. These networks certainly may promote your health, and there is impressive evidence that coordinated care provided in a network can be good for you. But it is unquestionably good for the health of the plans' bottom lines.

IS THE DOCTOR IN?

Keep in mind that MA plans have been around in their present form for only about a decade. But in this relatively short time, look at how greatly they've influenced the shape of the health care industry. Provider networks are a big reason, and are so important that Chapter 12 will deal separately with them.

For now, the key takeaway is that you should not, repeat, not purchase an MA plan unless your doctor and other preferred health care providers are in its provider network. You may not know whether he or she is, but your doctor will. Or, more accurately, your doctor's office staff. On second thought, make that your doctors' office staffs. I see a bunch of doctors for what ails me or threatens to ail me. I bet you do, too, as do most people who use Medicare. And if there's anything that's true about aging in this country, even so-called successful aging, it's that we will be seeing more doctors in the future, not fewer.

In theory, you also should know which hospitals and other providers are in the provider network of any MA plan you are considering. In practice, most people go to the hospitals where their doctors have privileges. You should ask your doctors not only if they're in an MA plan's provider network but if they are happy with their choices of hospitals and other facilities that they would have access to in the network. There may be other specialists you need to see, and MA plans often require that such care be coordinated through your primary care physician.

And Now for Some
Alphabet Soup

Private insurers sell a bunch of different MA plans. An individual insurer need not offer all types of plans, and some plans may not be sold where you live. The Kaiser Family Foundation maintains a useful state-by-state roster of MA plans.[3] The main differences among MA plans involve how their networks operate, the cost consequence of going out of network for care, and how they work with Part D coverage, remembering that most MA plans usually include such coverage.

Also, and this is key, these plans all must offer coverage at least as comprehensive as Original Medicare (Parts A and B). But they can, and often do, provide additional coverage for things such as dental, hearing, vision, foreign coverage when traveling, and even gym memberships. These services may be reflected in higher premiums and related plan expenses. You should spend some time *in advance* to decide which bells and whistles are important to you and what you're willing to pay for such things. And then, harking back to the self-reliance in Chapter 3 that is now required to use our health insurance system, you need to do some serious comparison shopping.

Nearly all MA plans are of two types —

either a health maintenance organization (HMO) or a preferred provider organization (PPO). These are known as coordinated care plans, or CCPs for short. Beyond being a primary differentiator from Original Medicare, CCPs will become more important as CMS intensifies its efforts to get care providers to form networks to provide more comprehensive and coordinated care to individuals.

The agency is also moving to create coordinated treatment programs within Original Medicare. For example, CMS began a big pilot program in 2016 to create what's called a "bundled payments" program for knee and hip replacements. The agency will pay a single price for the procedure, covering all services spanning the day of surgery and the following 60 days for covered care and rehabilitation. The point here is that all Medicare consumers are headed toward some form of coordinated care, whether we know it or not, and whether we like it or not.

INTRODUCING THE MAIN PLAYERS
Health Maintenance Organization — 67.5 Percent of MA Plans in 2016

HMOs generally require you to receive all your care in their networks and sock you with high out-of-network costs. Your primary physician needs to coordinate your care and is the gatekeeper for any referrals you might need. This is generally the cheapest MA plan, and has an average monthly premium in 2016 of $31, including Part D coverage. Keep in mind that this usually is in addition to the Part B Medicare premium, which is $104.90 a month for most beneficiaries. If you want Part D coverage and an HMO, they must come packaged together. In other words, you can't get an MA HMO plan and a stand-alone Part D plan. These plans have annual ceilings on out-of-pocket health costs. The national ceiling in 2016 is $6,700 but many plans have lower ceilings.

Point of Service
This is an HMO plan that provides some out-of-network access and includes some price protection for out-of-pocket costs. It tucks into the spectrum of plans between an HMO and the broader caregiver choices of a PPO (see next listing).

**Preferred Provider Organization —
25 Percent of MA Plans in 2016**
PPOs offer you broader access than HMOs to doctors and hospitals outside its network,

and you usually don't need referrals from your primary doc. If you want to go to a special hospital in another state for treatment, a PPO will let you do this. Of course, as with everything, this freedom usually costs you in terms of higher premiums and more out-of-network care charges. PPOs must have not one but two sets of annual limits — one for in-network and the second for out-of-network care. As with HMOs, if you want Part D, it can only come bundled with the PPO plan. Local PPOs include 23 percent of all MA plans in 2016. Including Part D coverage, they had average monthly premiums of $68. Regional PPOs, which feature broader network service areas, were the choice of 2 percent of all MA participants in 2016; their average monthly premium is $34 in 2016, including Part D coverage.

Private Fee-for-Service — 3 Percent of MA Plans in 2016

PFFS plans take the PPO concept and broaden it further. You don't even have to have a primary care physician in one of these plans (although why you wouldn't want one is beyond this mere mortal). These plans are moving toward using provider networks. But for those not in such network plans, you can see any doctor or health care provider who takes Medicare, assuming they agree to treat you. You don't need the approval of your PFFS plan to do so. And you must get benefit statements that are similar to those you see with Original Medicare. The plan must provide you with yearly limits on Part A and B costs. You can get a stand-alone Part D plan if you have one of these plans, and do not need to get it bundled with the plan. Medicare has been deemphasizing these plans, and they are expected to become increasingly scarce. Their average monthly premium in 2016 is $58.

Beyond these major types of MA plans, there also are special needs plans (SNPs) that are focused on caring for vulnerable populations — usually people with low incomes who qualify for Medicare and Medicaid, people in nursing homes or assisted living facilities, and people who suffer from serious chronic health conditions and need care that is tailored to their needs. These plans are not offered by all insurers. If you think you may qualify, talk to your doctor and use Medicare's Plan Finder[4] to locate SNPs where you live.

How Much Is That
Doggie in the Window?

I do not mean to suggest that MA plans are
dogs. After all, people love their dogs. I do
mean to provide you a primer here on how
to assess the costs of the health components
of MA plans. There is a companion primer
on Part D drug plan costs, which you can
find in Chapter 8. Because nearly 90 percent
of MA enrollees choose MA plans that
include a Part D plan (abbreviated as MA-
PDs), you should consider both cost components to truly *Get What's Yours for Medicare.*

Please remember that you usually need to
pay your Part B premiums before buying an
MA plan. For 2016, these premiums range
from $104.90 to $389.80, depending on a
measure of income called your modified
adjusted gross income, or MAGI, which
includes the adjusted gross income you
enter on your federal tax return *plus* any
tax-exempt interest income.[5] You can check
out Chapter 9 for more details on these
money matters. Most people, however, pay
the basic monthly premium of $104.90.

There are many so-called zero-premium
MA plans that tack on nothing to that basic
Part B premium. Roughly 80 percent of all
MA beneficiaries have access to zero-

premium plans, and they are a powerful draw, especially to beneficiaries with HMO plans. In 2015, nearly 60 percent of all HMO enrollees chose a zero-premium plan, with smaller percentages doing so in regional PPOs (38 percent) and local PPOs (18 percent).

Some MA plans go further, using rebates from CMS to actually reduce that basic Part B premium. In 2015, plans in 11 states (representing more than a quarter of the Medicare-eligible population) offered access to monthly premium reductions of $10 or more in their MA plans. In 2014, only about 250,000 enrollees chose such plans. Nearly 90 percent were in Florida, and half of them were in plans that reduced their Part B premiums by $80 or more.

Premiums may be the shiniest sparkling ornaments on the MA tree, but they should not be the only or even major thing you look at in evaluating the cost of an MA plan. Over time, in fact, both offerings and purchases of zero-premium and reduced-premium plans have declined. One of the reasons is that these plans were brand-new not so many years ago, but enrollees have gotten savvier over time about looking at copays and other costs of MA plans. Also, premiums vary a lot by location and plan type.

Beyond premiums, you also need to know about:

Deductibles. Medicare Parts A and B both carry annual deductibles. In 2016, these are $1,288 for Part A (and this is not an annual deductible but applies to each separate hospital stay a person has during a calendar year) and $166 for Part B. Does your MA plan require you to pay the full amount of these deductibles or does it pay some of them for you? If so, what are you still responsible for paying here?

Copays. What do you need to pay for visits to the offices of your doctors and other care providers?

Coinsurance. Original Medicare has a 20 percent coinsurance fee for most Part B–covered procedures and services. What does the MA plan you're looking at charge?

Out-of-network fees. You may have to pay more for care from providers who are not in your plan's provider network. If these are providers you really need, would you rather pay them or make them unhappy?

Annual out-of-pocket maximums. One of the strongest selling points of MA plans is that they put a cap on your maximum annual health expenses. The ceiling, as noted earlier, was set at $6,700 several years ago by CMS. Most plans set lower ceilings. However, the average out-of-pocket limit for MA plans has risen steadily, from $4,281 in 2011 to $5,257 in 2016. Ceilings will vary by location and plan type.

DO YOU REALLY LOVE ME? CHECK OUT MY RATINGS!

Once you have an idea about the type of MA plan you want, it's time to check out the CMS "star" ratings that measure the quality of MA plans. Plans receive from 1 to 5 stars, with some half stars in between. These ratings are being cleverly used by CMS. First, they give quick and easily understood guidance to consumers. Beyond this, however, they also represent powerful carrots and sticks for insurers.

Get low ratings repeatedly and CMS may not let you offer your plan for the next year. This literally can take insurers out of the MA business, especially smaller insurers who don't have a large number of plans in the first place. Get high ratings — 4's and 5's — and CMS will pay you a bonus. These funds can be used to help high-rated plans further improve their services, boost profits, or do a bit of both.

While plan ratings are important, consumer research shows that Medicare users and shoppers don't really use them. At least not yet. I suspect ratings will become more heavily used as people discover they are on their own when it comes to making smart Medicare choices. Chapter 11 has details about the explosion of other Medicare star ratings as well as broader health care rankings.

MA quality ratings are based on a large set of medical care indicators, measuring such things as whether patients in the plan are using Medicare wellness tests and staying healthy, how well the plans help manage patients with ongoing or chronic health issues, how patients feel about the care they've received, and how Medicare assesses plan performance. These variables are contested by many professional groups and practitioners. That's hardly a surprise. But in the interest of being consumer friendly myself, let me give you a few tips:

1. I'd favor MA plans rated 4 to 5 stars.
2. Medicare has upped the quality game so that today's 4-star plan is probably not so different from a 5-star plan of a year or two ago. Plans still push hard for higher rat-

ings, but the process of moving from a 4 to a 5 is so demanding that many plans seem content with 4 or 4.5 stars.

3. Plans with 5-star ratings get something else besides annual bonus payments. They get to sign up new members anytime during the year, and have a marketing edge over plans that can sell to existing Medicare beneficiaries only during prescribed enrollment periods (your mind may still be reeling from the extended explanation of these periods in Chapter 4). A note here: while you can sign up for a 5-star plan anytime during the year, you can't "plan hop" to other 5-star plans during that same year. You get to pick only one plan, although you are free to move into other plans or even back to Original Medicare during annual enrollment periods.

Would you like to see all the details of the more than 30 variables that Medicare uses to evaluate the quality of MA and Part D drug plans?[6] As the iconic financial writer George Goodman once advised someone enamored of an investment idea, please lie down until this feeling passes. Then, be thankful for book endnotes. This is a consumer guide, not the *New England Journal of Medicine.* Still, from the geek in me to the geek in you, Medicare relies heavily on three sets of health care evaluations: the Consumer Assessment of Healthcare Providers and Systems (CAHPS),[7] the Healthcare Effectiveness Data and Information Set (HEDIS),[8] and the Medicare Health Outcomes Survey (HOS).[9] If you would like hours and hours of captivating reading about these surveys and their use in the star ratings system, have at it!

TRADE-OFFS BETWEEN MEDICARE ADVANTAGE AND OTHER MEDICARE PLANS

David from Nevada:

> I take one expensive drug and three low-cost generics. I have always had a Medicare supplement plan (Medigap), but I'm considering an MA plan to save money. What do you think?

Well, first off, I'm assuming you also must have a stand-alone Part D prescription drug plan, because new Medigap policies don't cover drugs. So I'm guessing your real ques-

174

tion is whether an MA plan will cost you the same or less for the drugs you need, while its out-of-pocket annual maximum will give you catastrophic protection for less money than your Medigap plan. Based on your current health care needs, the answer is almost certainly yes — an MA plan with a bundled drug plan will be cheaper.

But you shouldn't stop there. What would happen if you needed a complex surgical procedure, faced an extended hospital stay, or had to start taking one or more really expensive drugs? If you wanted to see the best specialty surgeon in the country for what ails you, for example, would this be covered under your MA plan? You ought to check *before* you get the plan. Ditto with having that procedure in a hospital 1,000 miles away that is renowned for the specialty care you need. As for really expensive drugs, both stand-alone Part D plans and bundled MA drug plans have the same catastrophic coverage, and you never have to pay more than 5 percent of the cost of drugs once you reach this stage of any Medicare drug plan.

An Essential List Of Medicare Advantage Questions

This shopping list is just for MA health plans, not for MA plans with drug coverage. If you already have an MA plan, you should read the annual plan documents the plan sends you. These are called the annual notice of change (ANOC) and the evidence of coverage (EOC) that plans must send out by the end of September each year. They will never win awards for ease of use, but with some effort on your part, they can be useful in helping you understand whether you should stay with your plan or pick a new one during Medicare's annual open enrollment period, which runs from October 15 through December 7. Chapter 13 has all the open enrollment details you'll need.

1. Is your primary care doctor in the provider network of the plan? How about your specialists? What about the hospitals or outpatient surgical facilities where your doctors would perform additional services?

2. If the plan has a provider network, must you use only providers in the network or can you request an exception from the plan to cover the out-of-network care you and your

doctors want? (You are always free, by the way, to go out of network if you're prepared to pay all the costs yourself.)

3. If you go outside the network, what will you be charged?

4. Pick some surgeries — a knee or hip replacement, say, plus a heart bypass operation or extensive treatment and perhaps surgery for a life-threatening form of cancer. If you needed any of these and wanted to use the best provider in the United States that you could find, how would you request an exception to see if your plan would cover these expenses?

5. What is the plan's maximum out-of-pocket expense for the coming calendar year? Is this *only* for in-network services or does it also include out-of-network expenses?

6. PPO plans require two out-of-pocket annual maximums — one for in-network expenses and the second for out-of-network costs. What are these totals for the plans you're considering?

7. Beyond covering everything that Original Medicare covers (which

MA plans are required by law to do), are there additional things such as vision or dental coverage that you want and which, if any, do plans in your area offer?

8. When you call the plan for additional information, are its representatives helpful, knowledgeable, and friendly? If not, how do you think they'll behave *after* you're a customer?

NEXT STOP: PLAN FINDER

What should you do to Get What's Yours for MA? Compare several plans offered in your ZIP code. If you already know whether you want an HMO or a PPO plan, compare two or three HMOs or two or three PPOs. You may want to look at another type of plan, of course, but HMOs and PPOs represent more than 9 out of every 10 MA plans purchased by Medicare beneficiaries.

Remember when I said the Internet is essential to make informed health care choices? Medicare's Plan Finder tool was uppermost in my mind. You can call each MA plan and, assuming you have nearly limitless time and patience, find answers to your questions. Or, you can go online to Medicare.gov, call up its Plan Finder tool,[10] and answer many — but hardly all — of your questions in 15 or 20 minutes.

I'd also suggest that you not be in a hurry. Plan Finder can be an extremely helpful and valuable online tool, but it is complicated at best, and impenetrable at worst. Try out the video tour that Medicare offers. If you are stumped, call a local office of the State Health Insurance Assistance Program (SHIP).[11] SHIP, as I've earlier noted, is a federally funded program whose trained volunteers can, among other things, walk you through Plan Finder and help you with other Medicare questions. The Medicare Rights Center[12] is another terrific and free source of Medicare knowledge that you can use. And you always can call Medicare directly at 1-800-MEDICARE (1-800-633-4227).

For starters, you can enter your ZIP code into Plan Finder and get plan information anonymously. That's how I would begin. Later, once you are pretty sure about what you want, and you are actually close to signing up for Medicare, you can enter personal information and set up a password-protected account. This will allow you to return to your account and do follow-up work.

Plan Finder is designed to combine your

search for MA with Part D drug coverage. If you know that you want an MA plan with Part D coverage bundled in, you should hold off using Plan Finder until you've read Chapter 8. It covers the Part D aspects of Plan Finder in detail, especially how to navigate plan formularies — the lists of drugs offered by different plans.

For now, I'll skip the Part D details, other than to note that Plan Finder gives you three plan choices for your area: MA health plans only, MA-PD plans that combine health and drug coverage, and stand-alone Part D plans.

Using the general ZIP code access, begin by entering your five-digit ZIP. Next, you'll see a screen that asks you two sets of questions. To keep things simple for now, just click on these two answers:

◉ I don't have any Medicare coverage yet
◉ I don't know

Plan Finder will then ask you which drugs you take. For now, skip this stage by clicking on the "I don't want to add drugs now" response. Plan Finder will want to make sure this is your intent and display a pop-up window. Just click on "Skip Drug Entry" and proceed to the fourth and most important step of the process.

On this screen, you'll see all the plans offered in your service area. (Remember that not all types of plans are offered in all areas.) You'll also be offered a large number of filters on the left side of the screen. These will let you pare down the overall list of available plans according to things like what they charge in monthly premiums, their star ratings, and plans offered by specific insurers. There also are some filters related to drug plans here. You can and should click on different sets of filters to see how they affect your plan choices.

When you see the set of plan choices that you think might work for you, you can select up to three at a time and Plan Finder will display them side by side in a comparative list. Look at the key cost variables mentioned above — premiums, copays, coinsurance, out-of-pocket maximums, and estimated annual plan costs to you.

After you've spent time with filters and various sets of plan choices, you'll still need more information on the plans than Plan Finder provides. For example, seeing that a plan offers some dental, hearing, or vision coverage is hardly enough information on which to make a purchase decision. You'll need coverage details from the plan. You also may have questions about whether your preferred doctors and other health care providers are in a plan's provider network. Make a list of these questions and then hit the plans' websites, call them, or both. Their phone numbers are listed in the display screens linked to the plan name at the top of each plan entry.

Before you call the plans, make a promise to yourself that you are not going to purchase a plan on one of these calls. You may be tempted. Remember how much these plans loved you when you turned 65? But you should still go through at least one more round of your personal "due diligence." Talk to friends and perhaps family members as well. Call SHIP or the Medicare Rights Center again if you need to.

Most people will be combining their MA choice with a linked drug plan, so check out the next chapter for what you'll want to know about the Part D part of this process.

I won't try to kid you. Making the best possible choice of an MA plan takes time and effort. But what's at stake is nothing less than your health and wealth, plus the satisfaction of knowing that you are doing as much as you can to take care of yourself and, well, to get all of what's yours.

And now, from the frying pan of MA, we

jump next into the fire of Part D drug plans. This chapter is not only at the physical center of *Get What's Yours for Medicare.* It's also at the heart of what you need to know to get the most health care from Medicare for the least possible amount of money.

8

MUGGED AND DRUGGED
PART D PRESCRIPTION PLANS

Take all the consumer frustrations about Medicare and sort them into two piles — one for prescription drug complaints and the other for every other real and perceived Medicare slight. I'm betting the Rx pile will be the larger of the two. We may appreciate our prescription drugs but there is no love lost on the companies that make them or the complex insurance system we must navigate to get them.

Lost somewhere here is the fact that we receive more than $110 billion a year in government subsidies to help pay for our Medicare drugs. You could assemble a long line of seniors and few if any would have a clue that they get so much federal largesse. It's also true that today's state of affairs is far, far better than it was before passage of the Medicare Prescription Drug, Improvement, and Modernization Act (MMA) of 2003, which created Medicare's Part D drug plans. Prior to that law, many seniors could not afford drugs and either skimped on prescriptions or simply went without medications.

Things are better today. Research finds fewer than 10 percent of Part D enrollees still cannot afford drugs and either cut up their pills themselves to economize or go without their meds. Of course, this still represents millions of people. What's also increasingly true is that Part D plans have turned into an enormous financial bonanza for the pharmaceutical industry. The 2003 law led to the federal government being the guaranteed payer of last resort for many drugs that Medicare beneficiaries cannot afford to buy. And it did so while tying the hands of Medicare by forbidding the agency from being able to use its enormous buying power to negotiate lower drug prices.

Today, if a drug is approved as medically necessary and Medicare agrees to pay for it, price literally is no object. The surge in miracle drugs — with equally miraculous price tags — has created rising pressure to change the way drugs are priced in the United States. We boast the unenviable record of having the world's highest drug prices. Even if these revenues are needed to provide incentives to researchers and their employers to continue discovering and producing breakthrough medications — and many people do not accept this premise — surely it is not fair that Americans must shoulder such a disproportionate load in paying for them. The same drugs we pay in full to buy are sold for less in other nations. There are many reasons for this but none so compelling as the fact that drug companies often are up against national governments around the world when it comes to pricing. Not here.

Leaving this rant for another day, let's focus on the Part D plans that 40 million seniors purchase every year. As we noted in Chapter 4, Part D plans are voluntary. But voluntary or not, if you are late in enrolling for a plan, you may be hit with lifetime penalties.

If you do get hit with Part D penalties, let me once again repeat them: 1 percent a month tacked on to the basic Part D premium for each month you're late in enrolling. For someone who comes four years late to their Part D plan, by way of example, that would be a 48 percent upcharge each and every month for the rest of your life, applied to that year's monthly benchmark premium for a typical Part D plan. The benchmark usually rises each year, and is

$34.10 in 2016.

There are two pathways into a Part D plan. Both require you to first get Original Medicare. You can then buy a stand-alone Part D plan, often called a PDP. Or, you can purchase a Medicare Advantage (MA) plan, most of which come bundled with a Part D plan, usually abbreviated as an MA-PD plan. Details on how the plans work follow, including what they cost, how to get help paying for them, the drugs offered by the private insurers who run Part D plans, the shifting role of pharmacists in providing drugs, and the details of how to use these plans to *Get What's Yours for Medicare.*

DRUGS FROM COLUMNS A, B, AND D

Before descending into the depths of Part D, it may be helpful to keep in mind that it is not the only Medicare program that helps pay for drugs. Drugs may also be dispensed in the hospital, where they will be covered by Part A of Medicare if you're an inpatient or even Part B if you're an outpatient. Likewise, some drugs provided to you in your doctor's office or other outpatient settings may be covered by Part B of Medicare.

There are separate annual deductibles for

Parts A and B. And 20 percent coinsurance rules may apply for Part B drugs. So don't assume that all your drugs are covered by your Part D plan. Ask *before* a drug is administered. The answer may not dissuade you from taking a drug, but at least you'll know what you're in for. Drug costs already are included in the payments that hospitals receive for treating you as an inpatient. But if you're an outpatient your drug costs will be billed to you separately, and could be higher than what you would pay through your Part D plan. If so, try to use your Part D plan, not Part B's insurance.

Also, remember that these Part A and Part B rules are included in MA plans as well. MA plans may have different deductibles and coinsurance. And MA-PD plans may be in a better position to help you keep track of which part of Medicare is covering your drugs in different situations. Again, it's important to ask first and not receive an unpleasant surprise later when your plan statement arrives.

OF MONEY, COVERAGE GAPS, AND DONUTS

Part D plans usually charge a monthly premium. There is an annual deductible as well, meaning you must pay all of the cost of drugs covered by your plan until you've met the deductible. In 2016, the maximum annual deductible allowed by Medicare is $360. Many plans charge less, although more plans are using the maximum deductible in response to higher drug prices.

After the deductible has been reached, your insurance kicks in and pays its share for covered drugs. You usually pay a share as well, which may be called a copay or coinsurance.

Then, in a departure from sanity, your insurance coverage just stops after you've reached a certain level of spending. This level includes the total of your annual deductible and what you and your plan have paid. At this point, you have entered the infamous coverage gap. It's also called the donut hole — a phrase that makes less sense every time I encounter it.

The spending level that triggers the coverage gap changes every year to reflect medical inflation. In 2016, it is $3,310. The coverage gap has an annual end point that also shifts each year. In 2016, it is $4,850. So, while in the donut hole, you must use drugs costing $1,540 before your insurance coverage resumes.

While in this gap, you have to pay all of the costs for your covered medications. Only you really don't. You will pay less for both branded and generic drugs. The percent reductions are different for the two. In one of many Medicare quirks, your savings on branded drugs are credited back toward what you have spent in determining the end point of the gap, while discounts on generic drug spending do not trigger this favorable credit.

Once you reach the end of the gap, you've reached the "catastrophic" phase of Part D coverage. Is this fun, or what?

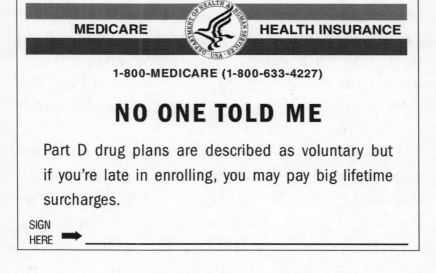

MEDICARE   HEALTH INSURANCE

1-800-MEDICARE (1-800-633-4227)

NO ONE TOLD ME

Part D drug plans are described as voluntary but if you're late in enrolling, you may pay big lifetime surcharges.

SIGN HERE ➡

LIKE THE WICKED WITCH, THE DONUT HOLE IS SHRINKING AWAY

The Affordable Care Act, passed in 2010, created a series of annual changes to the coverage gap that will eventually eliminate it in 2020. Here's how your annual drug payments will change in future years once you're in the gap:

	2016	2017	2018	2019	2020
You'll pay this percentage for brand-name drugs in the coverage gap	45	40	35	30	25
You'll pay this percentage for generic drugs in the coverage gap	58	51	44	37	25

The 25 percent payment levels reached in 2020 match the normal coinsurance payments you must make throughout the year in Part D plans until you reach the catastrophic phase of plan coverage.

CATASTROPHIC PAYMENTS ARE A CATASTROPHE FOR UNCLE SAM

Payments in the catastrophic phase of Part D plans are capped. You will pay only a few dollars per prescription or no more than 5 percent of the cost of the drug — whichever amount is *higher.* Catastrophic payments are often zero for people receiving financial help with their Part D expenses. Still, for most beneficiaries, 5 percent charges can mount in the case of really expensive drugs. Now, Part D plans often market themselves based on their annual out-of-pocket limits

191

on your drug expenses. Ceilings differ by plan and can be a major factor in choosing a plan in the first place. But these ceilings *do not* protect you from those 5 percent charges.

However, the bigger news in the catastrophic phase is not what you pay. If you pay no more than 5 percent, who pays the remaining 95 percent? Well, the Part D insurer must pay all of this, *except* (and it's a big except) the plan will receive a reinsurance payment from Medicare equal to 80 percent of the cost of the drug. This means the plan must pay, on net, only 15 percent of the cost of the drug.

Of course, it can take only a single expensive drug to blow through all of the stages of Part D coverage to trigger catastrophic payments. Rising drug prices are fueled by the surge of new costly drugs coming onto the market. But even generics and other longtime drugs have been jacking up their prices. Why? Because they can. With the pharmaceutical industry's pipeline full of literally thousands of such drugs, Uncle Sam's legal obligation to pay 80 percent of all catastrophic drug costs can't continue for long.

The financial imperative for change likely will be preceded by congressional action on all drug prices, driven by public outrage over not only prices for new miracle drugs but enormous increases on the prices of existing drugs, including many generics. The pace of congressional hearings had picked up steam by the time this book went to press. I'd like to say the current system will be replaced with one that is easier to understand, more transparent, and fairer to Medicare beneficiaries and taxpayers. Ha! How naïve of me.

PRICES FOR POPULAR STAND-ALONE PART D PLANS IN 2016

There's no doubt that rising drug prices are also making Part D plans more expensive for most people. Here's a look at the 2016 changes in the nation's most popular stand-alone (PDP) prescription drug programs, courtesy of Avalere Health, a consulting firm. People with Original Medicare (Parts A and B) buy stand-alone plans. These 10 plans enroll more than 80 percent of all Medicare buyers of stand-alone plans:

NAME	CURRENT ENROLLMENT	2015 AVERAGE PREMIUM MONTHLY	2016 AVERAGE PREMUIM MONTHLY	PERCENT CHANGE
AARP MedicareRx Preferred (UnitedHealthCare)	3,487,742	$50.18	$60.79	21
SilverScript Choice (CVS Health)	3,298,354	$23.21	$22.56	-3
Humana Preferred Rx Plan	1,709,973	$26.40	$28.39	8
Humana Walmart Rx Plan	1,510,530	$15.87	$18.40	17
AARP MedicareRx Saver Plus (UnitedHealthCare)	1,387,909	$28.00	$35.23	26
Humana Enhanced	1,142,405	$52.81	$66.25	25
Cigna-HealthSpring Rx Secure	927,930	$31.33	$36.39	16
WellCare Classic	871,781	$31.46	$32.06	2
Aetna Medicare Rx Saver	668,500	$24.40	$26.22	7
First Health Part D Value Plus (Coventry)	602,645	$38.92	$33.91	-13

These averages can be misleading. According to a Part D study[1] by the Kaiser Family Foundation, there are big swings in premium shifts among these popular plans depending on where you live. Looking at the three most popular plans, Kaiser found that the AARP Medicare RX Preferred premium increases in individual states ranged from 9 to 37 percent. The swing for SilverScript was even wider, from a 36 percent drop to a 24 percent hike. Premiums for the Humana Preferred plan fell 18 percent in some markets while rising 29 percent in others.

TOURING THE LANDSCAPE OF OUTRAGEOUSLY EXPENSIVE DRUGS

As noted, Uncle Sam pays much of the bill for top-priced specialty drugs. The "good" news, if you want to call it that, is that Medicare consumers' out-of-pocket share for such drugs is usually less than 10 percent of their cost. Here's a look, again by Kaiser, at 2016 Medicare Part D drug plan costs for a dozen expensive meds:

DRUG	COST MEDIAN ANNUAL	OUT-OF-POCKET MEDIAN ANNUAL
Sovaldi	$84,925	$6,608
Harvoni	$95,541	$7,153
Viekira Pak	$82,936	$6,516
Avonex	$64,074	$5,979
Copaxone	$73,922	$6,448
Tecfidera	$69,393	$6,235
Orencia	$38,407	$4,413
Humira	$42,059	$4,864
Enbrel	$41,499	$4,872
Revlimid	$182,973	$11,538
Gleevec	$122,804	$8,503
Zytiga	$97,025	$7,227

Costs for these drugs don't vary much among the plans checked by Kaiser. That was the case as well with popular branded and generic drugs. But Kaiser did find that drugs available but not listed in plan formularies often carried large mark-ups.[2]

NEIGHBORHOOD PHARMACISTS VS. THE MACHINE

The insurers who run Part D plans don't like high drug prices, either. Even though their cost exposure is only 15 percent — remember, you pay 5 percent at most and Uncle Sam pays 80 percent — they would like it to be 15 percent of the smallest number possible. And it's not Big Pharma that takes the calls and emails from unhappy Part D customers. The heat is directed at the plans. So, to become as efficient as possible, and with Medicare unable to negotiate lower drug prices, the health plans have stepped up to try to boost their leverage with drug companies.

Pharmacies have become an important part of this strategy. Pharmacy benefit managers (PBMs) have become nearly as large as the Part D insurers themselves. Health plans and pharmacies have done more than just partner. UnitedHealthcare even went out and acquired its own PBM. CVS Health is moving the other way, using its powerful pharmacy network as the channel to provide an expanding array of health services.

As a result, Part D plans usually include a preferred pharmacy network. Filling prescriptions through the network generally will be cheaper, especially for mail orders, than going outside the network to another pharmacist. This trend makes it important for you to understand the pharmacy rules in any Part D plan you are considering. Are you restricted to a certain pharmacy provider for your plan's prescriptions? What happens if you want to fill a prescription elsewhere?

From a business standpoint, insurer-pharmacy networks also can boost bargaining power with pharmaceutical companies. Now we have only a handful of big health insurers, all of whom have tightened their pharmacy supply chains. Novartis, Roche, Pfizer, and other Big Pharma firms are seeing fewer and more powerful customers across the negotiating table.

The push toward big and preferred networks of pharmacies is hard on many independent neighborhood pharmacists. They don't have the efficiencies and scale of PBMs or larger pharmacy chains. Increasingly, they don't have the powerful information tools that big chains and PBMs are using. From 2004 to 2014, the number of independent pharmacies dropped nearly 10 percent to about 22,500, according to the National Community Pharmacists Association. It says there is no doubt independents are being hurt by industry consolidation and the growth of proprietary pharmacy networks.

NEW HEALTH CARE MANTRA: PREDICTIVE ANALYTICS

Express Scripts, based in St. Louis, is the nation's largest independent PBM, and fills prescriptions for more than 85 million health plan customers in and out of Medicare. Express Scripts knows what drugs these people are being prescribed and, over time, knows which drugs they take and which they don't. It has assembled individual profiles of each of these 85 million consumers, and tracks 400 variables that not only reveal what people have done with their prescription meds but also, the company believes, predict what people will and won't do, and their future health outcomes.

The company says it "weighs dozens of factors — ranging from a patient's age, geography, and marital status, to prior prescription records and physician's profile — to determine with 94 percent accuracy whether that patient will take his medication as prescribed. By comparison when asked, patients themselves correctly predict their own future nonadherence just 10 percent of the time."[3] It also analyzes speech patterns in its call-center traffic to identify follow-up needs. Other PBMs have similar "predictive analytics" capabilities.[4]

WHAT HAPPENS WHEN YOU DON'T TAKE YOUR MEDS

Part D plans and their pharmacy networks also hate high drug prices because of the strong relationship between drug expenses and how well people follow their prescription instructions. Higher prices lead to higher non-adherence, and non-adherence, of course, leads to less healthy Medicare beneficiaries. Over time, people who don't take their meds, or don't take them in the proper doses or frequencies, not only will hurt themselves but also can generate higher health care costs and lower profits for insurers.

Here's a look at the worse non-adherence "offenders" in 2014, based on Express Scripts' research: heartburn or ulcers, 54–68 percent; asthma, 55 percent among adults; mental and neurological matters, 42 percent; depression, 40 percent; and, diabetes, 39 percent.[5]

FINDING THE RIGHT FORMULA(RY) FOR YOUR DRUGS

What good is a drug plan if it doesn't include the drugs you and your doctors think you need? A plan's list of drugs, called a formulary, is one of the first stops you should make in evaluating a Part D plan. Individual plans are required to send their formularies to you if you request one. This is usually something you can accomplish online. Be persistent. Links to plan formularies may be hard to find. In the Notes you will find the formulary links that big Part D insurers provided me for the 2016 open enrollment process: Aetna,[6] Anthem,[7] Cigna,[8] Coventry (part of Aetna),[9] Humana,[10] Kaiser Permanente,[11] and United-Healthcare.[12,13]

Instead of looking through what often can be a 200-page document, you could call each insurer and ask if the drugs you take are included in a plan's formulary, and what the plan charges for each drug you take by name and dosage. Again, you can get this information in most cases by using tools on each plan's website, but Medicare's Plan Finder[14] is the easiest way to see how all the plans in your ZIP code handle your drugs.

Plan Finder permits you to enter your

formulary information once and then the software will sort through available plans and tell you roughly what a year's worth of these drugs will cost you. You can set up a password-protected account to do this. It will take a bit more time than general research but you then will be able to return to your account, change your drug list as needed, and run a comparative analysis of available drug plans in a snap. Make sure you include your preferred pharmacy choices here, so that you can see whether a plan works with your pharmacy and how this may affect costs.

Drug plans also have star ratings from Medicare,[15] as mentioned in the last chapter. These ratings can guide you to the best plans. Even if you don't base your purchase decision on such quality ratings, they can help you pare down the number of plans that you seriously evaluate.

FORMULARIES MAY CHANGE, EVEN WITHIN A PLAN YEAR

Rick from Vermont says that one of his drugs will not be covered on his plan next year.

My plan sent me its complete formulary that was dated last October, but when I went to renew my plan in late November, Medicare's Plan Finder said it was not covered. Can the company decide to not cover a drug this way?

Unfortunately, usually it can. Medicare drug plans are not supposed to remove drugs from their plan during the year. But there are many grounds for changing their formularies on short notice. Perhaps a cheaper generic version of the drug becomes available. Or the drug's maker raises its price, causing the plan to favor a cheaper alternative. Or the drug is in short supply. And while the formulary may have been dated October 1, odds are it was filed with Medicare the previous spring.

However, you have the right to appeal this change. Should your prescribing physician attest to the clinical need for you to continue taking this particular drug, the plan may have to cover it, even if it has been removed from the plan formulary. Further, plans just can't cut you off cold turkey. They are supposed to provide you a transitional supply of any drug that has been removed from the plan.

WHY WE'RE ALL IN THE INSURANCE POOL TOGETHER

Janice, who lives in Illinois, is part of a rising tide of people of all ages who are fed up with high drug prices.

> I'm totally tired of overpaying for my prescription drug coverage right now and for the last four years. I currently use only three cheap generics. I'm thinking of dropping Medicare Part D coverage entirely and going with a retail pharmacy discount plan with a $20 annual enrollment fee.

Healthy people with insurance wind up subsidizing sicker people with insurance. That's the concept and reality of putting people into large risk pools, which is what Medicare (and the Affordable Care Act) do. Otherwise, only sick people would get insurance and their rates would be unaffordable. Having said that, I'm with you, Janice; drug prices are out of hand and it's time for Congress to give Medicare stronger tools to negotiate with pharmaceutical companies over prices.

For now, however, I would advise you not to end Part D coverage. If you do, you will face potentially stiff premium surcharges should you ever need Part D again. And, as you get older, the odds grow that you will need this coverage. These surcharges will raise your Part D premiums by 1 percent for each month you've been without Part D coverage. These surcharges can be substantial if you've been without a plan for a long time, and the surcharges last for as long as you have a Part D plan. Instead of leaving Part D, use this year's open enrollment period to find a plan with lower premiums. So long as your drug use remains modest, you will pay less, and by staying in Part D, you won't later incur any of those nasty surcharges.

WHY PART D PLANS MOVE US TO TIERS

Drug plans generally have to provide at least two drugs in every major drug category, Medicare says, including "almost all drugs within these protected classes: antipsychotics, antidepressants, anticonvulsants, immunosuppressants, cancer, and HIV/AIDS drugs." In other categories, the choices of which specific drugs they can offer usually are up to the plans.

Although Medicare is banned from negotiating with pharmaceutical companies about prices, drug plans do negotiate, as mentioned earlier. There is no set price for these meds. So, different plans will have different drug costs, and they may reflect these differences in the prices they charge members of their drug plans.

The plans have created multiple pricing categories called tiers within their plans. They assign drugs to different tiers and charge different copays within each tier. This is the key takeaway here for beneficiaries. (That's you, by the way, although in some cases I'm sure you wonder what the heck you're benefiting from.)

Usually, the first or lowest tier contains widely prescribed generic drugs that often have no copay requirement. Next up is a second tier that often contains what are called nonpreferred generics (nonpreferred usually equals more expensive). Tier three would be for preferred brand drugs and tier four for nonpreferred brand drugs. Tier five would contain those expensive specialty drugs — the ones that threaten to bankrupt you and sink Medicare's financial boat as well. Some plans even have a tier six that contains still more-rarefied specialty drugs.

Here's a look at a typical set of Medicare drug plan tiers from UnitedHealthcare:

	PREFERRED RETAIL 30-DAY SUPPLY	STANDARD NETWORK 30-DAY SUPPLY	PREFERRED MAIL ORDER 90-DAY SUPPLY
Tier One: Preferred Generics	$2 copay	$4 copay	$0 copay
Tier Two: Nonpreferred Generics	$5 copay	$10 copay	$5 copay
Tier Three: Preferred Brand Drugs	$40 copay	$45 copay	$115 copay
Tier Four: Nonpreferred Brand Drugs	$80 copay	$85 copay	$235 copay
Tier Five: Specialty Drugs	33% cost	33% cost	33% cost

This simple table, of course, is not so simple. It reflects the enormous price hits from more expensive drugs. And it shows the way plans are using pharmacy networks to control costs. Again, eternal vigilance is the message of the day.

Another crucial bit of consumer intelligence here is that different plans may place the identical drug in different tiers within their plans. This is their right. So, don't assume the different plans available where you live will adopt the same pricing approaches to the same drugs in their formularies.

YES, WE HAVE NO BANANAS (BUT FINE PRINT IS ALWAYS IN STOCK)

Once you know a plan has the drugs you need, and once you know what these drugs will cost, you might think you'd be done with your due diligence. Ha! No soup for you!

Plans have the authority to attach three major conditions that could affect using the drugs you want:

Prior authorization. The doctor or other health care professional prescribing your drug may be required to demonstrate to the plan that a drug is medically necessary before the plan will fill a prescription for the medication.

Step therapy. If your doctor prescribes a specific drug, the plan may require you to take a less expensive drug that has been shown effective for your condition. In some cases — mostly if you switch to a new Part D plan — Medicare rules say that the plan must first give you a supply of the drug your doctor prescribed, allowing you time to come up with a less costly substitute that is in the plan's formulary. If your doctor feels that only the prescribed drug will work for you, she or he can file a request for what's called an *exception.* If the plan grants the request, you can get the drug. If not, you can appeal this decision. In most cases, especially for conditions that are *not* immediately life threatening, you should expect to need to take the less expensive drug first, see how it works, and then file an exception request later based on your doctor's assessment that the cheaper drug is not doing the job for you.

Quantity limits. Plans can set limits on how much of a prescribed drug you actually receive. The most common reasons for such limits are if the drug is addictive or if the recommended treatment period is brief, such as for a course of antibiotics.

HERE'S ONE MORE NEW MEDICARE DRUG RULE

Beginning in June 2016, Part D plans can't pay for prescriptions unless they're written by a prescriber who has enrolled in Medicare or received an exemption from the agency. There are protections for consumers, including your right to a provisional supply of a medication prescribed by a non-enrolled provider. Still, this rule is likely to cause confusion. For example, it will apply to prescriptions from dentists and many other prescribers who don't regularly enroll in Medicare. Before you fill one of these prescriptions, ask the healthcare provider writing it if they are enrolled in Medicare.

ONCE YOU'RE SET, DON'T ASSUME YOU'RE SET

The formulary of a Part D plan this year can change next year, so don't assume a terrific plan for you in 2016 will be terrific in 2017. Medicare has an annual planning cycle aimed at requiring plans to create new editions of themselves every year. After insurers bid for the right even to offer Part D plans in the following year, they must work with Medicare on what their plans will look like. Plan specifics — rates, covered services, formularies, and other details — can and usually do change from year to year.

Medicare open enrollment begins each year on October 15 and extends through December 7. Every existing Medicare beneficiary can switch plans during open enrollment. In theory, it's a great way to maximize consumer choice and force plans to continually improve themselves. In practice, as noted earlier, people tend to stick with the plan they have, despite overwhelming evidence that they would be better off switching.

Even if consumers are slow to change their behaviors, this annual renewal cycle provides Medicare an effective mechanism to pressure plans to make improvements as well as institute the many changes in Medicare coverage and medical treatment rules that invariably occur each year.

By the time open enrollment rolls around, then, plans have locked into these specifics. And they gear their related marketing efforts to selling Part D plans during this period. Having set the terms of their coverage for the next calendar year, they are supposed to honor these terms and not make significant plan changes during the year. If you buy a plan during open enrollment, you are *supposed* to have a solid idea of the drug coverage you'll have the following year and what it will cost you. If you're wondering why *supposed* was italicized, read on.

ONCE YOU'RE SET AGAIN, DON'T ASSUME YOU'RE SET, PART II

Newcomers to Medicare and Part D plans do not sign up during open enrollment but during their own initial enrollment periods or, as we've seen, any number of special enrollment periods. These are defined based on when they turn 65, when their group employer coverage ends, or other qualifying events. And these periods seldom coincide with the open enrollment period.

If you are in this boat, you need to be aware that new drugs appear and existing drugs may move from branded to generic status. The same drug may move to a more expensive pricing tier. Plans battling outrageous drug prices may try to drop a drug from their formularies, although Medicare normally bans such midyear changes. New studies and cumulative results of drug consumption can change recommended prescription practices. This is not a static world.

Despite their best efforts, Part D plans may have trouble keeping up with the details of which drugs they actually include in their formularies and the pricing details of these medications. Even if this information is known and resides in a centralized database, a plan's public marketing materials may not always change quickly enough to stay current with plan changes. Its brokers and other plan sellers may not even be aware of all the changes.

My point here is not to scare you away from Part D plans or to cast these insurers or pharmacy benefit managers as bad guys. It's to emphasize that there are thousands and thousands of drugs in a typical plan's formulary, and that formularies are changing all the time. And it's especially to emphasize that you — and your doctors and those you turn to for medical guidance — need to be vigilant (there's that word again) before you buy a plan.

And your vigilance does not end here. If you buy a plan in, say, June, your insurer may have limited rights to change its formulary later in the plan year. But the odds are high that numerous formulary changes will be adopted in the formulary it publishes each fall for next year's open enrollment season.

To repeat if not belabor, just because a plan's formulary meets your needs this year does not mean it will meet them next year. Medicare does gives you the right to freely change drug plans every year. I'm urging you to take advantage of this right, and to make sure you have the best plan possible come next January 1. This decision often hinges on plan formularies.

WHY ARGUING OVER ADVERSE DRUG RULINGS IS A GOOD STRATEGY

If your plan makes formulary or other coverage changes during a plan year, and these changes adversely affect you, here are some things you can do:

If a plan does discontinue your drug it must give you 60 days' written advance notice.

If you and your prescribing physicians say you need expensive medications, or think you might, you should take advantage of your rights under Medicare to find out ahead of time if such drugs are covered by a plan. Ask your plan for what's called a "coverage determination." The plan must explain whether the drug you wish to take is covered by the plan, whether you've met any plan requirements to be eligible to take the drug, what it will cost, and, strangely enough, whether you and your prescribing doctor should seek a waiver of plan rules.

This waiver is called an exception and can be one of the most effective consumer rights that you have. You can ask for an exception to take a drug not included in your plan formulary, an exception to your plan's decision not to let you use a drug that is in their formulary, an exception to the plan's prior authorization or step therapy rules, and an exception to ask that it move your requested drug into a lower-cost plan tier.

Requesting an exception ahead of time is your way of effectively promoting your interests *before* getting embroiled in a more formal and extensive appeals process.

Plans and pharmacies approve an awful lot of exception requests. Competing insurers and plans would love to see this information. I've been trying for nearly two years to get hard data on exceptions but Medicare won't tell me, and individual insurers are not keen to part with it. If their exception approval rates were seen as low, they would get hammered for being heartless. If they were seen as being high, that might encourage more requests. I'm not saying anarchy would prevail in Plan D Land. But the plans just don't want to go there.[16]

Part D plans also have appeals procedures. I'll get into them in Chapter 10. But you should know here that there is a process for you to get expedited or fast appeals heard by your plan when it denies your request for coverage of a drug.

If you and your doctor feel this drug is essential to your health or even life, contact your Part D drug plan. You (and by "you" I mean you, your representative, your doctor, or whoever else might have prescribed the drug in question) have the right to seek a fast decision within 24 hours. The plan is supposed to honor this request if your prescribing physician tells the plan that waiting as long as 72 hours for a ruling could trigger serious adverse health consequences.

Part D plans also permit what are called "standard coverage determinations" that put the plan on the clock. Once it has received this form,[17] the insurer has 72 hours to let you know its decision about requested drug prescriptions and 14 calendar days if your determination request involves money you think your plan owes you. These determination requests also may be labeled exceptions to the plan's rules, and are often described as such.

MTMs FOR PDPs AND MA-PDs

The above initial-ese introduces the use of what are called Medication Therapy Management (MTM) programs for people with stand-alone Part D (PDP) and Medicare Advantage (MA-PD) drug plans who have multiple chronic conditions, take lots of meds for these problems, and take meds that in 2016 cost more than $3,507 a year. I bet that's what you thought, right?

Anyway, all Part D plans are required to offer an MTM, but I'm guessing the percentage of actual or prospective plan members who know about these programs hovers somewhere in the low single digits, if that high. The percentage of their doctors who know about them is, I hope, a lot higher. But I am not filled with confidence.

An MTM will, at no cost to you, do as its name suggests. It will coordinate all the drugs you are taking, make sure they're needed and working properly, make sure they don't have any damaging interactions, provide review sessions with doctors, pharmacists, or other care providers, and put it all in writing so that you know what meds you're taking and why you're taking them. And it will also address questions you might have about your program. Just to clarify, however, MTMs do not pay for your meds. That's still on you and your insurance.

Your Part D plan will enroll you in its program if you qualify. Unfortunately, but not surprisingly, the rules for qualifying are not the same among all Part D plans. They have different lists of qualifying chronic conditions and different thresholds for the number of drugs you must be taking to qualify. And that $3,507 spending floor is a number only a bureaucrat could love.

Still, MTM plans can be a real benefit, providing the kind of informed oversight that beneficiaries and their family members need to stay on top of what often are challenging juggling acts with medications. This is a great example of why SHIP offices, the Medicare Rights Center, area agencies on aging, and a host of other senior nonprofits are needed. Call or email them for more information.

HELP FROM STATES, PHARMACIES, AND DRUG COMPANIES

Rising drug prices are a growing national problem, if not a scourge. What good is it to have all these wonderful medications — and a development pipeline crammed with thousands of new specialty drugs — if the people whose lives they can extend or save can't afford to take them? Yet, we know this is the case. Many consumers, even those with Part D plans, can't afford their drugs. You've already read about the high human cost of non-adherence to prescribed drug routines.

Individual states may have safeguards that can provide you tools to improve your access to medications and help shield you from problems caused by the rules of your Part D drug plan. SHIP programs are a great resource here, as their roughly 15,000 volunteer counselors around the country are trained in state and local Medicare rules where you live. If you have any problems, call your local SHIP office.[18]

State Pharmaceutical Assistance Programs (SPAPs) exist in many states.[19] They provide a range of drug subsidy and discount programs.

Finally, many pharmaceutical companies have assistance programs to help people. Medicare has an online tool with extensive details on supports for individual drugs.[20] If your drug is not listed, contact its manufacturer directly to see if any assistance is available.

DISCOUNT COUPONS
NOT WELCOME IN MEDICARE

Readers of "Ask Phil" do not understand why Medicare will not accept the discount coupons that drug companies issue and which are otherwise widely accepted by pharmacies. I'm with them. If a drug company wants to subsidize the price that Medicare pays for a drug, and if the drug is medically appropriate and prescribed by your doctor, why not approve its use in Medicare?

Just so you know, drug discounts are viewed by Medicare as kickbacks and are therefore illegal. The logic is that such a discount could encourage a Medicare beneficiary to use a drug that costs more than a perfectly acceptable alternative. If Medicare thinks consumers or their prescribing health care providers will be improperly swayed by drug discounts, you'd think it could come up with other ways to deal with this problem. And don't even get me started on consumer drug ads. It is and should be a free country, but these ads bother me a lot. They can mislead consumers and create demand for expensive drugs of questionable therapeutic value. And don't forget: Uncle Sam may be paying 80 percent of the price.

There is nothing that requires you to use

your Part D plan when a prescription discount coupon could get you the medications you want for less money. Any money you spend on drugs in this situation will not, however, be part of your Part D record, and won't count toward satisfying annual out-of-pocket limits on drug spending within Part D.

MORE HELP WITH PART D DRUGS AND PRICES

There are loads of programs to help Medicare beneficiaries with drug needs that either can't be met by their Part D plans or consumers simply can't afford. If you're facing a 33 percent copay on a drug that costs thousands of dollars a month (or a dose!), it will not take long before your finances are drained, even with catastrophic insurance protection. A biopsy of your wallet quickly will confirm that it died of money starvation!

Medicare has large financial assistance programs. The main program for drugs is called Extra Help.[21] There is a broader set of Medicare Savings Programs[22] that help cover other Medicare expenses. These important supports are explained in depth in the next chapter, which deals with the enormous, and enormously complex, maze

of Medicare supports, income-based benefits, and premium surcharges. As always,
please join me and read on.

9
MEDICARE MONEYBALL
FINANCIAL HELP AND PITFALLS

With a basic understanding of Medicare taken care of, we can finally get to the money. Before digging in to personal pocketbook issues, there are important national Medicare pocketbook issues you need to understand.

MEDICARE'S GREAT RAID ON THE U.S. TREASURY

There is a myth afoot in the land that consumers have completely paid for their Medicare because they fork over 1.45 percent of their pretax wages in Medicare payroll taxes, an amount matched by their employers. The payroll taxes that go to Social Security actually do support all of that program, but in the case of Medicare, our payroll taxes come nowhere close to paying for program expenses.

During 2014, the most recent full year covered by official government reports, nearly $600 billion flowed into Medicare and an even larger amount flowed out — $613 billion. Of this $600 billion, how much do you think came from payroll taxes? If you said less than half, you get to keep playing the Medicare money game. Medicare collected $227 billion in payroll taxes in 2014, or about 38 percent of its revenues. That leaves $373 billion unaccounted for.

Premiums represent our dollars, too, so perhaps adding what we pay in Medicare premiums will justify the notion that we pay for Medicare. What do you think? Sixty percent? Fifty? Forty? Thirty? How about 21.5 percent, which translates into $80 billion in Medicare premiums.

It turns out that Medicare payroll taxes fully fund Part A hospital expenses (together with your share of uncovered Part A expenses) but that is literally where the buck stops. Expenses for Parts B, C (Medicare Advantage or MA), and D (prescription drugs) are paid mostly by Uncle Sam, to the tune of nearly $250 billion. And this is, by the way, not a fixed line item in the federal budget but more of a blank check every year.

So, while I not only support and respect seniors, and in fact have become a member of the seniors' club myself, please do not attempt to blow smoke on me or anyone else by saying that you've paid for your Medicare. You haven't, and I haven't either. I happen to think my tax dollars are *relatively* well spent by Medicare and that supporting the health needs of older Americans is one of the best things this country and government do. But it doesn't come close to paying for itself, and the gap will get larger and larger as baby boomers inevitably succumb to the realities of aging bodies and rising health care expenses. This doesn't mean I support cutting Medicare benefits. Far from it. Today's seniors deserve quality health care.

MEDICARE'S GREAT RAID ON WEALTHIER TAXPAYERS

If you are a wealthier taxpayer, you get a double Medicare hit. You pay more in Medicare payroll taxes because you earn more (recall that, unlike Social Security, there is no wage ceiling on Medicare taxes). But you also pay more in Medicare Part B and Part D premiums, and this enforced tithing will get worse, beginning in 2018.

In April 2015, Congress passed what was popularly known as the "doc fix" bill (its formal name is the Medicare Access and CHIP Reauthorization Act, or MACRA). It overturned a well-intentioned but ultimately unworkable effort to permit annual increases in Medicare's physician payment rates only if overall economic growth exceeded the rate of health care inflation. The thinking was that the earlier measure's use of what was called the "sustainable growth rate" would help restrain the upward pressure on doctors' rates and combat health care inflation. Instead, during the measure's nearly 20-year life, the economy seldom grew as rapidly as health care costs, and the law mandated annual cuts in doctors' Medicare payments. Rather than go through with the reductions, Congress each year would fashion a "doc fix" — an eleventh-hour funding bill to void the cut.

Getting rid of the fix did not come cheap — a projected $160 billion increase in federal deficits over 10 years, plus higher Medicare premiums for some beneficiaries, which are explained later in this chapter.

AND, OF COURSE, THE GREAT MONEY RAID ON YOU

We still are in the early stages of peeling back the many layers of the onion labeled "Medicare health care provider" costs. For the past several years now, the Centers on Medicare & Medicaid Services have released a growing inventory of Medicare claims information detailing what doctors and hospitals charge for various health procedures around the country. We also know how much money drug companies have been paying to physicians. We can see the relationships between these payments and the prescription patterns of physicians who receive Big Pharma payments. In the worst situations, they seem like payoffs, but much more work needs to be done here. These newly released databases are enormous, and as interesting as they are, they also lack many details needed to create truly actionable cause-and-effect linkages. However, it's just a matter of time before these linkages are established beyond a doubt.

As health care hurtles toward such game-changing capabilities, however, consumer empowerment lags far behind. To date, there is little evidence that we pay much attention.[1] Studies show that when consumers do know the true costs of health care, they don't engage in comparison shopping so much as simply cut back their use of health care.

For interested consumers, there are many health pricing tools. For starters, I recommend *The Wall Street Journal*'s "Medicare Unmasked" tools,[2] although they may be behind a paywall. The Health Care Cost Institute[3] is a health-insurer funded effort to compare the cost of various procedures around the country.[4] ProPublica, a non-profit news site, is one of several consumer sites that has used the CMS databases to build tools that are not exactly beloved by health care providers, including Dollars for Docs[5] and Surgeon Scorecard.[6]

Increasingly, CMS itself will be providing more pricing transparency. And individual state efforts are also underway, such as the Consumer Reports partnership with California to produce California Healthcare Compare.[7]

And now, on to Medicare Moneyball.

IRMAA — NOT A LADY YOU'RE LIKELY TO FORGET

IRMAA is the acronym for "income-related monthly adjustment amount," which is the set of income-based surcharges in Medicare Part B and Part D premiums.[8] These surcharges can take a real bite out of your income, especially for people who experience one-time surges in income from say, selling a home, and get snared in IRMAA's net.

The surcharges only affect higher-income earners, and perhaps we shouldn't shed too many tears for people whose taxable retirement incomes are above $170,000 a year ($85,000 for single filers). But I've heard from many frustrated readers who have been blindsided by these charges.

By way of background, the measure of income used in the IRMAA rules is called modified adjusted gross income, or MAGI. It consists of adjusted gross income (AGI), which taxpayers are used to seeing on their tax returns. Adding tax-exempt interest income (from, say, municipal bonds) to AGI produces MAGI. The other key thing about IRMAA is that any IRMAA charges this year will be based on your tax returns of two years ago. So, for 2016 IRMAA obligations, use your 2014 tax returns. This lag, by the way, reflects how long it takes Social Security to get and process IRS tax-return records.

Mike writes:

I am currently 59 and on Social Security Disability Insurance. I had lottery winnings in 2014 and now find my Medicare premiums are being raised a lot in 2016. Can they do this to me? Chop away my monthly payments because I won money? Is there anything I can do? If I don't win any money next year, will the government see this and reduce my premiums back to their regular levels? Since my Medicare Part B went up, will I be able to claim that as an expense on my itemized tax deductions?

The lottery is not good luck when it comes to Medicare premiums. Winning the lottery is normally not the basis for challenging an IRMAA surcharge.[9] Your higher Part B expenses *are* tax-deductible as a health care expense, but remember that the threshold for these deductions was raised from 7.5 percent to 10 percent of taxable income under the Affordable Care Act. But Mike's surcharges will disappear when his income returns to normal.

CURRENT IRMAA SURCHARGES FOR PARTS B AND D

Keep in mind that the basic 2016 Part B premium for people who are held harmless and earning less than $85,000 ($170,000 for joint filers) is $104.90. MA plans are free to reduce this premium if they choose, and some plans actually pay part or even all of your Part B premium to Medicare. There is no basic Part D premium, as drug plans are free to set their own premiums. However, whatever your Part D premium is, you will owe the additional monthly Part D amounts shown here.

2014 MAGI*	MONTHLY PART B PREMIUM	MONTHLY PART D** SURCHARGE
$85,001 to $107,000	$170.50	$12.70
$107,001 to $160,000	$243.60	$32.80
$160,001 to $214,000	$316.70	$52.80
$214,001+	$389.80	$72.90

There are separate brackets for married folks who file separate returns:

2014 MAGI*	PART B PREMIUM	PART D** SURCHARGE
$85,000 to $129,000	$316.70	$52.80
More than $129,000	$389.80	$72.90

*Double for joint tax returns

**Plus your Part D premium

AND SOMETHING NOT NICE TO LOOK FORWARD TO

Just to wring a bit more from those who have more, the 2015 MACRA law will apply the higher IRMAA surcharges to more people, beginning in 2018:

2016 MAGI*	MONTHLY PART B PREMIUM	MONTHLY PART D** SURCHARGE
$85,001 to $107,000	$170.50	$12.70
$107,001 to $133,500	$243.60	$32.80
$133,501 to $160,000	$316.70	$52.80
$160,001+	$389.80	$72.90

*Double for joint tax returns

**Plus your Part D premium

These projections assume no change from this year's Part B premiums. The actual surcharges will be linked to future rates of inflation and could be a bit higher. But these four brackets must continue to recover roughly 35, 50, 65, and 80 percent of Medicare expenses. So, if you are in a higher income bracket when 2018 rolls around, just take that year's basic Part B premium (the one that is $121.80 this year) and multiply it by 1.4, 2, 2.6, or 3.2, depending on which of the four brackets applies to you.

For good measure, as if any was needed, these IRMAA brackets are frozen until 2020. Wage inflation, of course, has not ended, meaning that more and more Medicare beneficiaries have been making IRMAA tithes. Which, of course, was exactly the goal when the Affordable Care Act froze the brackets beginning in 2011.

HOLD HARMLESS RULE MAY NOT
HOLD YOU HARMLESS AT ALL

I wish I could say with certainty that these IRMAA surcharges are in fact the ones that you will face in 2017. Unfortunately, if not unsurprisingly, there's that "hold harmless" rule that has thrown a big monkey wrench into annual changes in Medicare premiums.

In 2016, Part B premiums are all over the place. About 70 percent of Medicare recipients pay $104.90 a month in Part B premiums — the lowest possible amount — and *also* have these premiums deducted from their monthly Social Security payments. In fact, if you're using Medicare and receiving Social Security, the law says this is the way Part B premiums must be paid.

Social Security's "hold harmless" rule says Social Security payments generally can't decline from one year to the next. This is terrific financial protection for Social Security recipients, but it can play havoc with Medicare, and did so in 2015. That's because there was no consumer inflation. In fact, led by falling gasoline prices, the consumer price index for urban wage earners was lower during the third quarter of 2015 than during the third quarter of 2014. The lack of inflation meant that there was no annual Cost of Living Adjustment, or

COLA, for Social Security in 2016.

Normally, the COLA raises Social Security benefits enough to permit Medicare to collect higher Part B premiums while allowing net Social Security benefits still to increase. But when there is a zero COLA, that 70 percent block of Social Security recipients is held harmless. This meant they could not be asked to pay higher Part B premiums in 2016, so that $104.90 premium remained unchanged for them.

However, and this is the painful part, Medicare still is required by its rules to collect about 25 percent of total Part B expenses from beneficiaries. These expenses were expected to rise substantially in 2016. Because the agency could not recoup these higher expenses from folks who have been held harmless, it had no choice but to seek them from the other 30 percent of beneficiaries not held harmless.

This group includes higher-income beneficiaries who pay IRMAA surcharges. It also includes people new to Medicare in 2016. They couldn't be held harmless because they had no Part B premiums to deduct from Social Security in 2015. The unlucky 30, as I call them, also included people on Medicare who had not yet begun claiming Social Security. They paid their Part B premiums directly to Medicare and could not be held harmless, either.

In *Get What's Yours* — the Social Security companion to this book — my coauthors and I urge people to defer collecting Social Security benefits until they reach their maximum level by age 70. Many of our readers have done exactly that, only to see their financial planning efforts rewarded with a big boost in Part B premiums because they are not held harmless. This is a flaw in the Social Security–Medicare system.

So, here is what Medicare decided to do about 2016 Part B income brackets and premiums for people *not* being held harmless. Keep in mind that your 2014 tax return usually will be used to determine 2016 Part B premiums:

INDIVIDUAL RETURN	JOINT RETURN	MONTHLY PREMIUM*
$85,000 or less	$170,000 or less	$121.80
$85,001 to $107,000	$170,001 to $214,000	$170.50
$107,001 to $160,000	$214,001 to $320,000	$243.60
$160,001 to $214,000	$320,001 to $428,000	$316.70
Above $214,000	Above $428,000	$389.80

*per beneficiary

People who pay Part B premiums and decide also to sign up for an MA plan must still pay Part B premiums. In some cases, their MA insurer will rebate some or all of the Part B premium. Make sure you check with your MA insurer and understand exactly how your MA plan handles Part B premiums.

These higher Part B premiums eventually should recede. There were no COLAs in 2010 and 2011, either, and the hold harmless provision raised the lowest Part B premium from $96.40 a month in 2009 to $110.50 in 2010 and $115.40 in 2011. With the reinstatement of a COLA in 2012, Medicare was once again able to spread the financial pain for Part B expenses to everyone, and the premium dropped to $99.90 a month.

The 2017 COLA and resulting Part B premiums will be announced in October 2016. Look for details at the *Get What's Yours for Medicare* website.[10]

HOW TO DEFEND YOURSELF FROM UNFAIR IRMAA CHARGES

Ralph, a reader in Tennessee, ran into IRMAA the hard way, when he sold his home and, two years later, got hit with hefty Part B and Part D charges. Of course, by the time he got hammered, his income already had declined to its normal retirement levels. "If you sell your home to move to another state to retire, does that raise the cost of your Medicare Part B for that year, and how is that fair?" he wrote. "Why do the proceeds from your house, a one-time event, put you into a high-income category?"

This added income will be flagged at some point in the IRMAA calculations. I'm on Ralph's side here. Such one-time gains like this distort Ralph's true income situation. Of course, IRMAA should jack up his Medicare premiums for only a single year. But still, unfair is unfair.

MEDICARE   HEALTH INSURANCE

1-800-MEDICARE (1-800-633-4227)

NO ONE TOLD ME

Medicare does not cover nonmedical long-term care needs.

SIGN
HERE ➡

There is an IRMAA appeals process designed to help people whose current incomes are substantially *less* than their two-year-old MAGI figure. There are eight specific "change of life" factors that might qualify someone for reconsideration of their IRMAA:

- Death of spouse
- Marriage
- Divorce or annulment
- Work reduction
- Work stoppage
- Loss of income from income-producing property
- Loss or reduction of certain kinds of pension income
- Employer settlement payout

Work stoppage, to translate, can include retirement. So if you've retired and your income declines in subsequent years, this new lower income level can be used to argue against an IRMAA charge that was based on one of your higher pre-retirement earnings years.

Having a tax return that is inaccurate or out of date is also grounds for an appeal. But there is no reference to any relief when your IRMAA income surged because of a one-time event such as the sale of a residence.

The appeals process must begin by asking Social Security to reconsider its initial IR-

MAA determination of your Medicare premium. This is done by filing Form SSA-561.[11] In a moment of understated modesty, the form lists only 39 separate reasons why someone would question an agency decision. Last but not least on this list, listed on the form under Title XVIII, is "Initial determinations regarding Medicare Part B income-related premium subsidy reductions."

2020 MONEY CHANGES FOR MEDIGAP POLICIES

These changes were explained in Chapter 6 but bear repeating. There are two Medigap policies — letter plans "C" and "F" — that cover the annual Part B deductible, which is $166 in 2016. Beginning in 2020, policies sold to new buyers of these plans will no longer be able to cover this deductible. The stated logic for the change is that Congress wanted Medicare beneficiaries to pay these deductibles directly so that they would feel like they had "more skin in the game" in terms of their health care expenses. Of course, if premiums for these Medigap policies decline to reflect their reduced coverage, or rise because only older Medicare beneficiaries continue to renew them, it's not clear how this change will shape consumer attitudes toward health care spending or whether "C" and "F" plans will survive. In the meantime, anyone who buys or owns one of these policies by the end of 2019 will continue to have Part B deductibles paid for them so long as they renew their policies in future years.

BE WARY OF
OUT-OF-NETWORK CHARGES

If you have an MA plan or any other kind of Medicare policy with network providers and approved rate schedules, you need to look out for what you could be charged by care providers who are not in your plan network.

America's Health Insurance Plans (AHIP), the major lobbying group for private health insurers, took a look in 2015 at what physicians around the country charged compared with Medicare's approved rates.[12] It examined nearly 100 medical procedures and compared Medicare and out-of-network charges in the same geographic markets. To be as fair as possible to doctors, there can be a lot of reasons why they charge more than the admittedly modest fees permitted by Medicare. So, I'm not slamming doctors here. What I am saying is that you need to watch for pricey out-

238

of-network fees — preferably *before* you receive one of these services.

Here are the fee variations for the 10 most commonly performed procedures:

PROCEDURE	AVERAGE 2014 MEDICARE FEE	AVERAGE 2013–2014 OUT-OF-NETWORK CHARGE
Therapeutic exercise	$33	$65
Manual therapy	$31	$66
Subsequent hospital care	$106	$239
Emergency room visit—high severity	$176	$971
Office outpatient visit—40 minutes	$147	$260
Tissue exam by pathologist	$72	$227
Critical care—first hour	$279	$795
Chemotherapy IV infusion—1 hour	$136	$437
Ultrasonic guide for biopsy	$76	$517
Upper GI endoscopy with biopsy	$413	$1,062

The AHIP report includes details for each state, so you can get a solid idea of out-of-network physician charges where you live.

WHAT MEDICARE TAKETH AWAY, MEDICARE CAN ALSO GIVETH BACK

Now, after having dwelled on how Medicare helps relieve us of our money, let's switch gears and focus on all the programs that help lower-income seniors and disabled people pay for their Medicare. The first of these is called "Extra Help" and is a key feature of Medicare that millions of beneficiaries already use but which millions more could qualify for if they knew about the program and how to use it.

The Medicare Part D Low Income Subsidy program, otherwise known as "Extra Help," assists people in paying their Medicare prescription drug bills. Those bills are so expensive that nearly 12 million people with a Part D Medicare drug plan, or about 30 percent of all Part D participants, receive low-income subsidies — $21 billion to help pay for drugs in 2014 and another $3.5 billion for premium subsidies.

Medicare enrollees with low incomes — as defined in reference to the federal poverty level — who qualify for maximum Extra Help support usually pay no premium or deductible for their Part D plans. Their total payment for drugs in 2016 can be no more than $2.95 for generics and $7.40 for brand-name drugs.[13] Payments are higher for people whose incomes are above the federal poverty level but still low enough to qualify for Extra Help. Unfortunately, Extra Help is not available in Puerto Rico, the U.S. Virgin Islands, Guam, the Northern Mariana Islands, and American Samoa.

As big as the Extra Help program has become, the Centers for Medicare & Medicaid Services (CMS) has estimated that as many as 2 million more Medicare enrollees qualify for this help but either don't know about it, think it doesn't apply to them, or simply haven't bothered to ask. They, or you, as the case may be, shouldn't rule it out.

Having looked at the Extra Help details, I think that another reason people haven't applied for it is that the rules for qualifying are so complicated, even lower-income rocket scientists would be deterred from making the effort. I'm going to provide a lot of these details, because I am naïve enough to still cling to the notion that people can do things for themselves if the guidance is clear enough. In reality, you may need to turn to counselors at the State Health Insurance Assistance Program (SHIP)[14] or the Medicare Rights Center.[15]

To qualify, your annual income must be less than $17,655 a year ($23,895 for a married couple).[16] But you can get an unlimited amount of money to help you pay for household expenses — from relatives, friends, or others — and it does not count as income so far as Extra Help is concerned. This is not, I should stress, a number linked to MAGI or lagged by two years, as is the case with IRMAA payments.

Extra Help has both income and resource

tests. The income test, as noted, is linked to the official federal poverty level (FPL). The FPL changes every year and also varies with family size. Alaska and Hawaii have separate FPLs due to their high costs of living. You will first need to see how your income compares with FPL amounts,[17] and then calculate the size of any Extra Help subsidy, which is based on this table:

COUNTABLE INCOME	PREMIUM SUBSIDY
Up to 135% of FPL	100%
More than 135% FPL, but not more than 140%	75%
More than 140% FPL, but not more than 145%	50%
More than 145% FPL, but less than 150%	25%
150% FPL or more	None

The Extra Help resource test[18] exists because, in theory, someone with a zillion dollars in investments could have no wage income and would qualify for Extra Help if there was no resource test. Resource ceilings are modest but they do not include your home, car, or personal possessions.

Here are the 2016 qualifying resource amounts[19] for individuals and married couples:

2016 RESOURCE LIMITS
FOR INDIVIDUALS

INDIVIDUAL'S COUNTABLE RESOURCES	INDIVIDUAL'S COUNTABLE INCOME	AMOUNT OF THE PREMIUM SUBSIDY
$7,280 or less	At or below 135% FPL	100%
$7,280.01 to $12,140	At or below 135% FPL	100% but less help with copays or deductibles
$12,140 or less	More than 135% of FPL, but at or below 140%	75%
$12,140 or less	More than 140% of FPL, but at or below 145%	50%
$12,140 or less	More than 145% of FPL, but less than 150%	25%
$12,140.01 or more	Any amount	Not eligible for subsidy

2016 RESOURCE LIMITS FOR
MARRIED COUPLES

COUPLE'S COUNTABLE RESOURCES	COUPLE'S COUNTABLE INCOME	AMOUNT OF THE PREMIUM SUBSIDY
$10,930 or less	At or below 135% FPL	100%
$10,930.01 to $24,250	At or below 135% FPL	100% but less help with copays or deductibles
$24,250 or less	More than 135% of FPL, but at or below 140%	75%
$24,250 or less	More than 140% of FPL, but at or below 145%	50%
$24,250 or less	More than 145% of FPL, but less than 150%	25%
$24,250.01 or more	Any amount	Not eligible for subsidy

There are other exclusions to the income and resource cutoffs, so even if you think you're too well-off to qualify for Extra Help, you may not be. This note has a couple of examples from Social Security that walk you through the calculations.[20]

Social Security handles applications for Extra Help. You can apply online[21] or call Social Security at 1-800-772-1213 (TTY users: 1-800-325-0778).

If you do plan to apply for Extra Help (there is no cost or obligation), you should first round up your personal financial information, tax returns, and details of any Social Security benefits you are receiving.

Also, if you earlier paid for drugs after you qualified for Extra Help but before it was approved for you, you might get some of this money back. Medicare's Limited Income Newly Eligible Transition Program[22] (literalness is highly valued in government work), at 1-800-783-1307, is the place to call. You will need receipts of your drug purchases.

ALL THE COLORS OF THE RAINBOW

Also, Extra Help is automatically provided to people on Medicare who also are on Medicaid, or who also collect Supplemental Security Income from Social Security. If this applies to you, you should not have to apply for Extra Help. The program will reach out to you, or at least it is supposed to. Medicare must have been suffering from Extra Silliness when it set up the Extra Help notification program. There is a complex color key provided by Medicare that explains the overwhelming number of Extra Help notices the agency sends out.[23]

The best way to proceed with Extra Help is to first figure out if you might qualify for it and then use Medicare's Plan Finder to choose the best Part D plan. They all work with Extra Help. Once you find a plan you like, call a representative and discuss the plan's process for enrolling in Extra Help and any other requirements or benefits it has.

MEDICARE SAVINGS PROGRAMS (MSPs)

Medicare offers four Medicare Savings Programs (MSPs)[24] to beneficiaries of modest means. They pay varying amount of Medicare premiums, copays, and deductibles. Like Extra Help, there are income and resource thresholds, and the definitions are similar to those used in Extra Help. MSPs are not available in Puerto Rico and the U.S. Virgin Islands. Many recipients are also eligible for Medicaid. The figures here are for 2015; you can find updates here.[25] Before applying for the programs, you should contact a SHIP representative familiar with your state, and see if there are any related or additional Medicare subsidies provided where you live.

Qualified Medicare Beneficiary (QMB)

Individual monthly income limit: $1,001

Married couple monthly income limit: $1,348

Helps pay Part A and Part B premiums and other costs (like deductibles, coinsurance, and copayments)

Specified Low-Income Medicare Beneficiary (SLMB)

Individual monthly income limit: $1,197

Married couple monthly income limit: $1,613

Helps pay Part B premiums only

Qualifying Individual (QI)

Individual monthly income limit: $1,345

Married couple monthly income limit: $1,813

Helps pay Part B premiums only

Qualified Disabled & Working Individual (QDWI)

Individual monthly income limit: $4,009

Married couple monthly income limit: $5,395
Helps pay Part A premiums only

Resource limits: The 2015 resource limits for the QMB, SLMB, and QI programs were $7,280 for one person and $10,930 for a married couple. Resource limits for the QDWI program were $4,000 for one person or $6,000 for a married couple. Countable resources include money in a checking or savings account, stocks, and bonds. When you count your resources, don't include your home, one car, a burial plot, up to $1,500 for burial costs if you've put that money aside, furniture, or other household and personal items.

A Bit of Caution About Income-Based Medicare Rules

When your income or financial situation changes, you need to consider the possible impact of such changes on your eligibility for Medicare subsidies. I have heard from too many readers who lost some of this help because they did not consider how extra income would affect these subsidies. It is hard to give specific advice here. Your own circumstances will govern the best course of action. But please think about possible impacts. And remember: you are supposed to tell Social Security if your income changes in a material way. Even if you don't, such changes likely will be reflected on future tax returns, and the IRS shares this information with Social Security.

OTHER MEDICARE MONEY SCORECARD ITEMS

Part B pays for outpatient services in hospitals. Rates are related to local wages and other factors under Medicare's outpatient prospective payment system. This means the agency will pay different amounts to different hospitals for the same services.

Don't assume your copay is a fixed dollar amount or a set percentage. Make sure you ask ahead of time to avoid unpleasant surprises.

Medicare has caps on outpatient therapy. In 2016, they are $1,960 for physical therapy and speech-language pathology combined, and another $1,960 for occupational therapy. If your provider certifies that continued therapy is medically necessary, Medicare generally will cover its share of therapy expenses above these caps. If spending exceeds $3,700 on either of the two areas, you may get audited by a Medicare contractor to make sure the therapy was medically required.

Many of us like fast cars, but ambulance rides? Not so much. However, life happens, and so does the need for an ambulance. Medicare certainly covers emergency ambulance use but there can be a gray area where the ambulance is helpful but may not be medically necessary, or you might have been able to reach a health care provider using less costly transportation. Proceed carefully in these situations, as you could get tagged with the entire bill. If time permits, some ambulance companies may ask Medicare for prior authorization to make sure a previously scheduled trip is covered. If an ambulance company does not think your request is "medically reasonable and necessary," it must provide you what's called an Advance Beneficiary Notice of Noncoverage, or ABN for short. If you still want to take the ambulance, you may have to pay the full amount and the company is within its rights to ask for payment before you take the ambulance. Speaking of ABNs, pay attention to them whenever you run across one.

Who pays first? Coordination of benefits was discussed briefly in Chapter 5. If you are in situations where expenses are covered by more than one insurer, make sure you understand which policy pays first. This situation can arise when you have more than one coverage, such as Medicare and retiree health insurance. But it also occurs if there are health expenses associated with an accident involving your auto or home insurance, or another person's accident insurance. Medicare may still pay for some of these expenses but it also may expect to be repaid by another insurance policy, and the responsibility for making sure this happens could fall to you under certain circumstances.

Mastering Medicare Moneyball is a big part of *Getting What's Yours for Medicare*. Another enormously important part of this process involves knowing how to stand up for yourself. This is hard enough in any health care setting but especially so when the process is governed by rules that you never knew existed or could possibly need to know. The good news here, as you'll find in the next chapter, is that Medicare has extensive consumer rights and safeguards. Learning how to use them may be essential to your health.

10
WHEN YOU'RE MAD AS HELL
MEDICARE RIGHTS AND APPEALS

The stories I shared with you in Chapter 1 — about Glen and Margie, Carol and Ernesto, and Phyllis — could have turned out differently if these people had known more about how to stand up for themselves with Medicare. So might many of the tales of people who write to "Ask Phil," often with sad and angry pleas for help.

Medicare does have extensive rules to protect the rights of beneficiaries and make sure they have access to the care they need, are treated with respect, given the chance to understand the medical advice and care instructions they receive, and allowed to ask whatever questions they have to make sure they receive the proper care, in the proper setting, and at the proper price.

These rights, however, are not exactly sitting out in the open and broadcasting their existence. You need to know them, or at least know in general that such rights exist.

251

And for far too many people, the doctor is definitely not in when it comes to consumer knowledge of beneficiary and patient rights.

As part of the research for *Get What's Yours for Medicare,* I have worked extensively with the professionals who help manage the State Health Insurance Assistance Program (SHIP) and the 15,000 volunteers who help beneficiaries navigate Medicare. The Medicare Rights Center (MRC), another terrific consumer resource, has developed interactive online tools that are accessed some 40,000 times a week.

Maximus Federal Services in northern Virginia explained to me how the Medicare appeals process works, and sometimes doesn't work. Maximus is the sole Medicare contractor in charge of the initial external reviews of Medicare claims rejected by Medicare Advantage (MA) plans (Part C of Medicare) and Medicare prescription drug plans (Part D of Medicare). Consumer appeals in these plans are first handled by the private insurers who run these plans and, if consumers receive unfavorable decisions, they are then free to appeal these decisions to Maximus.

There is a separate contractor system for Original Medicare, operated by Medicare Administrative Contractors, or MACs, around the country. These companies serve at the pleasure of CMS and were shy to the point of invisibility when I attempted to interview their officials. However, you may need to know details about these companies should you encounter problems with how your Original Medicare claims are handled. So, I have put these details in an endnote.[1]

Consumers generally have only a vague understanding of what to do when they get bad news from either Original Medicare or a private Medicare insurance plan. The volume of complaints is tiny in relation to the enormous volume of Medicare claims that people file. And when an initial complaint or grievance is rejected, consumers often just give up. In many cases, according to Maximus, it's clear that they don't even know they have the right to appeal.[2]

For example, there are now roughly 40 million Medicare beneficiaries with Medicare drug plans. In all of 2013, Maximus received a grand total of 23,716 requests that it reconsider Part D plan rejections of consumer claims. This means that if you assembled 100,000 Part D subscribers in a stadium, only about 60 in the whole place would have filed such a request. Nearly 60 percent of these requests, by the way, involved consumer requests to take drugs that are, by law, excluded from the list of drugs that Medicare will cover in Part D plans.

In Part C, there were nearly 15 million MA beneficiaries in 2013 (there are now millions more due to gains in MA plan enrollments), and about 120,000 appeals to Maximus from plan coverage denials. This amounted to only about 800 appeals per 100,000 beneficiaries, but it is far higher than the rate for people in Part D plans. The major difference, Maximus officials say, is that reconsideration requests from Part C rejections are automatic, whereas the 2003 law that created Part D drug plans specifically disallows automatic appeals. Of course, nearly no consumers know that they must initiate Part D appeals — shades of Chapter 1's lament that "No One Told Me."

So, Job No. 1 here is to know your rights, which is what this chapter is about. However, even assuming you do, there are few more confusing and intimidating experiences than being surrounded by medical professionals who are telling you in no uncertain terms to do things you do not fully understand. It can be hard to disagree with doctors, hospitals, and other caregivers. They seem to hold all the cards.

What professionals in all walks of life often

fail to appreciate is that the things they do every day are things their patients and customers may do only once or twice in their lives. In health care settings, these professionals usually are intimately familiar with their surroundings, with medical devices and equipment, and with the health care terminology they use in discussing a patient's condition and care options. You, the patient, may have a Nobel Prize and an Einsteinian IQ. But you are on someone else's playing field, and it's a foreign experience.

I know this is complicated stuff. If you still have questions about your rights after reading this chapter, send an email to me.[3] I will post an answer at the *Get What's Yours* website.[4] I won't always be able to get back to you right away, so sending me a question while you're flat on your back on a gurney, hooked up to an IV, and on your way to the operating room is perhaps not the ideal recipe for success. Read on to learn how to get immediate help.

As you get into the particulars of your rights as a Medicare beneficiary, please keep some things in mind:

1. You may need to step up and speak out to exercise your rights.

2. If you're not willing, comfortable, or able to do this, find a family member or someone else who is.
3. Figure out what you need to know ahead of time. Your health care needs, and the financial implications of your decisions, are too important and usually too complicated for you or your caregiver to simply wing it.
4. You can and must do these things. And if you do, your odds of achieving the proper outcomes will be enhanced. Going back to Chapter 2, the stakes couldn't be higher — longer life and a higher quality of life.

THAT THING YOU'RE LOSING IS PROBABLY YOUR MIND

I want to expand on item 2 above. Please don't get offended by what I'm going to say, or at least not so offended that you stop reading. But the reality of nearly everyone who has turned 65 and begun receiving Medicare benefits is that we are literally losing a little bit of our minds every day. It's called cognitive decline, and while some 90-year-olds still perform amazing mental gymnastics, the futures that nearly all of us face will include a steady period of decreasing mental acuity. Our minds may still be steel traps, but they're missing some teeth and picking up rust.

I am 70 years old. I have already lived longer than my mom, and am quickly closing in on the age at which my dad died. I feel great most days and try to do the things the "experts" say I should do to boost my odds of not only living a long life but living it in good health. I believe this advice. What I've also learned is that I can't do this on my own. Most likely, you can't, either. We need friends and counselors whom we trust to help us navigate life and do everything we can to be as healthy as possible.

So, please believe me when I say that despite all the details about Medicare that I've learned while writing *Get What's Yours for Medicare,* I know that even I will need help navigating Medicare. In fact, it's because of all these details that I say this with such conviction. And the exact time when you require maximum mastery of its many details is, sadly, likely to be when you are at or near your most vulnerable state — fairly sick, or perhaps in an emergency setting and getting ready to take that scary gurney ride.

One of the most important rights you have

under Medicare (and other health care situations as well) is the right to have a formal representative who can help you make Medicare and related health care decisions. Once a Medicare dispute has arisen, this can lead to retaining an attorney. But you also have the right to appoint a spouse, caregiver, or friend to represent you. You will need to complete an Appointment of Representative form.[5]

While you're at it, you might want to complete a companion Social Security representative form.[6] Social Security administers a lot of things for Medicare and it may come in handy for your representative to also be able to speak with Social Security on your behalf. To be on rock-solid ground here, I'd also find a local attorney who can make sure these representational forms pass muster with state and local regulations. I know this will take time and some money. But if you believe in the "ounce of prevention" approach, as I do, it will not be a waste of either.

WHERE'S A MEDICARE BILL OF RIGHTS WHEN YOU NEED ONE?

Well, there is one, or at least a statement from CMS that comes pretty close. You can find it on page 127 of the 2016 *Medicare & You* guidebook.[7] This is what it says:

All people with Medicare have the right to:

1. Be treated with dignity and respect at all times.
2. Be protected from discrimination.
3. Have their personal and health information kept private.
4. Get information in a way they understand from Medicare, health care providers, and Medicare con-

tractors.

5. Have questions about Medicare answered.
6. Have access to doctors, other health care providers, specialists, and hospitals.
7. Learn about their treatment choices in clear language that they can understand, and participate in treatment decisions.
8. Get emergency care when and where they need it.
9. Get a decision about health care payment, coverage of services, or prescription drug coverage.
10. Request a review (appeal) of certain decisions about health care payment, coverage of services, or prescription drug coverage.
11. File complaints (sometimes called "grievances"), including complaints about the quality of their care.

If I had to remember only one of these rights, it would be No. 5: you always have the right to have your Medicare questions answered. Keep asking questions until you find out what you need to know to make an informed decision. If you do not receive clear and satisfactory answers to your

Medicare questions, and you are not in an emergency setting where your health and perhaps life are at risk, do not proceed with a treatment or procedure or medication. Your questions should include getting information ahead of time about what things cost, how this cost is covered by whatever kind of Medicare insurance you have, and what you are personally at risk for.

PSST! MEDICARE MAKES MISTAKES. LOTS OF THEM.

Every day, tens of millions of Medicare beneficiaries take prescription medications, or at least their health care providers and families hope they do. Smaller numbers are in hospitals or nursing homes, laid up at home recovering from illness or surgery, or trying out that fancy new wheelchair. All of these activities involve someone generating a claim for Medicare insurance coverage — *three million a day* and rising sharply just for Original Medicare alone. And so somewhere, someone is keying in or scanning one or more billing codes into some software product, and transmitting the claim to Medicare directly or to some largely digital claims processing repository at one of the private insurance companies that issue MA,

261

Part D prescription drug, and Medigap policies.

Last year, CMS introduced a new set of medical billing codes called ICD-10. The new codes generated lots of funny stories about their unbelievable specificity. Here's a sampling, courtesy of Sarah Kliff at Vox Media[8] and Maggie Fox at NBC News[9]: getting struck by an orca, being sucked into a jet engine, getting hit by a motor vehicle while riding an animal, acquired absence of unspecified greater toe, pedestrian on foot injured in collision with roller skater, contact with nonvenomous toads, crushed by an alligator (and, of course), crushed by a crocodile, and drowning and submersion due to falling or jumping from crushed waterskis.

Fun, yes, but there are nearly 70,000 codes in ICD-10, which is about *five* times as many as in the previous system (yes, indeedy, it was called ICD-9). Doctors, hospitals, and other care providers will be cursing the new codes and, quite likely, making lots and lots of billing mistakes as they wrestle with this new system.

The point here is that it should come as no great shock that some of your Medicare claims filed by others will contain bad information. Other claims may be correct but describe procedures and charges that are not at all what you expected. Eventually, beneficiaries receive reports on their use of Medicare, either from private insurance plans or, for Original Medicare, from one of those Medicare Administrative Contractors (MACs) I mentioned.

The MAC forms are called Medicare Summary Notices, or MSNs.[10] You can expect them quarterly, assuming you've had any covered health care expenses during that period. You also can create an online account at mymedicare.gov and track your claims. There's a helpful video walking you through an MSN.[11] In private insurance plans, your claims record may go by different names, but all of them are under an umbrella labeled an Explanation of Benefits, or EOB. These are the official records that are part of your Medicare claims history. Please read them.

When you think one of these reports is incorrect, you can and should take action. This is most likely to occur when Original Medicare or an MA or Part D drug plan has rejected your claim for coverage. Medicare has created multiple pathways for you to express your displeasure with something it or one of its contractors has done, or about something done or not done by the private plans that provide Medicare insurance.

As is often the case, the government's purposeful effort to be responsive can create more consumer confusion than satisfaction. For example, you can file an appeal, a complaint, a grievance, a request for determination, or an exception. All of these may involve the same thing from your perspective — "I want this procedure or piece of medical equipment or prescription drug covered." But to Medicare, these words can signal different processes, forms, and time frames. If you have trouble keeping them straight, and who wouldn't, just remember that fifth Medicare right, and keep asking questions.

Also, the front ends of the Medicare appeal processes work a little differently in the cases of Original Medicare and private Medicare insurance company plans. We're going to get to these details, but first, a word or, more accurately, a bunch of words, about mistakes that can't wait for some periodic report or leisurely adjudication.

UNDERSTANDING YOUR EMERGENCY AND EXPEDITED RIGHTS

Appealing a Medicare claim for medical treatment, equipment, or medication can take a long, long time to resolve. But there are situations when time is exactly what you don't have. This is one of the reasons, for example, that Medicare's normal rules for getting physician referrals and seeking care within your health plan's provider network are waived if you need emergency care. But the need for speed is not limited to such emergencies.

If you're in a hospital or seeking to be admitted to a hospital, and you receive a discharge notice that you feel is unwarranted, you have the right to request an expedited or "fast" appeal from Medicare. The rules say you must request a fast appeal no later than your scheduled hospital departure date. If you comply with this timetable, Medicare says, you will be allowed to stay in the hospital while you wait for your appeal to be heard. Your insurance will remain in effect, too, although you will be responsible for any copays or deductibles under your Medicare coverage plan. (This is a good place to remind you of the possible Medicare coverage and billing problems caused should your visit to the hospital be deemed an observational stay and not a formal admission. Check Chapter 5 for details.)

The people that hear your appeal are

required to be medical professionals, and they work under contract for Medicare for a mouthful of words called the Beneficiary and Family Centered Quality Improvement Organization.[12] Medicare uses this impossible-to-pronounce-or-remember acronym: BFCC-QIO. And now, I'm afraid, I will be BFCC-QIO'ing you to distraction, if not worse.

If you have been admitted to a hospital, it should within two days provide you a notice that is called "An Important Message from Medicare." It will spell out your patient rights and also provide contact information for the BFCC-QIO office and details for the fast appeal process.

The BFCC-QIO is supposed to notify the hospital that you have appealed the hospital's actions. The hospital then is supposed to provide you a "Detailed Notice of Discharge" by noon of the day after receiving the BFCC-QIO's notice. The BFCC-QIO then is supposed to give you its ruling within a day of receiving the hospital's detailed notice. If it rejects your appeal, you will have until noon of the next day to leave the hospital without facing any additional charges beyond your Medicare copays and deductibles.

You have similar rights for expedited appeals in other services covered by Part A of Medicare — skilled nursing facilities (SNFs), care from a home health agency (HHA), a comprehensive outpatient rehabilitation facility (CORF), and licensed hospice services. Appeal rights are limited, however, where the issue is a reduction in services and not their complete termination.

AND NOT TO LEAVE OUT YOU PART D FOLKS

Another major source of quick Medicare appeals involves claims for prescription drugs that are denied. This information also was included in Chapter 8 and, rather than send you back there, is repeated here:

If you and your doctor feel this drug is essential to your health or even life, contact your Part D drug plan. You (and by "you" I mean you, your representative, your doctor, or whoever else might have prescribed the drug in question) have the right to seek a fast decision within 24 hours. The plan is supposed to honor this request if your prescribing physician tells the plan that waiting as long as 72 hours for a ruling could trigger serious adverse health consequences.

Part D plans also permit what are called "standard coverage determinations" that put the plan on the clock. Once it has received this form,[13] the insurer has 72 hours to let you know its decision about requested drug prescriptions and 14 calendar days if your determination request involves money you think your plan owes you. These determination requests also may be labeled exceptions to the plan's rules, and are often described as such.

HAVE YOU HAD YOUR ABN YET TODAY?

On the Original Medicare game board, the space labeled ABN is probably not one you want to land on. These initials stand for Advance Beneficiary Notice of Noncoverage — an acronym seemingly devised by the same minds that decided that the Centers for Medicare & Medicaid Services should be short-formed as CMS and not CMMS. An ABN is what your doctor or ambulance company or other health care provider may give you when it thinks that Medicare will not pay for their services. Like the old *Let's Make a Deal* game show, you will have three doors to choose from should you get an ABN:

Door #1 — You understand the services

or items may not be covered but you want them provided to you anyway, even if you have to pay for them fully on the spot. You also can ask the provider to file a claim with Medicare. Filing such a claim is essential because it creates a basis, should the claim later be denied, for you to come back and appeal the denial.

Door #2 — Same as Door #1 except you ask the provider not to file a claim and, by doing so, you have no rights to appeal. If the provider wants you to pay right away for the items and services, you have little choice but to do so.

Door #3 — You decide not to seek the services or items and are not responsible for any payments — no services, no claim, no right to appeal.

If you get an ABN, make sure the provider accepts Medicare assignment — meaning they agree to be paid at the rates Medicare has approved for the service or item. Otherwise, you could get dinged with a higher cost and would still be responsible for some of these expenses even if Medicare later decides to cover the claim.

Now, you might logically assume that a service or procedure will be covered if you don't get an ABN. But Medicare assumptions, as I've warned repeatedly, can come back to haunt you or worse. For example, say a hospital orders an ambulance to pick you up for transport to the hospital. It's not considered an emergency and Medicare might not cover it. But the ambulance company is not going to issue you an ABN because it didn't order the service. You assume it's covered, of course, because the hospital ordered the vehicle. You don't discover the bad news until you get your next MSN (Medicare Summary Notice). After seeing the rejected claim, you get so mad that you might then actually need an emergency ambulance run!

There are other names for ABNs depending on the institution or care providers involved. These include a Skilled Nursing Facility Advance Beneficiary Notice of Non-Coverage (SNFABN), a Hospital Issued Notice of Noncoverage (HINN), and no fewer than three involving home health care: a Home Health Change of Care Notice (HHCCN), a Notice of Medicare Non-Coverage (NOMNC), and a Detailed Explanation of Non-Coverage (DENC).[14] Have you gotten into the swing yet of CMS acronyms and abbreviations? Don't forget to check out its list of 4,400-plus officially approved acronyms here.[15]

INSURANCE COMPANY MEDICARE HEALTH PLANS

These plans don't have quite the regulatory hurdles of Original Medicare. Instead of waiting to receive unpleasant news in your EOB (Explanation of Benefits), you should think about asking the plan first whether it will cover something you or your doctor think you need. Of course, we can't have a procedure simply called "Go Ask," so the formal name for this is called an "organization determination." If the plan says it won't cover what you've requested, you can then launch a formal appeal.

DANTE HAD NINE CIRCLES OF HELL. MEDICARE HAS ONLY FIVE.

See? I bet this makes you feel better, doesn't it? And we've already explained the first level, which is to seek redetermination from an Original Medicare Administrative Contractor (MAC) or review from an insurance company MA or Part D drug plan.

Level two of the appeals process also differs slightly, with Original Medicare beneficiaries seeking an external reconsideration of their appeal by another Medicare contractor called a Qualified Independent Contractor, or QIC.[16] In appealing a private insurance plan decision, your appeal (which can be called a reconsideration or redetermination request, depending on the type of plan) would go to another Medicare contractor called an Independent Review Entity (IRE).[17] As noted, Maximus is the sole IRE for Part C and Part D appeals. The QICs for Original Medicare are:

For Part A: Maximus in the eastern United States and C2C Solutions Inc. in the western United States.

For Part B: C2C Solutions for the northern United States and also for the southern United States.

(And, no, I have no clue why Part A splits the United States one way and Part B another. The states included in the two sets of regions are, by the way, identical: the North and West regions contain the same states, as do the South and East. Go figure.)

For DME (Durable Medical Equipment): C2C Solutions for the entire United States.

Following the second level of appeals, levels three through five are the same. All level three appeals flow into the Office of

272

Medicare Hearings and Appeals (OMHA)[18] and to a date with an independent administrative law judge. Level four takes you before the Medicare Appeals Council and level five moves you before a U.S. District Court. In reality, few consumers have the time, money, or desire to move deeply into the Medicare appeals process. Nearly all of them have called it quits by level two or three, leaving the field to institutional appeals where a big equipment or health care provider has enough money at stake to justify higher-level appeals.

If you are game for the appeals process, you need to keep careful records and it can help a lot to have contemporaneous accounts of treatment needs.[19] A statement from your doctor about why you needed a certain treatment or drug at the time you needed it is more persuasive than a report a year later trying to reconstruct or justify such a treatment.

In fiscal 2011, OMHA took an average of 121 days to process an appeal. Now, its statutory maximum is 90 days but, hey, no one's perfect and 121 days is not so bad. In fiscal 2013, however, that average processing time had nearly doubled to 220 days. And it has kept soaring since then. By 2015, the average was up to 572 days — more than a year and a half.

Indeed, its workload is so heavy[20] that it takes OMHA 20 to 24 weeks even to enter new appeals onto its docket, prompting this sobering if not shocking website notice to claimants: "If 22 weeks have not lapsed since you submitted your Request for Hearing, do not resubmit your request."

Medicare itself has added to the appeals workload by stepping up efforts to recover excessive billings.[21] State Medicaid offices have boosted their efforts to reduce their expenses and get Medicare to pay more money for claims involving people who are eligible for both Medicaid and Medicare. People on Social Security Disability Insurance are eligible for Medicare after a two-year waiting period, and the recession-induced boost in SSDI rolls is still being felt in appeals of Medicare claims. Last, lest we forget, the demographic wave of aging baby boomers continues to add millions of people to Medicare every year, further boosting workloads.

But as it turns out, nearly none of this caseload directly involves Medicare beneficiaries. Amanda Axeen, an OMHA program official, says, "Although we have this enormous backlog, the appeals filed by individual beneficiaries represent a very small percentage of those cases — perhaps about one percent." Now, it's true that appeals involving medical providers could have a trickle-down effect on consumers. But in most cases, the providers' interests are aligned with consumers'. Both are seeking money or more money from Medicare.

And that 572-day processing time and 24-week intake lag? Axeen says OMHA policy is "We're moving anything filed by the beneficiary to the front of the line." There is a dedicated mail stop within OMHA for consumer appeals. "We open those on a same-day basis," she says. Here's that address:

HHS OMHA Centralized Docketing
200 Public Square, Suite 1260
Attn: Beneficiary Mail Stop
Cleveland, OH 44114-2316

Beneficiaries need to have enough financial skin in the game to qualify for OMHA and court proceedings — $150 for OMHA's administrative law judge reviews and $1,500 for judicial review. Given health care costs, such thresholds are easily met.

Each appeal level has separate compliance time frames. Adding them up for all five levels yields a total of 780 days — easily more than two years — between the time a beneficiary receives an MSN or EOB and a federal district court is asked to hear the final appeal. Of course, OMHA delays alone have blown this timetable out of the water.

It is only slightly in jest to suggest that Medicare beneficiaries need to be in good health before initiating a serious appeal. In fact, while a congressional committee was looking into appeal backlogs in 2015, it was informed of the death of a 92-year-old appellant who died before his appeal could be resolved.[22]

So, there you have it — rights and appeals wrapped nicely in a bow, albeit a large and intricate one. Life would be simpler, of course, if you never had to make a Medicare appeal. One way of minimizing that unpleasant possibility is by making wise choices up front about your Medicare insurance plans and health care providers. The next chapter explains the explosion of health care ratings and online tools that can help you make these important decisions.

11

SO MANY STARS IN THE SKY
HEALTH PROVIDER QUALITY RATINGS

Star ratings, popularized for mutual funds by Morningstar, have come to health care and Medicare with a vengeance. There has been an explosion of data- and user-opinion-driven and anecdotally based ratings sites for hospitals, nursing homes, doctors, and other health care providers. Wherever big data is found in health care, it seems, one or more provider ratings tools has sprung up as well. But as with Medicare health plans themselves, the sheer amount and complexity of all this provider performance information threatens to overwhelm the very consumers for whom it is intended.

When you encounter these tools, make sure you know exactly what is being rated and understand the results that are displayed. Easier said than done, I know. And with new rankings appearing all the time, making sense of them likely will become more difficult. But as was the case in making sense of all the private Medicare insurance plans that are offered to us, reducing complexity can make these rankings more useful. Simplification done poorly, however, may be worse than no simplification at all, and can raise its own set of challenges.

People are touchy about being judged, of course. While hospitals and others with blue-chip scores often will trumpet their ratings, less favored providers may carp until the cows come home. My read, and it's just that, is that they often are offended at the thought that any outsider even has the right let alone the expertise to evaluate them. But it's politically incorrect to say this. So they meet the evaluators' big data with their own big data, creating extensive studies to discredit ratings they don't like, all the while saying they welcome transparency and consumer empowerment.

Meanwhile, those doing the judging — from the Centers for Medicare & Medical Services (CMS) to the many private organizations with health provider ratings — have endless and endlessly detailed explanations in defense of their efforts. The result is a flurry of dueling studies and reports, all in the interest of the public good but providing little enlightenment to users who don't have a medical background or a degree in statistics.

Further, despite their rapid expansion, health care ratings cover only a sliver of the actual care situations faced by Medicare beneficiaries and their families. CMS and other national ratings providers may spew out a huge and growing amount of health care data. But in terms of hospitals, doctors, and other care providers, this information is only as good as the specific surgical procedures, disease treatments, and other care situations it covers. So, unless you see a rating for your specific health needs, don't assume that a hospital with high overall ratings will be the best one for you.

Even if you can find your specific need covered in one or more health ratings, proceed with caution. Not all ratings are created equal, and some may contain serious flaws. But it's a start. Also, don't forget to consult your state insurance department and other consumer groups. There are some terrific health care ratings provided at the state level. California, in particular, stands out.

I'm going to tell you about some of the major ratings tools and how you can and should use them to get the best possible health care — care that Medicare generally does a good job of helping you use and afford.

A DIFFERENT RATING
FOR EVERY OCCASION

Your use of ratings should be driven by your medical needs. Let's follow a hypothetical couple of Medicare beneficiaries as they engage with various health provider ratings. Our couple is named Spin and Marty. Each is 73 years young, and they may have nothing or everything in common with the fictional Walt Disney television characters whose names they share.

Spin and Marty are trying to decide whether to change Medicare insurance plans in the upcoming open enrollment season that begins October 15 and extends through December 7. They have been using Original Medicare and a Medigap plan so far. They like the freedom it provides them to use the services of any doctors, hospitals, or other Medicare-participating health care providers they wish. But Marty, a longtime smoker, has heart and lung problems. He was hospitalized twice last year, and while his Medigap plan helped with some of the expenses not covered by Original Medicare, he still had big out-of-pocket medical expenses. Spin and Marty have heard that they might be able to save a lot of money with a Medicare Advantage (MA) plan and still get excellent health care. Spin might still want to keep Original Medicare, but he, too, wants at least to check out the different MA plans offered in their ZIP code.

Fortuitously if not fortunately, Spin and Marty are old friends of mine, and I've shown them rough drafts of *Get What's Yours for Medicare.* They immediately head to Plan Finder,[1] plug in their ZIP code, and begin looking at their local MA plans that have built-in Part D drug plans (so-called MA-PD plans). They also enter their prescription drug needs to see how their meds are covered by their locally available plans.

IT'S STILL ALL ABOUT
THE NETWORK

Spin and Marty find 17 MA-PD plans that cover their drugs. They next check out the plans' star ratings. CMS, which developed and provides these ratings, lists nearly 60 variables on which each plan is rated.[2] These individual variables are available but they also have been boiled down into a single star rating. It ranges from one to five stars and includes half-star increments. CMS has been trying to weed out low-performing plans, and fully 14 of the 17 plans have at least a 4-star rating. However, only 7 have either 4.5- or 5-star ratings, and these are the ones that Spin and Marty decide to research further.

In doing so, they realize that these seven plans all require members to use health care provider networks of doctors, hospitals, and other providers chosen by the health plan. There's no readily available list of these network directories on Plan Finder, so instead of contacting all seven plans, the pair decide to further limit their comparative assessment to the two 5-star plans available where they live. They call these plans, using the phone numbers listed on Plan Finder, and ask to see the plans' provider networks in their ZIP code. The networks include some of the doctors and hospitals they have used, but not all of them.

Spin and Marty then use CMS's Physician Compare[3] to find out more about the physicians in the two plans' provider networks. CMS and private organizations are trying to beef up physician ratings, including allowing consumers to see comparative ratings of multiple physicians and also create tools permitting users to see which MA networks work with which physicians. To Spin and Marty, Physician Compare in its present form is a useful but incomplete reference to find out more about area doctors in the two plans' networks. They identify four primary care doctors (PCPs) and six specialists they want to know more about. Spin takes the four PCPs and Marty looks at the six specialists who deal with his heart and lung issues.

They enter these doctors' names one at a time in an Internet search engine. The resulting avalanche of hits causes them to want to return to bed and save this work for another day, but they plow ahead. They don't see any yellow or red lights from this review, but it's not a great help, either. So they then call their own doctor's office. The pair's own primary care physicians are in the same group practice and in both their networks as well. They speak with an office administrator and ask for help in evaluating the other doctors on their list. At the end of the day, and it's been a long one, this is the information that is most useful to them.

While on the phone with their doctor's office, they also asked about the hospitals in the two plan networks and whether their doctors use these hospitals and what they think about them. Marty in particular wants to make sure the hospital he used last year will still be available to him should he sign up for MA. They then use CMS's Hospital

Compare,[4] which lets them compare three hospitals at a time, based on six or seven groups of performance data on things such as patient experiences, in-hospital complications, readmission rates, and financial information.

Based on their reviews of the doctors and hospitals in the two plans' provider networks, Spin and Marty are comfortable moving ahead with their MA-PD choice.

WHAT CHANGES WHEN THE SCALPELS COME OUT

Spin and Marty decided to both go with the same new MA-PD plan. While they might have been a bit better off individually with different plans, the hassle of dealing with two different health insurers was too unappealing.

So far, so good. But then real life intervened, as it often does. Marty's heart problems worsened and his doctor sent him to an in-network surgical specialist who recommended inserting a stent to improve blood flow to his heart and reduce his worsening chest pains. Around the same time, Spin faced having to give up tennis unless he replaced his deteriorating left knee. He, too, received a recommendation for a surgeon who could do the job.

These procedures immediately raised the health care stakes for both men. The CMS Physician Compare site was not useful, at least in its current form. Its Hospital Compare site did have surgical complication information for hip and knee replacements, plus general findings about complications following surgery. Hospitals also were rated based on measures of patient experiences, timely and effective care, readmissions and deaths, use (or overuse) of medical imaging tests, and the overall payment and value of care. These were helpful for Spin and Marty but not enough on which to base a decision. The men looked for additional ratings information on stent and knee replacement surgeons and on the hospitals where their surgeries could be performed.

They found a list of local hospital performance on heart bypass and knee replacement surgeries at *U.S. News & World Report*.[5] They then took a further look at Hospital Compare to see what it had to say about the best-rated *U.S. News* local hospitals. Lastly, they did some more homework on the performance of the surgeons in their health plan who were recommended to do this work. *Consumer Reports*[6] has a well-respected set of hospital ratings that key on patient safety, with a special emphasis on hospital-acquired infections. Unfortunately, the advertising-free site is available only to paying subscribers. A one-month online subscription was only seven bucks, so the men accessed these ratings to see how they compared with others. HealthGrades[7] and The Leapfrog Group[8] also provide ratings.

A leading professional journal, *Health Affairs,* looked at these four providers (*Consumer Reports,* HealthGrades, Leapfrog, and *U.S. News*) in a 2015 article and found that their hospital ratings almost never agreed.

"Leapfrog and HealthGrades agreed most frequently (48 hospitals, 55 percent); *Consumer Reports* and *U.S. News* agreed on none of the hospitals they rated as high performers," the article said. It acknowledged there were major differences in the goals and methodologies of the four sets of ratings, but said consumer decision making would be improved through standardization and greater transparency of their ratings. Because the goals of these ratings systems do vary, however, *Health Affairs'* findings not only aren't surprising but are to be expected. All Spin knew is that after looking at all this information, his head was, well, you know, spinning.

ProPublica, a foundation-supported investigative journalism site, has a Surgeon Scorecard.[9] It's been criticized by doctors' groups, among others, and has generated lots of those learned papers mentioned earlier. I wouldn't rely solely on this rating tool, or any other, but would use them collectively to get a better sense of surgical and hospital quality. It's also important to note that we are still at an early stage of health care provider ratings, and that the tools will become better over time.

ProPublica processed an enormous amount of Medicare data for its scorecard, and in fact, third-party provider ratings often rely on big data sets released by CMS. Still, ProPublica began by reporting results of only eight surgical procedures — knee replacement, hip replacement, laparoscopic gallbladder removal, 2 lumbar spinal fusions (posterior and anterior), a cervical spinal fusion, prostate removal, and prostate resection.

Spin found the ratings helpful. Marty had to keep looking for information on stent procedures. Physician Compare allowed him to find local cardiac surgeons. *U.S. News* identified local hospital rankings for heart conditions and surgeries. He also looked at the *Consumer Reports* and Leap-Frog hospital safety scores. He then looked at which of these doctors and hospitals were in his health plan network and called his primary care physician for feedback. If this sounds like an unrealistic amount of homework, imagine if you were going to get a stent placed in your body. Suddenly, doing this research does not seem far-fetched.

Marty's doctor told him that unless he could find out the relative health and riskiness of these doctors' surgical patients, he shouldn't base his choice of a surgeon on either specific surgeon or hospital ratings. Even within the same hospital, it might be possible that one doctor did more high-risk surgeries than another. Even if this doctor was a superior surgeon (and doing higher-risk surgeries might actually be an indicator of better skills), he or she might have worse patient outcomes than other surgeons. While his doctor applauded Marty's effort to be well informed, he cautioned him against using any single provider of surgeon performance or hospital safety information to choose health care providers.

Okay, that was not really Marty's doctor speaking there. It was me. I have toiled in the trenches of health care ratings. They are, literally, all over the place. So, use them to narrow your choices of providers. But then talk to your doctors, their nurses, other health care professionals, and friends who've faced similar health needs or know people who have.

Here are the questions to ask a prospective surgeon: In general, how many of the surgeries I need have you done during the past 12 months, and what's your record in terms of deaths, complications, and how quickly patients return to their usual activities? Also ask the same questions as they apply to patients similar to you in terms of age, overall health, and other risk factors. You should also pose these questions to any hospital you're considering for your surgery, procedure, or care. They have this information and know that this is increasingly what patients want to know.

WHEN A HOSPITAL STAY LEADS TO A NURSING HOME

Marty's stent surgery was successful but required a recovery stay in a nursing home. He didn't know this, but technically he needed to go to a skilled nursing facility (SNF) that participated in Medicare in order for his stay to be covered by Medicare. There are about 15,500 nursing homes in the United States and all but 1,000 or so participate in Medicare and Medicaid. Nearly all are regarded as SNFs, and are evaluated in CMS's Nursing Home Compare tool.[10] Yikes, CMS does compare a lot of things, doesn't it? No wonder Spin has that issue with his head. If Marty wished, he could see a detailed list of items on which CMS bases its nursing home evaluations.[11]

They fall into three buckets — health inspection results, facility staffing, and quality-of-care measures. All are important, but the last two are based on self-reported data from SNFs. Only the first measure is based on external reviews and it generally is considered the most important of the three measures. So, while each home has an overall star rating, it's important also to check out the star ratings within each of these three buckets. ProPublica has put inspection results into a tool that compares the incidences of inspection deficiencies.[12]

CMS has been beefing up its efforts to push quality improvements at nursing homes, including singling out facilities that make heavy use of antipsychotic drugs to control patient behavior.

New homes will not have star ratings until they've had two annual inspections. Because of the way the ratings are compiled, ratings on homes within the same state can be directly compared, but comparing ratings of homes across state lines can produce misleading results.

Spin found three top-rated nearby homes for Marty to consider — Marty being otherwise occupied having a stent placed in his chest. Only two of them were in their MA plan's provider network and, as it turns out, the hospital Marty was in preferred sending him to one of these homes. Spin made an appointment to visit that facility and liked what he saw. He earlier had used Genworth Financial's annual Cost of Care survey[13] to research the range of local SNF costs, and satisfied himself that this particular SNF was not out of line in its fee structure. He then called a Medicare counselor at the State Health Insurance Assistance Program (SHIP),[14] who put him in touch with his state's nursing home ombudsman. He asked for any relevant details on the facility. There were no yellow or red lights from that call, so he recommended to Marty that he use this SNF for the care he needed before returning home. While this may sound like a lot of research, it actually took Spin only an hour of time plus the visit to the SNF.

How to Get Comfortable with Home-Based Care

Once Marty got home, he needed some continuing care. Spin and Marty both learned that Medicare does not cover so-called custodial care but will cover home-based care that is medically necessary. Marty's doctor agreed with that assessment and Spin helped Marty get in touch with their MA insurer to make sure it would cover such care. Once they got a positive response to that request, they then needed to find someone to provide the in-home care. They got a list from their health plan of a dozen in-network agencies and a smaller list from their doctor and the nursing home where Marty had received skilled care. There were still five providers on all the lists, so they set off to do some more home-work.

This homework, by the way, is going to be increasingly common for Medicare benefi-ciaries. As the Genworth Cost of Care survey illustrates, in-home care can be cheaper than care in a skilled nursing facil-ity. Insurance companies often tilt toward in-home care on cost grounds as well. And consumers prefer in-home care nine-to-one versus being in a nursing home. In the case of medically required in-home care, using an agency makes sense because relying on a single caregiver can be dicey when that person, for whatever reason, can't make it to your home. More to the point, Medicare won't cover in-home care expenses unless they're provided by an agency registered with Medicare.

Spin and Marty checked out the five recommended providers on, you guessed it, CMS's Home Health Compare site.[15] Be-cause there are different patient needs, CMS includes half a dozen care categories — nursing, physical therapy, occupational therapy, speech therapy, medical social services (such as counseling for emotional issues or finding community resources to help patients cope), and home health aides who can provide nonmedical help. They looked at the star ratings and backup details on all five and found two that seemed best for Marty. They then made appointments for each agency to visit Marty at home. There still were no clear winners, so they wound up flipping a coin to decide.

WHEN THE STAKES ARE VERY HIGH

Readers might recall that this chapter is based on different care needs, which I'll summarize here as routine, serious, and life-threatening. When everything is on the line, the stakes for finding the best solution become high. The process changes and, often, the time frame of making a decision becomes compressed and pressured.

At this time, your penny-pinching approach to health care may fly out the window. If you can afford the best care, and even when you can't, you will do everything to find it, and worry later about the financial consequences. The financial planner in me says this is an awful way to fly. The human in me says it's the way real people fly.

If you have Original Medicare, it will cover the hospital and doctor of your choosing, and nearly all participate in Medicare. If you have a Medicare Advantage plan, you must check on which hospitals, surgeons, and other care experts are in its provider network. Of equal or perhaps even greater importance, you must find out — *ahead of time* — its rules for out-of-network care. MA plans often permit out-of-network care in emergencies without socking you with steep out-of-network prices. Other plans, particularly MA fee-for-service plans, have more tolerant rules for out-of-network care. As we saw at the beginning of this book, this is a crucial bit of research.

When Marty's weakened heart began failing him, it became clear that his life would end soon unless he received a new heart. Spin dropped everything when he heard this news, and began searching for the best place for Marty to get care. While individual surgeons are always important here, the hospitals where they operate become the focus of care decisions.

U.S. News rates hospitals in 16 specialties for patients whose medical needs are especially challenging. One is cardiology and heart surgery (actually a combination of medical heart conditions and cardiovascular procedures and surgeries). Its ratings have their critics, as do all health care ratings. Their use of peer "reputation" ratings strikes some as a popularity contest that can be overly influenced by motivations of reciprocity. However, as a decision-making aid, they are a valuable and influential tool. Beyond a hospital's reputation with other cardiologists and heart surgeons, the ratings include statistics on patient survival, safety, volume of procedures (you want to go somewhere where they do a lot of whatever you need), and several other factors. (Personal disclosure: I spent five years writing articles on retirement, health, and aging for *U.S. News.* Am I biased toward their ratings? Probably.)

Spin consulted the list, entering his ZIP code and looking first at ranked hospitals within 25 miles of his location. He had to widen the radius to 250 miles to find a hospital ranked in the *U.S. News* top 10. Marty's doctor knew medical-school classmates there, secured a short list of transplant surgical practices that used the hospital, and agreed to call Marty's health plan and see if it would permit use of this hospital even though it was not in the plan's provider network. The plan agreed.

Marty looked at details of the various doctors' groups that worked with the hospital, using other ratings services and even social media sites such as Yelp. He and Spin talked to friends, and friends of friends, and, after a few intense days, made their selection. Again, with his plan's approval and the medical recommendation of Marty's doctor, they made an appointment with the doctor. Like many highly rated hospitals, this one was a research and teaching hospital. The other members of the doctor's cardiac team agreed that Marty, even at 73, was a good candidate for a heart transplant. He was then registered as a transplant candidate with UNOS, the United Network for Organ Sharing.[16] Then Marty and Spin waited, joining roughly 125,000 other people also registered with UNOS and hoping to receive an organ transplant to extend their lives.

AND DON'T FORGET

CMS also provides comparative ratings for people needing kidney dialysis. It has the snappy name of Dialysis Facility Compare.[17] Like its other tools, this site lets you enter your ZIP code and access a list of nearby dialysis facilities. You can filter the list by distance, star ratings, types of dialysis offered, and even sites that are staffed in the evenings so you can have your dialysis after work.

The various CMS health ratings sites will never be confused with private-sector sites that are often better designed and easier for consumers to use. However, over time, I will put my money on the CMS ratings tools. First, they are getting better all the time, albeit slowly. Second, nearly all private-sector ratings sites are based largely on the same Medicare and other government-agency databases used by the CMS sites. Third, CMS is transparent in terms of explaining ratings factors, often at excruciating length. The downside is that you have to do lots of work to access this supportive information. It's one of the main reasons CMS is pushing hard to develop overall star ratings that consumers can use to make quick quality assessments. I support making Medicare as simple as possible. But I remain leery of basing critically important health care decisions on a single set of stars, no matter how brightly they shine.

Further, as Spin and Marty found, a lot of their decisions about the best health providers for their medical needs were influenced by the health care provider network their insurance plan used. These networks — of doctors, hospitals, and other care providers — are becoming all-important considerations in the decisions of more and more Medicare beneficiaries. Too often, however, it is way, way too hard to see inside these networks and to understand how they work. This murky task will be tackled in the next chapter.

12
FUZZY RECEPTION
HOW TO SEE HEALTH CARE PROVIDERS AND NETWORKS CLEARLY

Medicare has oodles of pilot programs, large-scale tests, and experimental approaches to coordinated care. Critics, of whom the agency has no shortage, say that while these efforts might have laudatory goals and be couched in clinically appropriate "medical-ese," they amount to little more than throwing ideas against the wall and seeing which ones stick. Despite being more than 50 years old, Medicare is still a work in progress. And its efforts to change health care have created a messy, messy process. So, one of the things I can say with certainty here is that the snapshot of Medicare that exists now does not look like the picture taken a year ago, or one that will be taken a year from now.

What will remain the same is that Medicare is under incredible pressure to improve your health care while spending less money to do so than it did last year, all the while devising plans to spend even less money the following year, and the year after that. Health care demographics are great on one level — more and more Americans are joining the ranks of 65-year-olds every year. So, at least in terms of longevity, we have achieved great gains, because more and more of these 65-year-olds are becoming 75-year-olds and 85-year-olds and, well, you get the picture.

As this aging of America takes place, it is inevitable that it will also produce many more chronically ill older Americans. As I'll explain in Chapter 14, successful aging doesn't mean avoiding illness and frailty. In fact, the longer we live, the bigger our health care bills will be. This certainty is the 800-pound gorilla in the health care room. It makes health care economics look scary, if not horrendous.

Longevity means rising government tabs for Medicare and Medicaid that simply can't be sustained. Yes, the Affordable Care Act triggered improvements in Medicare's financial sustainability, adding a good number of years until the Medicare trust fund is projected to run out of money. But a future of rising health care costs has only been deferred, and as I've noted before, the Medicare trust fund is not the real problem

here. Rather, it's the blank check Uncle Sam
has to write each year for unfunded Medicare expenses that are not supported by the
trust fund.

So, Medicare has little choice but to
tighten the financial screws on health care
providers while it searches for more cost-
effective ways to deliver high-quality health
care. Insurance companies, hospitals, doctors, medical equipment makers, and drug
companies see these cost pressures all too
well. To make money in the changing world
of Medicare, more costs are shifted to
consumers. The plans also have to get more
efficient and, in many cases, get bigger. Doing so may create economies of scale. But
increased size also permits these bulked-up
for-profit and nonprofit organizations to use
their national and, especially, local-market
dominance to drive better business terms
with their suppliers.

Medicare has triggered much of this shift
in the health care landscape. Its policies can
be seen at work in the merger wave of health
insurance companies. They also explain an
awful lot of the jockeying that's taken place
in local health care markets. Hospitals have
formed growing alliances with doctors and
physician groups, often hiring them outright
to secure improved access to the flow of

patients they need to prosper. Bigger health insurers have bulked up their pharmacy networks so they can bargain for better drug prices with pharmaceutical companies. Bigger hospital-doctor networks strive to bargain more effectively with the insurers, while also developing the abilities to provide the greater levels of coordinated and "team" health care to patients that Medicare increasingly is demanding. Some health care providers have actually taken the plunge and themselves formed health insurance organizations.

The Centers for Medicare & Medicaid Services (CMS) has, as noted, been busier than the proverbial health care bee in trying new things. It's even setting up pilot projects that connect care provided by hospitals and doctors to nonmedical factors that influence people's health, including their housing and social services.

You, as the patient or consumer or Medicare beneficiary, depending on who's doing the talking, are provided lots and lots of lip service here. Virtually all of these changes are described as being based on what's best for you. But this just isn't true, or at least represents a motivational goal that is often not achieved in practice. In all too many cases, you and your health profile are reduced to a set of numbers. And in today's all-consuming world of "big data," it is these numbers and not your needs that may drive your treatment under Medicare.

THE SICKER YOU ARE, THE MORE YOU WILL COST SOMEONE

In Medicare Advantage (MA) plans, people have individual risk scores that are supposed to measure their health, or at least measure their health related to future health care costs. This information is laid out by CMS in its Medicare Managed Risk Manual (CMS has a manual for nearly everything).[1] Here's what the agency has to say:

> Risk adjustment allows CMS to pay [insurance] plans for the risk of the beneficiaries they enroll, instead of an average amount for Medicare beneficiaries. By risk adjusting plan payments, CMS is able to make appropriate and accurate payments for enrollees with differences in expected costs. Risk adjustment is used to adjust bidding and payment based on the health status and demographic characteristics of an enrollee. Risk scores measure individual beneficiaries' relative risk and risk scores are used to adjust payments for each beneficiary's expected expenditures.

Whether you know it or not (and you almost certainly do not), private Medicare insurers analyze your health records to produce a numerical risk score. Believe me here that mere mortals cannot figure out how this is done. The process begins with your health diagnosis codes provided by hospitals, doctors, and other caregivers. Doctors get paid by health plans for contributing to these profiles, according to Fred Schulte, who has done eye-opening journalism on this topic for the Center for Public Integrity.[2] Then the information gets massaged by enough factors to impress even the most imaginative bureaucrat. We are managing a big health care economy here, people! And it's hard and complex work.

When it's all done, Medicare will adjust its payments accordingly. The practical translation of that paragraph I quoted above may have escaped you at the time, so let me make it clear: plans with members (remember, that's you) who have higher risk scores get more money to treat them. Does some of this money flow down to the plans' bottom lines as profit? You bet. Do some plans try to game the risk system to inflate the perceived ill health of their members to get higher Medicare payments? Of course they do. Is your care affected by this risk score that you don't even know exists? In many cases, it is, although the case also can be made that you are the better for it, whether you know it or not. Lastly, might you like to know how sick your doctors and other health care providers think you are? Good luck with that.

Some MA plans promote their wellness services, including sending health care professionals to your home at no cost to you to see how you're doing. On the surface, this seems wonderful. But should those visits turn up any health problems — and they often do — your risk score may increase and so will the revenue your friendly health plan derives from having you as a customer. Is this wrong? Again, that's a judgment call. But it certainly is not transparent.

THE LONGER YOU STAY, THE MORE YOU COST HOSPITALS

Hospitals are, to cite safecracker Willie Sutton's memorable insight about banks, where the money is. About a third of all health care spending stems from hospital stays, of which there were a whopping 36.5 million in 2012, lasting an average of 4.5 days each at an average daily cost of nearly $10,500.[3] The way Medicare pays hospitals for their services is of more than passing interest.

For starters, Medicare pays them different amounts for different surgeries and illnesses. This makes sense, as does further adjusting these payments depending on factors such as the local costs of doing business where the hospital is located, the type of care it provides, the mix of its patients, and even whether it's a teaching hospital with educational overhead costs.

CMS has created a set of diagnosis-related groups, or DRGs, to manage these different payments. There are more than 700 of them,[4] and while you don't know what they are, your hospital certainly does. It's all public, too, so you could look at the charges for each DRG for each hospital near you, including how many times each hospital provided each DRG surgery or treatment.[5] It's an enormous amount of data and, while it might be helpful to an eagle-eyed patient with lots of time on their hands, the odds are you would either be dead or miraculously recovered by the time you read enough to make a more informed treatment decision.

As part of the DRGs, Medicare has developed a detailed understanding of typical in-hospital admission stays. When it pays a hospital under one of these codes, it pays an amount that reflects this typical patient stay. Here is where it gets really interesting. If a hospital provides treatment under a DRG code with an average inpatient stay of, say, four days, that's what it gets paid, regardless of how many days the patient (again, remember that this could be you) actually stays in the hospital. So, if your stay is shorter than this average, the hospital likely will make more money. And if you stay in the hospital longer than this average? Well, your doctors might get paid more, but the hospital won't. Hospitals thus have strong incentives to hustle you out as quickly as they can. How this affects your health is a tough question to answer, but at the least, what's best for you is subject to financial pressure.

While there are more than 5,000 hospitals in the United States, fewer than 10 percent of them qualify to provide long-term medical care to Medicare patients. For these hospitals, Medicare has a different compensation system that actually can boost payments for longer stays, but only up to a point. When those time limits are reached (and these limits once again are linked to a patient's underlying condition), the payments no longer rise. Only a cynic would suspect that the discharge rates of these long-term care hospitals would rise sharply one day or two days after stays were no longer producing higher hospital revenues. Well, in a cynic's world, this is what researchers discovered.[6]

Now, if you were being admitted to a hospital for care, and you asked for the DRG that would be used to bill for your care, and the duration of stay associated with that DRG, you would quickly become one of that hospital's least favorite patients. But these are the Medicare rules that can have a big impact on the costs and often the quality of your health care.

THE MOVE TO PAYMENT FOR PERFORMANCE

If there's a holy grail in health care, it will be found where better care intersects with lower costs. Many experts, including leaders of CMS, believe the path to that goal involves the use of health care provider networks, the development of coordinated care plans for patients, and the movement away from fee-for-service medicine to payment-for-performance health care. This certainly is a mouthful, but it's an important mouthful, so let's break it down.

Fee-for-service health care, of course, is

another name for Original Medicare. You generally can choose whatever doctors and hospitals you want, and Medicare will pay them to treat you, even if the treatment is not successful. Over time, this has become an expensive way to deliver health care.

One of the reasons CMS has supported MA plans is that they make extensive use of health provider networks to deliver care. As Chapter 7 explained, costs can be less in a network. On paper, this will allow the plans to deliver care more cheaply than Original Medicare. That's one ingredient of the holy grail quest. (An attendant problem, of course, is whether insurers pocket too large a share of those savings for themselves and their shareholders.)

But the other thing provider networks potentially can do is provide coordinated care to a patient. If done properly, co-ordinated care should lead to healthier patients. That's because your health needs will be overseen by a defined team of providers. Your doctors, specialists, pharmacists, hospitals, and other providers will all have access to your medical records and will have an agreed-upon plan of care for you.

To encourage networks to work together, Medicare has implemented and aggressively enforced a series of "carrot-and-stick" rules that reward providers for desired patient outcomes and punish them for bad outcomes. These tools often lack the nuances that exist in the real world of health care, but they're getting better with experience (and a whole lot of provider squawking). The point here is that provider networks, and not individual providers, are becoming the focus of such efforts. To borrow a well-worn political phrase, it does take a village to provide coordinated care and better patient health. In Medicare, this village is called a provider network.

CMS has been aggressively expanding the idea of health networks to Original Medicare, too, through what are called Accountable Care Organizations (ACOs). Provider compensation is linked to patient outcomes, not just performing medical procedures and prescribing tests and drugs. ACOs have had many growing pains but they, or something like them, will be a growing part of the health care landscape.

The passage of the Medicare Access and CHIP Reauthorization Act of 2015, known as MACRA for short, empowered CMS to develop new programs to accelerate the move toward such value-based medicine. You can expect the implementation of MACRA to be messy on occasion — three steps forward and two steps back — but over time, you will receive more care from provider networks regardless of the type of Medicare you have.

IT'S ALL ABOUT THE NETWORK

For Medicare Advantage users then, and, increasingly, other Medicare beneficiaries, understanding your provider network is essential. For starters, you need to know who is in your network. Begin with your primary care physician and spread out from there to other specialists and providers you rely on the most.

Your doctor's office may not have all these details. I keep reminding myself that I want my doc to be an expert in my health care, not in Medicare administration. MA plans must give you this information but there have been lots of growing pains in developing better ways to build networks and communicate their details to plan members. Many provider directories have been badly out of date, spurring a movement toward Internet-based real-time directories that are easily updated by health plans. As of late 2015, plans with unreliable provider directories began facing fines from CMS.

Finding out who's in a network can be difficult. As the next chapter on open enrollment explains, MA plans must tell you every fall which providers will be in their plan networks during the coming calendar year. And if you already have an MA plan, it must tell you at that time about changes to its network. At any time of the year, it must tell you promptly if your doctors are no longer in its network, and give you time and options for finding other doctors who remain in the plan. You can find details on how to access online provider networks of the nation's six largest MA insurers in this endnote.[7]

Another headache with networks is that the agreements that health plans have with their providers frequently do not align with the calendar-year commitments that plans make to beneficiaries. You might sign up for a health plan in October that takes effect next January. But in February, your doctor drops out of your plan's provider network. Such network changes not only happen but are more likely these days because of the competitive pressures on plans, doctors, hospitals, and others to form and re-form health care alliances that reshape the landscape in terms of provider networks.

Right now, your plan may let you continue seeing your doctor and paying in-network rates, but usually only if you are under active treatment for a serious health problem. But the Medicare rules (despite how many there are!) are still inadequate to safeguard consumer rights and to make it easier for people to sign up for a new Medicare plan when their provider network no longer includes the providers they have been seeing.

Last but hardly least, the prices you pay for services often are higher for non-network providers than for your health plan's in-network caregivers. While it's not hard to make sure you work with in-network providers for most health needs, this can be difficult when you face emergency care in a hospital. Even if your primary physician is in your health plan network, what about all those other doctors running in and out of your operating room or hospital room? Whom do they work for? This is a problem likely to get worse before it gets better. Family members need to be particularly attentive to out-of-network charges, as you, the patient, may be forgiven by the slight distraction of worrying about your health if not your life.

Many outside analysts, including those at the U.S. Government Accountability Office (GAO),[8] have raised alerts about the need for better policing and improved consumer protection for Medicare Advantage plan provider networks. To repeat the obvious, which I know I do a lot, you need to do your provider network homework.

WHAT TEAMS ARE YOUR DOCTORS AND HOSPITALS PLAYING FOR?

The growth of provider networks, and the growing muscle of private Medicare insurers who control them, has spurred hospitals and doctors to form their own networks. This gives them more power to negotiate with private insurers, of course, but it also raises questions about how much such a doctor's care decision is driven by your needs versus his or her business relationship with a hospital.

Studies in the journal *Health Affairs* have found that higher prices occurred in local markets where hospitals own physician practices and in places with higher concentrations of large physician practices.[9] Physicians also are more likely to direct their patients to hospitals with whom they have business ties. Of course, there can be logical explanations for these observations beyond a raw exercise of market clout. But the lesson is clear for Medicare beneficiaries and their families: it can pay a lot to shop around for the best prices for care in markets increasingly characterized by provider networks. And in this exercise, your private insurance plan might actually become an ally.

FOLLOW THE BOUNCING BILL

I have repeatedly lamented that Medicare is not allowed to negotiate with pharmaceutical companies about the prices they charge Medicare beneficiaries. Medicare is, however, very involved with negotiating favorable prices with doctors, hospitals, equipment companies, and other health care providers. Just ask a doctor how "happy" he or she is with the rates they get from Medicare.

You normally benefit from these rates

whether you know it or not. Roughly 19 out of 20 doctors are what's called "participating providers" in Medicare. This means they have agreed to "accept assignment" with their Medicare patients and will accept Medicare's fees as payment in full. Further, they will collect these fees directly from Medicare or from an MA plan and not from patients. You owe only copayments and perhaps other charges based on the terms of your Medicare coverage.

The other few percent, according to a 2014 Kaiser Family Foundation report,[10] are what are called nonparticipating providers. They can charge you more than Medicare charges and your Medicare insurance may not cover these excess amounts. This practice is called "balance billing." Additional consumer safeguards have made balance billing a relatively minor problem for most beneficiaries. But you should ask about your physician's billing practices up front.

In Original Medicare, according to an example provided by Kaiser, a $100 doctor's bill involving a participating provider would cost you a 20 percent copayment, or $20, after Medicare's 80 percent payment under Part B insurance rules.

If you were, instead, seeing a nonparticipating provider, Medicare would first reduce its allowable fee for the service by 5 percent, from $100 to $95. If your doctor agreed to assignment here, Medicare would cover $76 of the $95 bill (its 80 percent payment) and you would pay the remaining $19.

But if the doctor did not accept assignment, he or she would be able to charge you up to 115 percent of the reduced charge. In our example, this would total up to $109.25 (115 percent of $95). Medicare would still pay $76. But now you would pay not $19 but as much as $33.25. In the real world, of course, especially if the doctor involved was performing surgery, you would be multiplying this $100 many, many times over. And balance billing could definitely unbalance your budget.

Remember here that Original Medicare has no caps on your upper exposure to claims. Two Medigap letter plans — C and F — will cover balance billing charges. Balance billing is prohibited in most MA plans but is permitted in MA physician fee-for-service (PFFS) plans.

This is especially true for a small percentage of doctors — less than 1 percent in 2014 — that have opted out of Medicare entirely. They can charge you whatever they wish and you may be on the hook for the entire bill, not just the normal Medicare co-payments.

The implications of health provider networks, in terms of pricing, access to health care, and the quality of that care, have slowly become clearer to consumers and watchdog groups. Still to come, I hope, are the development of consumer safeguards and tools to help Medicare beneficiaries and their families make the right health care decisions. I liken this to the state of consumer auto safeguards fifty years ago when crusader Ralph Nader began taking on Detroit.

One area where consumers do have lots of Medicare clout is the annual open enrollment period. It, too, has a lot in common with automobile shopping, as you'll see in the next chapter.

13
OPEN ENROLLMENT
HOW TO FIX A MEDICARE LEMON

If Medicare were an automobile, you would be a happy driver. Every year, you would have the chance to lease a new car with better styling, performance, fuel economy, and safety features. It wouldn't necessarily cost more than your last car, and might even cost less. If this year's car turned out to be a lemon, you would need to live with it at most for a single year.

Each fall, a new batch of cars would hit showroom floors. Before they could be approved for use, they would have to meet basic performance standards. The quality of every model would be evaluated and these grades would be freely available to all potential drivers. The sellers couldn't gouge you on prices, either. In fact, they could sell you their products only after submitting their prices to a review panel, which has the power to ban cars from even being sold if they are judged too expensive.

Okay, this last example stretches even my credulity, and I wrote it. Of course, the auto industry does not work this way, and we must now part company with this analogy.

But Medicare has an annual open enrollment period and it does work this way. In fact, it does so in a manner that tilts the odds even further in favor of consumers *IF* — and it's an IF that merits its capitalized letters — *IF* consumers know how the system works.

The ability to literally get an annual "do-over" for your Medicare coverage is so important and potentially so valuable that you should read this chapter every year.

Open enrollment does not have to be an annual morass that gets you so stuck that you cannot move and you wind up doing nothing. By this point in *Get What's Yours for Medicare* you are close to being a Medicare pro, so don't fail to take advantage of this pro-consumer opportunity. Remember those behavioral horror stories about Medicare complexity from the beginning of the book? Don't let such attitudes derail you.

Open enrollment begins each year on October 15 and extends through December 7. There are other enrollment periods as well, and they are covered in Chapter 4. But taking advantage of open enrollment is essential. It will help you get the most from Medicare. And it is a powerful way consumers can have a big group say by rewarding the best plans with more business and helping rid the market of poorer plans.

THE COMPLEXITY CONUNDRUM

First, let's return to the complexity issue, so I can attempt to put a stake through its heart once and for all. People who already have Medicare plans tend to stick with them. The perceived complexity of Medicare is akin to having a tooth pulled, and who would want to volunteer to have that done year after year?

I used to feel this way about all insurance. But a long time ago, the experts I interviewed for stories would tell me that consumers needed to shop around for their best deal. We certainly do this for big-ticket items like homes and cars. Once we have an insurance policy, our comparison-shopping "gene," for lack of a better word, seems to shut down. But this doesn't have to be the case.

Every year, your Medicare insurance providers must by law tell you by the end of September about meaningful plan changes that will take effect the following January. These documents, while long, are not complex if you know what to look for, and where to find it. The point of this chapter, indeed the point of the entire book, is to reduce Medicare's complexity so that you can feel confident changing your Medicare coverage when it's in your interest to do so.

When it comes to open enrollment decisions, here are the variables you should focus on:

THE "MONEY" PARTS

Premiums. What's the monthly premium of the plan? How does it differ from this year's? People will need to pay more than normal attention to their Part B premiums. These premiums have been on a roller coaster due to the Social Security consumer protection measure it calls its "hold harmless" rule, as explained in Chapter 9. You'll find current Part B premiums under the Updates tab on the *Get What's Yours for Medicare* website.[1]

Deductibles. These are the annual amounts you must pay before your Medicare insurance kicks in. Medicare changes its annual Part A and Part B deductibles each year. They were $1,288 for Part A in 2016, $166 for Part B, and $360 for Part D. Again, some Medicare Advantage (MA) plans will absorb some of these costs, as will some Medigap plans for people using Original Medicare.

Copays and Coinsurance. How much will you need to fork over to a doctor or other health care provider for appointments and covered services? Is it different from this year's? How about your Medicare plan's coinsurance requirements?

Donut Hole. The coverage gap for Part D drug plans is shrinking each year. It will be eliminated by 2020, but we're stuck with it until then. In 2016, the gap began at $3,310 and ended at $4,850. For 2017 updates, check the *Get What's Yours* website or "Ask Phil." In 2017, you'll have to pay 40 percent of the cost of brand-name drugs and 51 percent of the cost of generic drugs while in the gap. By 2020, both payment levels are slated to drop to 25 percent, which is the standard coinsurance payment for all drugs.

Drug Tiers. Is your Part D plan moving the drugs you take from one pricing tier to another? Most plans have five tiers. They place more expensive drugs in higher tiers, and beneficiaries are asked to pay larger co-pay amounts and coinsurance percentages in these tiers.

Out-of-Pocket Maximums. One of the great appeals of MA plans is that they cap your annual health care spending. In Original Medicare, you need to buy a Medigap policy to accomplish the same thing. Part D plans also have annual spending caps that protect most people from all but relatively small prices for prescription drugs should you be in what's called the "catastrophic" zone of Part D coverage. However, you're still obligated to pay 5 percent of drug costs in this zone, so if you take really expensive medications, you could face steep Part D payments.

Keep in mind here that if you have an MA plan that includes a Part D plan, as most MA plans do, you will have *two* annual caps, one for health coverage and the second for prescription drug expenses.

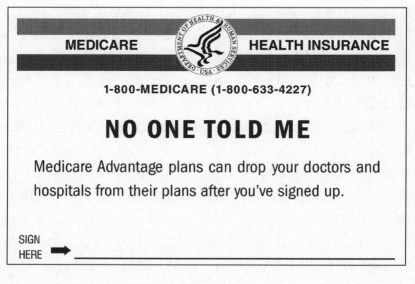

MEDICARE   HEALTH INSURANCE

1-800-MEDICARE (1-800-633-4227)

NO ONE TOLD ME

Medicare Advantage plans can drop your doctors and hospitals from their plans after you've signed up.

SIGN
HERE ➡ _____

The Non-Money Parts

Provider Networks. As the last chapter detailed, understanding the workings of health care provider networks will be increasingly important for all Medicare beneficiaries. For now, it's especially important for folks with MA plans. So, make a list of the doctors you need to keep seeing, and make sure they're included in your plan's provider network. Ditto for hospitals and other care providers. If they aren't, it's time to find another plan that does include them. If there are no MA plans that include your primary doctors, and you want to keep seeing them, you need to consider whether you should switch to Original Medicare during open enrollment.

Drug Formularies. The second major non-money issue is whether your prescription drugs are included in your plan's formulary for next year. If not, you should get ready to spend some time with our old friend, Medicare's online Plan Finder.[2] (Go back to Chapter 8 if you need a Plan Finder refresher.) You can review MA plans with both bundled-in drug plans and stand-alone Part D drug plans. Keep in mind that most MA plans require you to get a bundled Part D plan. This means that if a key medication is not offered by your plan, or is offered at a price far in excess of what you would pay in another plan, you will face the challenge of changing more than your drug coverage. You will need to look for another MA plan available where you live.

MEDIGAP PLANS

You can switch Medigap plans during open enrollment, or even get a plan for the first time should you switch from MA to Original Medicare. However, you need to proceed carefully here. Remember our discussion of Medigap's guaranteed issue rights in Chapter 6? You may lose these rights if you no longer are within your "protected" sign-up window for Medigap. This means that insurers can charge you more money, possibly expose you to larger future rate increases, and even impose a six-month period where any preexisting conditions you have are not covered by the policy. (These conditions will, of course, still be covered by Original Medicare, but during this six-month period your Medigap policy would not cover the 20 percent coinsurance requirement of Original Medicare.)

The loss of guaranteed issue rights for Medigap can occur if you already have a Medigap plan and want to get a different one. Or, if you have had Original Medicare but not a Medigap policy, you may no longer have guaranteed issue rights if you now want Medigap. There are more safeguards for people who wish to get a Medigap policy when they are switching from Medicare Advantage to Original Medicare. But there can be complications even here.

Because Medigap policies are regulated at the state level, you should call a State Health Insurance Assistance Program[3] counselor in your state and review your options *before* making a decision. It also might help to take a refresher "course" by rereading Chapter 6, especially the part about the different types of insurance rating rules used by Medigap insurers. It's not enough to find a plan that meets your needs *next* year — you need to find a plan that will meet them for *many* years.

ARE YOUR ANOCS AND EOBS AWOL?

If you are an existing Medicare beneficiary and have private insurance, your Medicare Advantage and Part D drug plans should send you legally required annual notices by the end of September. They're called the annual notice of change (ANOC) and Explanation of Benefits (EOB) for MA and Part D plans. There is a shorter Medigap notice that must disclose any upcoming premium changes.

For the MA and Part D plans, the ANOC is the shorter of the two. It lists the important changes occurring in the coming calendar year. The changes are presented in sections that closely track the money and non-money items listed above. These are not hard to follow or fathom. You will see changes in premiums and copays, additions and deletions to what the plans cover, changes in their drug formularies, plan tiers, and related copays.

If the plans make meaningful changes to their networks of participating doctors, hospitals, and other health care providers, they must tell you. Ditto for changes in the pharmacy networks they use to fill your prescriptions and provide preferred pricing terms.

Changes in plan formularies and provider networks should be accompanied by detailed lists, either as part of the plan documents you are mailed or on the insurer's website.

Once you've highlighted year-to-year changes in the ANOC that are important to you, you can look at related details in the longer EOB document. Consider it your backup resource for official health plan coverage terms.

Medigap plans' coverage requirements are set by law and the individual letter plans (A, B, C, etc.) must offer coverage identical to the same-letter plans offered by other insurers. So, the only annual variable is the price that insurers charge. This notice is provided in a document called the "Annual Notice of Rate." As described earlier, beginning in 2020, newly issued letter C and F plans will no longer be able to cover the annual Part B deductible.

WHAT TO DO NEXT

Realistically, if your doctors and hospitals are still in your provider networks, your drugs are still covered, and your prices have not gone up by what you consider unreasonable amounts, you probably will stick with what you've got. If so, you need do nothing during open enrollment. If your plan does not hear from you, it will renew your insurance plan for the next year.

If your plan's health care provider network has changed, however, you have two choices.

First, your plan is legally obligated to work with you to identify other doctors or hospitals in its network that are acceptable to you. If this happens, you can evaluate these alternatives using the star ratings and other provider ranking tools described in Chapter 11. If these new providers are acceptable to you — and no other big plan changes are occurring — you can stick with this plan.

Second, you can call your doctor's office and ask for his or her other health plan affiliations. In most cases, your doctor's preferred hospitals will also be your first choice. So, if your doctor is still in your plan's network but her or his preferred hospital is not, ask if other plans do work with both or if the plan's hospital is acceptable to your doctor.

Once you have these details, you can use Plan Finder to evaluate these plans and compare them with the one you have.

Plan Finder is also where you should turn if your existing plan alerts you to any pricing or changes in its prescription drug coverage next year that raise red flags in your mind. You can look at pricing and drug availabilities in other plans that will be offered in your ZIP code next year.

If you want to see the complete lists of your plan's provider network and its drug formulary, the plan must mail them to you and most likely will have them on its website as well. Here are these online links for large Medicare insurer formularies.[4]

Finally, of course, these same comparison-shopping tools are available to you if you've become unhappy with your plan during the year and want to change plans next year.

Even if you've reviewed your alternatives earlier in the year, you need to refresh plan details in the fall after insurers have posted their new plan offerings before open enrollment begins on October 15.

You need not rush. Any changes made during open enrollment, even those made at the December 7 deadline, will take effect on January 1.

So, to recap, pay attention to these three shorthand "P's": Prices, Prescriptions, and Providers.

As I've been saying: simple.

Now, please take a deep breath or perhaps as many as you can without hyperventilating. Because the next chapter is not simple at all. It involves some of the toughest choices you and your family members will make about Medicare: what kind of health care do you want near and at the end of your life?

14
WHAT'S YOUR ENDGAME?
GETTING READY TO NOT BE HERE

Planning for the end of life, you ask? What a colossal conceit. I don't even know what I will be doing in the next day or even hour! Now you ask me to flash ahead many years and figure out what I want the end of my life to look like? Really?

Yep, I do.

This is my third book dealing with various facets of longevity. Since 2008, I have written more than one thousand articles on aging, health, retirement, and the financial implications raised by these topics. I've also heard innumerable heartfelt stories from friends, readers, and others. And I've been fortunate enough to live my own three score and ten. Aging and views of my own swan song are less and less academic subjects and more what I see in the mirror each morning, assuming I can locate my glasses to help me see anything at all.

Along the way, I have watched my own

parents die at what now seem terribly and unnecessarily early ages. Perhaps because of this, I've listened closely to the stories told by my more fortunate friends, now in their 50s and 60s, whose parents have lived on well into their 80s and 90s.

It has come as a big surprise to me that their common refrain is not how lucky and blessed they are by their parents' longevity. Instead they say how hard it has been for them to care for one or more aging parents, how it has broken their parents' nest eggs and also cracked their own, stolen precious time from their own lives, and left them exhausted, and, truth be told, occasionally resentful of a burden they never sought.

I doubt they would respond well to even a gentle suggestion that such efforts are a bargain in exchange for having one or both parents for 20 years longer than I had mine. But before rushing to judgment, let me also point out that these stories are coming from good people. They are the ones who have stepped up, out of love and family obligations. They did not turn their backs or look the other way. They have stayed the course.

HAVING LOTS OF COMPANY IN THE POORHOUSE

The point I want to make, and by this point in *Get What's Yours for Medicare,* you know I am not a subtle guy, is that this course can be a tough one to navigate. Here's a sobering look at what's in store for us, drawn from a Kaiser Family Foundation assessment.[1]

Between 2010 and 2050, the United States population ages 65 and older will nearly double, the population ages 80 and older will nearly triple, and the number of nonagenarians and centenarians — people in their 90s and 100s — will quadruple.

As adults live into their 80s and beyond, they are more likely to live with multiple chronic conditions and functional limitations, and this combination (compared to having chronic conditions only) is associated with a greater likelihood of emergency department visits and inpatient hospitalizations as well as higher Medicare spending for inpatient hospital, skilled nursing facility, and home health services.

If you are or soon will be using Medicare, or are the adult child or perhaps just a friend of such a person, you must not close your mind to the inevitable health and financial issues that play a large role in the final stages of life. Reading this chapter will not make those final years a walk in the park, either for you or the people who love you. But it just might make it an easier walk for everyone.

By paying close attention to a manageable list of later-life situations, older Americans and their relatives, friends, and caregivers can create better outcomes near and at the ends of their lives. They can get better health care, possibly spend less money, and feel better emotionally as well as physically.

IT'S THE INSURANCE, STUPID

There is an understandable focus on money when it comes to Medicare and health care in general. That's fine, up to a point. But there is a reason Medicare is called insurance, and one of the major things that insurance can do is protect people from serious financial loss. That's what we do with home and auto coverage. It's why we get life insurance. The same thing is true with Medicare. Viewing Medicare as insurance protection and not just as an expense item makes more and more sense as we age.

Health care expenses have become a major if not the major financial concern of

336

people in their retirement years. They are a big source of personal bankruptcies[2] and the ultimate wild card in retirement planning. You can budget for housing, food, and utilities. How the heck do you budget for unsuspected diseases and operations at unknown points in your future?

Studies regularly tell us that the average 65-year-old couple faces future out-of-pocket health costs ranging between $250,000 and $300,000 in today's dollars. This excludes the cost of long-term care, which averages close to $80,000 a year in a nursing home, and can easily top six figures a year in some locales. These are averages, it should be noted. If you look at the distribution of such expenses over the entire population of older people, you will see lots of million-dollar-and-up health care bills.

Original Medicare has an enormous coverage gap. It pays only 80 percent of Part B covered expenses. It's true that closing this gap with a Medigap policy can seem like a big expense. But as the odds of ruinous medical bills rise as we get older, it makes less and less sense to roll the dice by "saving" money on Medicare insurance premiums. You need to protect yourself.

If you cannot afford a Medigap plan, you should adopt a defensive insurance posture,

337

especially as you enter your later 70s and 80s. Medicare Advantage (MA) plans have caps on annual out-of-pocket spending for health and drug expenses. You could consider them as catastrophic policies. However, catastrophic does not mean free. MA patients with expensive and complex health needs — a group heavily weighted toward older beneficiaries — often switch out of MA plans back to Original Medicare.[3] While the reasons for the trend need further study, consumers need to find out more about how MA plans cover the kinds of multiple medical conditions that often afflict the elderly.

MEDICARE: A PROGRAM FOR THE AGED, IF NOT THE AGES

At the same time, don't kid yourself that Medicare or any other kind of insurance will cover all of your expenses. If your spouse is seriously ill and in the hospital, are you really going to park them in a room with one or more other patients if you can afford a private room? Medicare doesn't cover private hospital rooms, or private duty nurses, or lots of in-room amenities that hospitals offer. When it's your loved one hooked up to tubes and monitors, you're going to want them to have the best possible care.

Traditional Medicare expenses rise with age. Here's more from Kaiser, based on 2011 expenses:

AGE	ANNUAL PER CAPITA MEDICARE SPENDING
70	$7,566
75	$9,760
80	$11,618
85	$13,466
90	$14,745
95	$15,732
100	$15,411

Not many people make it to 95 or 100, or course, but if you do, your Medicare use will rise. Also, these are average program expenses, not out-of-pocket spending. But rising Medicare expenses often are associated with higher out-of-pocket spending, especially in Original Medicare.

Kaiser also looked at average Medicare spending by age for people who died in 2011. Again, these are program expenses, and Medicare certainly will cover much of them. These numbers actually are higher for younger Medicare beneficiaries. That's not surprising, given that efforts to heal people and extend lives often are more aggressive for younger patients. Here's a look at those numbers:

AGE AT DEATH	ANNUAL PER CAPITA SPENDING
All	$33,486
70	$42,933
75	$40,372
80	$35,794
85	$32,431
90	$26,687
95	$21,993
100	$20,318

Even after toting up your maximum out-of-pocket expenses that are covered by Medicare, you need to have a reserve fund to handle things that are *not* covered. If you own a home, consider using your home equity as a piggybank for such expenses. If you don't have a home, think about setting aside retirement funds for medical expenses.

If you do not yet need Medicare and are covered by employer group insurance, see if you can enroll in a high-deductible health plan and make tax-free contributions to a health savings account (HSA). Then, do your best *not* to spend these dollars. Unspent balances can roll over from year to year. These funds can be placed into investment accounts like 401(k)s. Better yet, if you spend them on qualifying medical expenses, you won't pay taxes on them when they're withdrawn. Properly planned and managed, an HSA is a marvelous rainy-day fund for unanticipated medical expenses when you're older.

MEDICARE HEALTH INSURANCE

1-800-MEDICARE (1-800-633-4227)

NO ONE TOLD ME

Medicare does not cover ambulance service if the patient dies before the ambulance arrives.

SIGN
HERE ➡

OUR BIGGEST HOLE IN LATER-LIFE CARE

This has been noted before but it bears repeating here: Medicare does not cover long-term stays in nursing homes, assisted living facilities, and other custodial care providers. These places can be expensive, and there is a 70 percent chance that someone aged 65 and older will require long-term care services at some point during the rest of their life. Of course, not all long-term care stays are all that long. But extended stays can cost a small fortune. The point here is that most people don't know what's in store for them other than a two-in-three chance that they'll need such care.

Genworth Financial, a long-term care insurer, produces an annual long-term care cost survey.[4] It looks at costs in some 440 geographic markets across the country, so you can get an accurate idea of costs near your home, or perhaps the home of an adult child or other family member who might agree to be your primary caregiver. In its 2015 survey, Genworth presented the median (Geek Alert: median is the midway point between the highest and lowest costs; it is not an arithmetic average) *annual* rates of these six care services:

Homemaker services: $44,616
Home health aide services: $45,760
Adult day health care: $17,904
Assisted living facility (one bedroom, single occupancy): $43,200
Nursing home (semiprivate room): $80,300
Nursing home (private room): $91,250

If you are fortunate enough to be healthy

and physically independent as you enter your 80s, the top-of-the-line choice for many seniors is a private continuing care retirement community (CCRC). There are different business models for CCRCs. More expensive ones will sell you an apartment for $250,000 or more (often a lot more), and then bill you thousands of dollars a month for your meals and other costs associated with living in the CCRC.

However, a full-service CCRC will provide you meals, a range of activities and, perhaps most important, a guaranteed roof over your head for the rest of your life, including assisted living services and nursing home care for especially ill or frail residents. Some even provide on-site dementia care. Couples often can continue to live in a community even if one of them no longer can live independently. It all costs money, lots of money. And while Medicare will continue to provide coverage at CCRCs, this represents a small share of total community expenses.

Private long-term care insurance can defray a substantial share of long-term care costs but it is expensive and the insurance industry has had a tough time making acceptable profits from long-term care insurance. Low interest rates are poison to life and health insurers, robbing them of safe and profitable places to park money for long periods. Many companies have left the business or cut back. Most have raised rates and there has been little stability in the outlook for the industry or product.

(By way of personal disclosure, I once worked at Genworth, which has been buffeted just like other carriers. I also have a long-term care insurance policy, as does my wife. We are lucky to be able to afford them. Our lifetime premiums will easily exceed $150,000 if we are fortunate to live long enough. I will be a happy guy if we never have to use these policies. That's what insurance is for, as I keep saying.)

Only a small percentage of seniors buy long-term care insurance. The wealthy self-insure and can afford to pay these expenses. People of lesser means roll the dice and hope they will not need long-term care. The real irony here is that many seniors who do buy the product drop it in their later years after they've already paid out many thousands of dollars in premiums. That money is wasted, just at the time when their likelihood of needing care is greatest. Money woes are most often cited as the culprit, which just further emphasizes the need for end-of-life financial planning.

Medicaid is the default provider of long-term care. People have to spend down just about all of their assets before Medicaid will pay for their custodial long-term care. But this is the closest thing we have to a national "plan" for long-term care.

Not surprisingly, most nursing home residents are poor women. This is a sad longevity dividend for them. As a nation, we are badly failing older residents who do not have enough money to pay for their own care. Yes, there's Medicaid. But there are lots and lots of holes in that safety net. More worrisome is the certainty that Medicaid and our nursing homes will be overwhelmed with the financial and care demands of all the aging baby boomers who will need long-term care and be unable to pay for it. This enormous problem gets larger by the day, and no amount of whiz-bang telemedicine or home-based care is going to solve it.

PLAY YOUR MARBLES WHILE YOU STILL HAVE SOME

I earlier alluded to the inevitable cognitive decline that begins to affect most people in their 60s and 70s. This is the normal course of events when it comes to aging, not the outlier. And what it means is that when it comes to making the right decision, anticipating future needs, and engaging in complex financial and health care planning and management tasks, your ability will fall off.

Roughly half of those older than 65 admitted to a hospital are unable to make their own care decisions and need a friend or relative to be their health care decision maker, or proxy.

Leaving your future health care planning needs to some undefined and distant *mañana* is a bad idea on multiple fronts. Here, I'll only reinforce the notion that you need to make these plans while you still can. They may have lots of moving parts, which I'll turn to momentarily. You need to be at the top of your game mentally to put them together in the best possible way.

There is no shortage of reasons why we fail to put end-of-life plans in place. After all, who likes to dwell on their eventual decline and demise? Our aversion to the topic has improved since Elisabeth Kübler-Ross wrote *On Death and Dying* in 1969. But not nearly enough.

Then there are family issues. They can always get in the way. For the rising share of older Americans who live on their own and have no or little family support, this vacuum likewise serves as a deterrent to wise planning.

THIS TALK IS DEFINITELY
NOT CHEAP

Whether you have a close, extended family or just your weird nephew Bob who lives on the other side of the state, it is essential to begin talking about your end-of-life needs, and to keep talking. Repeat conversations are a good idea. And make sure all your kids are included and on board. If they are not, or you don't have family to call upon, enlist friends. I know this is hard and often uncomfortable, especially at the start. But you and your family can benefit in so, so many ways.

Now, I am a big believer in taking the best possible care of myself, and I hope you are, too. Research shows that we can live longer if we do this. But more than living longer, we can spend more of our time leading active lives. Becoming frail and physically dependent is, I'm afraid, one of the less publicized consequences of longevity. My goal is to stave off my inevitable decline for as long as I can. The scientific term for this, which I mentioned earlier in the book, is "compressed morbidity." Being a fan of most things morbid, I love it. Compressed morbidity has become my mantra for aging.

Regardless of how compressed your own morbidity may be, you really can't escape it. Sure, many of us may hope we pass away quietly in the night, with no pain or regrets or things unsaid or paths not taken. Our realities are likely to be quite different. We will need more and more help taking care of ourselves, first by friends and family and, later, by health care professionals. The costs and complexities of these decisions will grow. And grow and grow.

To prepare for these times, you need to put together "Team You" — a group of family members and friends who will be there for you when you need them. There are many sources of help in putting together such a team. One such helpful site is called Prepare[5] and has easy-to-follow videos.

All of these efforts need to begin with "the conversation," a phrase that is deservedly credited to journalist Ellen Goodman, who for the past several years has been the face of a program called, not surprisingly, the Conversation Project. Its purpose is to support end-of-life discussions and planning. Along with other voices, it is making a difference.

Having the conversation means sitting down with one or more people and talking about end-of-life issues. The group has what it calls a starter kit[6] that can be downloaded from its website. Here are some of the key questions it suggests you discuss:

When you think about the last phase of
your life, what's most important to you?
How would you like this phase to be?

Do you have any particular concerns
about your health? About the last phase
of your life?

What affairs do you need to get in order,
or talk to your loved ones about? (Personal finances, property, relationships.)

Who do you want (or not want) to be
involved in your care? Who would you
like to make decisions on your behalf if
you're not able to? (This person is your
health care proxy.)

Would you prefer to be actively involved in
decisions about your care? Or would you
rather have your doctors do what they
think is best?

Are there any disagreements or family ten-
sions that you're concerned about?

Are there important milestones you'd like
to meet if possible? (The birth of your
grandchild, your 80th birthday.)

Where do you want (or not want) to receive
care? (Home, nursing facility, hospital.)

Are there kinds of treatment you would
want or not want? (Resuscitation if your

heart stops, breathing machine, feeding
tube.)

When would it be okay to shift from a
focus on curative care to a focus on
comfort care alone?

HEY, DOC? ABOUT
THOSE PEARLY GATES . . .

Medicare began in 2016 to pay doctors to
have end-of-life conversations with patients
and their families. This is a big deal within
a big deal, and a long-needed improvement
in Medicare benefits. Advocated by many
medical and patient groups, the broader
topic of end-of-life care was derailed by a
puffed-up "debate" over whether the Affordable Care Act would lead to the creation
of "death panels." The scare tactic du jour
was that the law would allow some faceless
bureaucrat to decide that some seniors
would be denied essential health care if their
condition was too far advanced to benefit
from additional treatments. This was, is, and
will be a bogus issue.

End-of-life discussions should, if anything,
have the exact opposite goals. What kind of
health care do you want? What does your
physician think about the best types of care
for you, given your age and medical issues?
What's hospice really like? Have you ever

heard of palliative care? Are your family members aware of your preferences and are they on board with them? Is there someone in your family, or perhaps a close friend, who will agree to serve as your health "proxy" — a legally appointed person who can make medical decisions for you should you be unable to make them for yourself?

In *Being Mortal,*[7] physician and writer Atul Gawande speaks movingly about coming to terms with death in his own family and of how doctors and patients alike are uncomfortable and unprepared to discuss death. But the payoff for doing so can be enormous. "People who had substantive discussions with their doctors about their end-of-life preferences were far more likely to die at peace and in control of their situation and to spare their family anguish," he wrote.

These are enormously important matters, and these end-of-life doctor sessions might — emphasis on *might* — provide the perfect setting to address them. Amy Vandenbroucke, an advocate for strong patient tools to ensure that their end-of-life wishes are carried out by doctors and other health care workers, passes on one tech-appropriate tip in today's wireless age: bring along a smartphone and make a video recording of the meeting. This will create a needed record for you and, perhaps of greater importance, for family members who aren't present. "Seeing a video of Mom saying she never wants to be hooked up to a machine is very powerful," she notes.

FINDING THE RIGHT DOC AS YOU GET OLDER

Doctors, as Gawande and other informed observers have noted, may not be particularly well-equipped or interested in having helpful end-of-life discussions. More to the point, doctors in general appear to be a shrinking breed. And geriatricians — doctors specifically trained to care for aged patients — are very, very hard to even find. Only about 7,000 now practice in the United States, serving a population of older Americans well north of 30 million. Do the math.

As we age, finding the best possible physician with whom to grow older should be a priority. If you can't find a geriatrician, look for a doctor who is not only competent but listens to you — not one so pressed for time that they are checking their watches or smartphones after your appointment has exceeded a few minutes.

TRANSLATING YOUR WISHES INTO BINDING INSTRUCTIONS

Having the conversation and talking with your doctor about end-of-life issues can prepare you to create a set of legally binding documents to turn your preferences into instructions that your family, doctors, and other caregivers will follow when the time comes. This stage of the process has long been a stopper for many people. The idea of needing to hire lawyers causes many folks to proceed no further. Identifying a family member or friend to be your medical surrogate can also be a tough go. Lastly, there seems to be a regular flow of horror stories about people who did all these things and whose wishes were *still* denied by a health care system based on doing everything possible to keep patients alive.

Increasingly, however, you will not need an attorney to create what's generally referred to as a set of advance directives. Most often, these directives include two components.

Health Care Proxy. (Also called a health care power of attorney or durable power of attorney.) This authorizes your health care decision makers to make medical decisions on your behalf should you be unable to speak for yourself. Whether you feel like

Superman or Superwoman today, odds are that one or more children or friends will be needed to help you make crucial decisions when you are ill and perhaps confused by the array of challenging medical care decisions that must be made — often in a hurry and nearly always during times of great personal stress.

Living Will. This spells out the types of medical care you want in an emergency situation. Do you want doctors to do everything possible to keep you alive? Do you want ambulance medics and other health care professionals to try to resuscitate you should you stop breathing? Do you want to be hooked up to a machine and intubated so that you can stay alive while doctors try to restore your health?

A number of states have online forms that can be filled in to create advance directives that will be accepted by hospitals and doctors. Hospitals are required by law to provide you a blank advance directive form that you can fill in and sign, and which would be legally binding upon them.

You can find the state-specific forms for both the health care proxy and the living will at www.caringinfo.org. There are also a few states where there is a statewide registry of advance care planning documents. Check this endnote to see if your state has one.[8]

Increasingly, these documents are moving online, where they can be accessed on a timely basis by care providers. Keep in mind that one state's forms might not be binding if your health issues occur when you are in another state.

Here's another key asterisk: your health, your end-of-life priorities, and the people you trust to help you may well change, and then change again, before you confront the actual health issues that required all this advance planning in the first place. So, do not think having these conversations and executing the proper documents is a "one and done" event. Have new conversations and draft new documents as needed.

A nonprofit called Aging with Dignity has created a simple set of advance care preferences called Five Wishes that is now accepted by nearly all states.[9] Here are the wishes:

Wish 1: The Person I Want to Make Health Care Decisions for Me When I Can't

Wish 2: The Kind of Medical Treatment I Want or Don't Want

Wish 3: How Comfortable I Want to Be

Wish 4: How I Want People to Treat Me

Wish 5: What I Want My Loved Ones to Know

The American Bar Association has a smartphone app called My Health Care Wishes[10] that will permit your end-of-life documents and wishes to be accessible from your phone so that you or your health care decision maker can show them to doctors and other health professionals on a timely basis. More such apps are appearing all the time.

ONE LAST THOUGHT ABOUT LAST THOUGHTS

Having advance directives is a necessary part of having your end-of-life wishes recognized and followed by care providers. But it may not be enough. Advance directives are not medical orders, so, for example, emergency medical technicians (EMTs) are not legally able to follow them. Instead, they are legally required to do everything possible to try to save your life. Likewise, if you have a life-threatening health situation, hospital personnel may feel morally and often legally obligated to keep you alive. Advance directives are reviewed at the hospital with your surrogate and used to make treatment decisions. But general medical care preferences, even if expressed in a directive or a living will, may not encompass the specific care decisions that they must make.

To deal with this reality, advocates have been working to develop state-by-state acceptance of what are known collectively as Physician Orders for Life-Sustaining Treatment (POLST); they go by different names in some states.[11] These orders are signed by a physician (or in some states, also nurse practitioners, advance practice registered nurses, or physician assistants) and the patient (or his or her representative). The POLST form is completed based on the specific medical issues involved in your end-of-life care situation and your goals for care. As a result, POLST documents often are not signed until a patient is ill or frail, and facing important care decisions.

Unlike an advance directive, Vandenbroucke explains, a POLST is a specific medical order that must be followed by health care professionals, including EMTs. All but three states (Minnesota, Mississippi, and North Dakota) have a provision for an out-of-hospital do not resuscitate (DNR) order, which allows the patient to determine what kind of care would be provided, or not provided, by an EMT.

POLST programs are available in more and more states, and in some locales these forms have also been integrated into patients' electronic health records. Again, a POLST signed in one jurisdiction may not be binding upon health care providers in another.

MEDICARE'S EXPANDED HOSPICE BENEFITS

As explained in Chapter 5, Medicare has extensive hospice benefits that are being used by more and more beneficiaries. Hospice is offered under Part A of Medicare, and the benefits are the same for Original Medicare and MA users.

Hospice care at home has become the preferred place that people want to spend their final days. I don't need to rehash these benefits here. But I do want to make sure you're aware of a new Medicare pilot program for hospice.

To many people, the biggest problem with hospice is that the patient has to cease what's called "curative" medical care in order to use Medicare's hospice benefits. Traditional hospice provides what's called palliative care, to help relieve pain and make the patient as comfortable as possible. But it does not permit caregivers to continue efforts to cure the underlying medical condition that has threatened the patient's life.

This can seem like giving up — a tough concession for many patients and their families. Medicare launched a pilot program in 2016 to offer participants the chance to use hospice and continue receiving curative medical care. I know that patients and their families will support this effort. What I don't know is whether such a program will be too costly for Medicare to expand to all beneficiaries.

WHERE IT ALL COMES TOGETHER

Jane deLima Thomas is a geriatrician and palliative care physician at the Dana-Farber Cancer Institute in Boston, where she also teaches other doctors about end-of-life care situations and care.

If you are not clear on exactly what palliative care is, here is the National Cancer Institute's definition:

Palliative care is care given to improve the quality of life of patients who have a serious or life-threatening disease, such as cancer. The goal of palliative care is to prevent or treat, as early as possible, the symptoms and *side effects* of the disease and its treatment, in addition to the related psychological, social, and spiritual problems. The goal is not to cure. Palliative care is also called *comfort care, supportive care,* and *symptom management.*[12]

That's okay as far as it goes. Dr. Thomas's description of what she does fills in some essential pieces that are missing, and also cements the role of intrafamily communicating as a vital way to help patients and families navigate the difficult times that many if not most families face when a loved one is ailing or dying.

Dr. Thomas sees patients in the hospital, not in a clinic or other outpatient setting. "I meet them when they are sick and sometimes in a crisis," she says. "The physician's role [on a palliative care team] is to really learn very carefully and rigorously the medical facts of the patient. . . . The second piece is to really get to know the patient and the family well, including what's important to them. This is a key step in helping me guide them to an appropriate path forward for the care the patient should receive."

Religious, cultural, and other personal beliefs are an important part of patient and family attitudes and preferences toward end-of-life care. Learning these things requires conversations among all parties —

patient, family members, and the physician.

"The thing that palliative care brings to the center of the conversation is, 'Who is this patient? Who is this family?' " Dr. Thomas says. "It is what we remind the medical profession as a whole to bring into the center of the conversation."

While advance directives are important, she readily agrees, they are static documents written on pieces of paper, often months or years removed from whatever medical emergency has created the care situation faced by her patients. "Having a conversation is essential so that the family and the patient's physician understand why what's written on that piece of paper" was done in the first place.

"Families can be tortured when they have not had these conversations," she says. "That's a terrible position in which to put a family member. I've seen family members who have just become undone, because they just don't know what to do."

Discussing these issues can provide comfort and closure to everyone. Without such understanding and consensus, the default standard of medical care will be aggressive. Dr. Thomas is quick to note that aggressive care may, in fact, be exactly what's called for. But it might not. In such settings, aggressive treatment can be a lose-lose-lose situation, exposing the patient to physical suffering, leaving their family emotionally devastated, and costing a lot of money.

Palliative care is often provided within a hospice setting but is also available to patients with serious illnesses and pain who are not considered terminally ill. It has been shown to improve the quality of life for patients near the end of their lives. Moreover, for many patients, the effort to make them comfortable, reduce pain, and provide quiet time at home with family members can also extend their lives compared with continued hospital treatment.

At the end of life, the quality of your death will matter tremendously. Certainly, it will matter to you. But, perhaps even more important, it will matter to your surviving family members. Knowing that you've left them in as peaceful and accepting a state as possible, in turn, will be of great importance to you. All of us would prefer a good death that leaves us at peace on many levels. Medicare has the tools to make this possible. It's up to you to use them.

ACKNOWLEDGMENTS

During a professional life spanning nearly fifty years, the highlight reel of my working life is populated with many anecdotes, a few nuggets of wisdom, and, fortunately, a still-smaller number of "there but for the grace of God" lessons from mistakes that I somehow managed to survive. Fifty years is long enough to accommodate a lot of mistakes, and I wasted little time assembling my personal record of fallibility. So it is with certainty that I say there may be mistakes and, likely, omissions in this book. They are my fault and responsibility. And there would be many, many more were it not for the efforts of so many people who are enormously talented and informed. And patient.

When you come across a suspected mistake within the covers of this book, I hope you will let me know. I am sure your suggested corrections will be pleasant and constructive. Such cordiality is, of course, today's Internet communications standard. I don't even know why I bother to note these things. In any event, send your observations to me at medicarephil@gmail.com. I will post updates and corrections on the *Get What's Yours* book website.[1] When you visit the site, you'll see that this book shares digital shelf space with the 2015 book I coauthored: *Get What's Yours: The Secrets to Maxing Out Your Social Security.* Feel free to leave comments about that book and any questions you have about Social Security as well. If I can't get to them, I will seek help from my Social Security coauthors, noted economist Laurence Kotlikoff and accomplished PBS economics correspondent Paul Solman.

There would be no journalists or writers without readers, so my initial and broadest appreciation goes to you and your ilk. When writing a consumer guide, the writer needs guidance as well. And there is no better source than the experiences, the observations, and, just occasionally, mind you, the rants of readers. They were invaluable for our Social Security book and have proven so once again for this book about Medicare. Just when I might think I had seen or heard everything there was to know about some arcane Medicare topic or rule, a reader email invariably would pop up in my inbox to let me know of yet another situation I had not thought to ask about. I know that thanking readers can be an author's bromide. But not in this case. I am not the best or even appropriate judge of how accurate, complete, and helpful this book is. But I am confident that it would have ranked lower in all three respects were it not for the thousands of Medicare questions I have received.

Many of these questions have been answered in the weekly "Ask Phil" column I write for the *PBS NewsHour*'s Making Sen$e website. If these pieces have been even occasionally lucid, please credit my editors, Simon Pathe and, more recently, Kristen Doerer. Writers are constitutionally required to bridle at the audacity of editors who, well, edit. But there is no substitute for a fresh set of eyes partnered with questioning and curious minds. They make our work better, although I will deny this in any public setting. Their boss, in turn, is the aforementioned Mr. Solman. He has been an unflagging champion of "Ask Phil," as well as a craftsman of superior headlines. And while Paul is not a coauthor of this book, he has without doubt placed his stamp on it. Larry is not a coauthor of this book, either. Yet Paul and Larry deserve my thanks, and yours, for this book as well. The three of us were active contributors and sounding boards in our Social Security book. Unbeknownst to them, perhaps, they played the same virtual roles in this book. As I reported and wrote, I had countless constructive if imagined conversations with them, both individually and collectively. I am thankful for all the virtual help they have provided me. (And, of course, I will be sure to send them virtual royalty payments.)

Larry and Paul also have been core members of what came to be known as Team Get What's Yours, or just Team GWY, at our publisher, Simon & Schuster. The good news for me is that all these other team members have stayed on the job for this second Get What's Yours book, beginning with my principal editor at Simon & Schuster, Bob Bender, and a bunch of good and supportive people: Johanna Li, Sarah Reidy, Stephen Bedford, Ebony LaDelle, Taline Najarian, Sumya Ojakli, and I am sure, others who should be included here save for my feeble memory. Also on the team, in her role as nonplaying captain, has been my agent, Alice Martell. The first time I met Alice, she had taken a train from New York to Boston to meet with me and Larry to talk about the Social Security book. Being nothing if not a mature individual, I stood at the top of the train station stairs holding an ALICE MARTELL sign that I had hurriedly hand-lettered. Agents are used to dealing with such people, and Alice has had my number, and my back, ever since.

It should go without saying, but won't, that this book relies upon the generosity of hundreds of people who gave me their time and shared their views and expertise about Medicare and related health care issues. It is an unavoidable reality of today's communications environment that journalists are seldom welcomed inside government agencies and health care companies with open arms, if welcomed at all. There is little perceived upside to speaking to a stranger whose professional responsibilities include finding out things you don't want them to know, and sharing these tidbits with the public, competitors, and regulators who can make your life even more challenging. In truth, many doors were not opened to me. Fortunately, others were, although often not as widely or frequently as I hoped. This shout-out is to all of you who did open doors. Your contributions are greatly appreciated, and doubly so when they were offered against what may have been the better wisdom of your colleagues.

The Centers for Medicare & Medicaid Services (CMS) is the ultimate source for just about everything Medicare, and has become increasingly transparent about its programs and the massive amounts of data it collects on how well or poorly Medicare beneficiaries are treated by health care providers, insurers, medical equipment companies, and others. Still, it is an enormous bureaucracy whose communications efforts often seem more directed at those providers than the Medicare beneficiary. If you have enough time and a good Internet connection, you can find just about everything you need to know about Medicare. Or, you can get lost. Thanks to Lauren Shaham, Lorraine Ryan, and other members of the CMS communications team for doing what they could to help guide me. Carla Daniels, at the U.S. Department of Health and Human Services, also provided me background on Medicare appeals, as did Amanda Axeen. If I had only one call to understand a key Medicare coverage situation, it would go to David Santana at CMS. I especially appreciate being allowed to attend Medicare training sessions for counselors who field beneficiary questions and problems about Medicare. It is easy to portray big government bureaucracies as, well, big government bureaucracies. But at a personal level, it is clear that there are thousands upon thousands of people who care deeply about older Americans and want to help them navigate Medicare.

The largest such organization is called the State Health Insurance Assistance Program (SHIP), which is funded by the government and coordinates a volunteer force of some 15,000 SHIP counselors around the country. Christine Phillips at SHIP has been funneling my "Ask Phil" Medicare questions to SHIP counselors for nearly two years now. Thanks to her, and to them. There also are other terrific Medicare advocacy organizations. Mitchell Clark at the Medicare Rights Center also fielded "Ask Phil" questions and patiently answered my questions about how Medicare benefits worked, as did Casey Schwarz. David Lipschutz at the Center for Medicare Advocacy provided expert gardening advice when I was getting into some serious Medicare weeds. Thanks also to Jack Hoadley at Georgetown University's Health Policy Institute and Judi Lund Person at the National Hospice and Palliative Care Organization for reviewing parts of the manuscript for accuracy; ditto to Ben Harder and Avery Comarow at *U.S. News &*

World Report, and journalist Ellen Goodman on behalf of the Conversation Project.

The Kaiser Family Foundation is far and away the most knowledgeable and user-friendly provider of Medicare facts and wisdom on the planet. It produces a stream of highly informative Medicare reports and public opinion polls, under the leadership of senior vice president and Medicare program director Tricia Neuman. During repeated meetings and phone calls, much of what little knowledge I retained about Medicare was valiantly put forward by her and colleagues Christina L. Boccuti, Juliette Cubanski, Gretchen Jacobson, and Craig Palosky.

Original Medicare is administered by largely anonymous Medicare Administrative Contractors, or MACs. Despite my repeated efforts, these MACs will remain anonymous within these pages. With only one exception, they did not wish to be interviewed or discuss their immensely important work in helping to manage the insurance needs of nearly 70 percent of those Medicare beneficiaries who use Original Medicare. I wish they had. Medicare needs to be more sensitive to consumers and the MACs should be in the lead here. The exception was MAXI-MUS Federal Services, which oversees the early stages of all appeals involving Medicare Advantage and Part D drug plans. Thanks to Thomas Naughton, Barbara Yakimowicz, Marc Remillard, Jane Kjoller, Laura Church, Maddy Gruber, Marci Chodroff, and Janice Eidem.

Mercer, the big benefits consulting firm, operates a private health exchange that works with many retiree health plans around the country. It graciously opened the doors of its call center in Norwood, Massachusetts, and let me interview representatives who spend their days, and often their evenings, helping people with Medicare questions. Among all the people I've spoken with about consumers and Medicare, call-center reps became my gold standard. Better than almost anyone else, they know how confusing Medicare can be to people, and they have developed wonderful communications skills. I really appreciate the time and wisdom of Brad Ashburn, Anne Hart Davies, Dick Powers, Lorraine Trubia, and Kurt Wasserman-Beal. And thanks also to Bruce Lee for making it all happen.

Express Scripts, the nation's largest pharmacy benefits company, let me into its St. Louis–area offices and provided me extraordinary access to many of its talented people and the wealth of information it has derived from managing the pharmacy needs of some 85 million Americans. I appreciate the informed and patient explanations provided by Rebecca Rabbitt, Rochelle Henderson, Michael Looney, Dr. Lynne Nowak, and Maureen Downey. Thanks also to communicator Susan Haber and a special thanks to public relations manager Jennifer Leone Luddy. The wealth of information gathered by Express Scripts, and other "big data" Medicare firms, is producing smarter and smarter health care services. If we ever hope to flatten the financially unaffordable arc of rising health care prices, we will need all this knowledge and then some.

I knocked on the doors of all the big private Medicare insurers, over and over and over again. I hope there is an ICD-10 billing code for bruised knuckles! These large companies are all cordial but generally not keen on placing their executives on skewers for media grilling. Aetna and Cigna provided help and interviews. Anthem and Humana did not. A big and most welcome exception was United-Healthcare, the nation's largest health insurer. The company generously provided access to top health executives, marketing teams, and sales representatives, both at their headquarters in Minnetonka, Minnesota, and elsewhere.

Appreciation to UHC's health care leaders Steve Nelson, Susan Morisato, and Tim Noel; marketing leaders Brad Hunt, David Shapiro, Mark Phillips, and Terry O'Hara; sales managers and agents Michael Vayette, George Puchovich, and the Edwards, Diana and Zach; and communicators Matt Burns and Sarah Bearce, with special thanks to Sarah for yeowoman scheduling, fact-checking, and document procurement duty.

Finally, boundless thanks and continued love to my wife, Cheryl Magazine, herself a journalist and the temperate sounding board for all the problems, questions, ill-conceived ideas, and awful writing that initially went into this book. If only modest amounts of these flaws remain in the finished version, the credit goes to my remarkable partner and better half in all things.

GLOSSARY

There are tens of thousands of terms associated with Medicare. As mentioned, the feds' new medical coding and billing system introduced last year (ICD-10) has nearly 70,000 all by itself! Here are terms you will frequently encounter, drawn from knowledgeable public and private sources.

Administrative Law Judge
A hearings officer who presides over appeal conflicts between providers of services, or beneficiaries, and Medicare contractors.

Advance Beneficiary Notice of Noncoverage (ABN)
A notice that a doctor or supplier should give a Medicare beneficiary when furnishing an item or service for which Medicare is expected to deny payment. If you do not get an ABN before you get any scheduled service from your doctor or supplier, and

375

Medicare does not pay for it, then you probably do not have to pay for it. If the doctor or supplier does give you an ABN that you sign before you get the service, and Medicare does not pay for it, then you will have to pay your doctor or supplier for it. ABNs apply only if you are in the Original Medicare plan. They do not apply if you are in a Medicare managed care plan or private fee-for-service plan.

Advance Coverage Decision

A decision that your Medicare Advantage (MA) plan makes on whether or not it will pay for a certain service.

Advance Directives

A written document stating how you want medical decisions to be made if you lose the ability to make them for yourself. It may include a living will and a durable power of attorney for health care and can be supplemented with other documents, including a physician order for life-sustaining treatment (POLST). Some states have different names for these documents.

Annual Notice of Change (ANOC)

A document that MA and Part D plans must send customers each September to explain how their plan will change in the coming year. This is one of the most valuable and least-read Medicare documents.

Approved Amount
The fee Medicare sets as reasonable for a covered medical service. This is the amount a doctor or supplier is paid by you and Medicare for a service or supply. It may be less than the actual amount charged by a doctor or supplier. The approved amount is sometimes called the "approved charge."

Assignment
In Original Medicare, this means a doctor agrees to accept the Medicare-approved amount as full payment.

Authorized Representative
An individual authorized under state or other applicable law to act on behalf of a beneficiary or other party involved in Medicare decisions and appeals. An authorized representative has all the rights and responsibilities of a beneficiary. Examples of an "authorized representative" include a court-appointed guardian, an individual with durable power of attorney, and an individual designated under a state health care consent statute.

Balance Billing

A situation in which private fee-for-service providers (doctors or hospitals) can charge and bill you more than the plan's payment amount for services.

Beneficiary and Family Centered Care Quality Improvement Organization (BFCC-QIO)

This is a type of quality improvement organization (see also QIO) that reviews beneficiary complaints and quality of care for people with Medicare. The BFCC-QIO makes sure there is consistency in the case review process while taking into consideration local factors and local needs, including general quality of care and medical necessity.

Benefit Period

The way that Medicare measures your use of hospital and skilled nursing facility (SNF) services. A benefit period begins the day you go to a hospital or skilled nursing facility. The benefit period ends when you haven't received any hospital care (or skilled care in a SNF) for 60 days in a row. If you go into the hospital or a skilled nursing facility after one benefit period has ended, a new benefit period begins if you are in the

Original Medicare Plan. You must pay the inpatient hospital deductible for each benefit period. There is no limit to the number of benefit periods you can have.

Capitation

A specified amount of money paid to a health plan or doctor. This is used to cover the cost of a health plan member's health care services for a certain length of time. For example, MA plans receive varying amounts of money from Medicare to pay for beneficiary medical expenses, keyed to an individual's health condition as reflected in a personal health risk score.

Capped Rental Item

Medicare rules allow suppliers in some circumstances to rent durable equipment to beneficiaries rather than selling it to them outright. Over a period of time, such rented items will become the property of the beneficiary. Capped rental rules can be tricky to navigate should a beneficiary move from one insured location (a nursing home, for example) to another (back home or into a hospice program). Make sure such changes of venue don't adversely affect your access to rented equipment.

Coinsurance or Copay

Your share of medical expenses covered by your Medicare plans. Medigap policies cover some of these costs for people with Original Medicare. Check with your MA or Part D plan for its schedule of such payments.

Conditional Payment

A payment made by Medicare for services for which another payer is responsible. For example, Medicare may pay health expenses you incur due to an auto accident but expects to be reimbursed by your auto insurer (or the other driver's auto insurer if that driver was at fault in the accident).

Coordination of Benefits

A program that determines which plan or insurance policy will pay first if two health plans or insurance policies cover the same benefits. If one of the plans is a Medicare health plan, federal law may decide who pays first.

Coverage Determination

The initial decision by your Part D drug plan of whether it will cover a drug, how much it will charge you, and whether it will make an exception to its rules should you request a certain drug. If you disagree with the plan, you can initiate an appeal. The first level of Medicare's five-step appeal process will be handled by your drug plan, but all other appeals go to outside parties.

Creditable Coverage

If you reach 65 but are still covered by an employer group plan (with more than 20 members) you usually do not have to sign up for Medicare. However, if your drug coverage is not "creditable" — meaning not at least as good as that offered by a typical Medicare Part D drug plan — you will need to get a Part D plan, which means you also need to get Medicare Part B and perhaps other Medicare insurance as well. Employers are required to certify their drug coverage creditability each plan year. "Prior creditable coverage" is a phrase used to describe when a person's previous health insurance justifies shortening or even eliminating a waiting period before Medigap will cover that person's preexisting medical condition.

Custodial Care

Nonskilled personal care — help with activities of daily living including bathing, dressing, eating, getting in or out of a bed or chair, moving around, and using the bathroom. In nearly all cases, Medicare doesn't pay for custodial care.

Deductible

The amount you must pay for health care before Medicare begins to pay, either for each benefit period for Part A, or each year for Part B. These amounts can change every year. MA plans usually have their own deductibles, but they cannot be higher than those required under Original Medicare.

Determination

A decision made by a Medicare insurer or contractor to pay in full, pay in part, or deny a claim.

Diagnosis-Related Groups (DRGs)

Hospitals that participate in Medicare accept fixed payments for inpatient hospital procedures and treatments, as specified by roughly 700 DRG codes. These payments are the same in each DRG (adjusted for local economic conditions and certain hospital characteristics) regardless of what it actually costs the hospital to provide such care.

Donut Hole

Medicare Part D plans stop covering your drug costs after payments have reached a certain level each year, and then resume coverage once additional spending has reached a certain level. In 2016, the donut hole begins at $3,310 and ends at $4,850, when catastrophic coverage kicks in that limits your spending to a few dollars per prescription and never more than 5 percent of a drug's cost (but 5 percent of a really expensive drug can still set you back). Under terms of the Affordable Care Act, the donut hole is becoming smaller and will disappear entirely in 2020.

Drug Tiers

Part D drug plans group their covered drugs (formularies) into several groups, and charge different amounts and copays for drugs in different tiers. Tiers often start with preferred generics, generics, preferred brand drugs, brand drugs, and a higher tier for costly specialty medications.

Durable Medical Equipment (DME)

Medical equipment that is ordered by a doctor for use in the home. These items must be reusable, such as walkers, wheel-chairs, or hospital beds. DME is paid for under both Medicare Part B and Part A for home health services. Unnecessary use of some types of DMEs, particularly power wheelchairs, has led to tightened oversight of such items. Further, in late 2015, the Centers for Medicare & Medicaid Services (CMS) issued rules[1] to create a master list of 135 other types of DME that have been overprescribed, and said these items would require prior authorization before it would provide insurance coverage.

Employer Group Health Plan

People who are still working at age 65 (and their covered spouses of Medicare age) generally do not have to sign up for Medicare until their active group coverage ends, usually because they have retired. However, people who work for employers with fewer than 20 employees usually have to sign up for Medicare when they turn 65 because such small-employer plans become the secondary or backup payer of covered Medicare expenses at that time. For disabled workers, the employer-size cutoff is 100 employees.

Enrollment Periods

Medicare has multiple and potentially confusing enrollment periods during which people can sign up for different types of Medicare health plans. These include initial enrollment periods, general enrollment periods, open enrollment periods, and special enrollment periods. Check the Medicare.gov website for details.

Exception

Drug plans may grant a formulary exception and approve coverage for a drug not on their plan formulary. They also may move a drug from one tier to a less expensive tier. So, don't just give up if your plan does not cover the drug you need or you think it charges too much for it compared with other plans.

Excess Charges

If you are in Original Medicare, this is the difference between a doctor's or other health care provider's actual charge (which may be limited by Medicare or the state) and the Medicare-approved payment amount.

Extra Help

This is Medicare's low-income support program to help people pay their Part D drug costs.

Formulary

The list of drugs covered by a Part D prescription drug plan.

Free Look

The period, usually 30 days, during which you can use a Medigap policy and cancel it at no cost should you change your mind. Because Medigap policies are regulated at the state level, it's a good idea to check with your state insurance department to see if it provides other consumer safeguards for Medigap policies.

Grievance

A complaint about the way your Medicare health plan or Medicare drug plan is giving care. For example, you may file a grievance if you have a problem calling the plan or if you're unhappy with the way a staff person at the plan has behaved toward you. Grievances are different from appeals, which involve a plan's refusal to properly cover (in your view) a service, supply, or prescription.

Guaranteed Issue Rights

Rights you have in certain situations when insurance companies are required by law to sell or offer you a Medigap policy. In these situations, an insurance company can't deny you insurance coverage or place conditions on a policy, must cover you for all preexisting conditions, and can't charge you more for a policy because of past or present health problems.

Guaranteed Renewable
A right you have that requires your insurance company to automatically renew or continue your Medigap policy, unless you make untrue statements to the insurance company, commit fraud, or don't pay your premiums.

Health Maintenance Organizations (HMO)
A type of MA plan where a group of doctors, hospitals, and other health care providers agrees to give health care to Medicare beneficiaries for a set amount of money from Medicare every month. You usually must get your care from the providers in the plan.

Health Risk Scores
Medicare assigns health risk scores to beneficiaries that are used to help set the annual level of capitated payment that some Medicare insurers receive each year to provide insurance services.

Hold Harmless Provision

A Social Security rule that may have the effect of limiting the annual dollar increase in the Part B premium to the dollar increase in an individual's Social Security benefit. Should Part B premiums rise by more than a person's Social Security benefit, which usually would occur if the Social Security's annual cost of living adjustment (COLA) was zero or small, a person held harmless would not have to pay the higher Part B premium. However, other Part B users who are not held harmless would pay a disproportionate amount of the increase. This group includes new Medicare beneficiaries, higher-income beneficiaries (see the entry for IRMAA), and people on Medicare who have not yet begun taking Social Security.

Hospice

Hospice provides care to people who are terminally ill, including respite care for family caregivers. It includes physical care and counseling. Hospice care is covered under Medicare Part A hospital insurance.

Independent Review Entity (IRE)

This is the firm hired by Medicare to handle the second level of the appeals process for

Medicare Advantage plans and Part D drug plans.

IRMAA (Income-Related Monthly Adjustment Amounts)

People with higher incomes must pay higher premiums for Part B and Part D insurance. These amounts change each year. IRMAA brackets and amounts for 2016 may be found in Chapter 9. It takes Social Security two years to use your tax return as the basis for any IRMAA charges. In 2017, for example, IRMAA surcharges will be based on your 2015 federal tax return.

Long-Term Care (LTC)

Custodial care in a facility or the patient's home. Medicare does not cover long-term care.

Medically Necessary

This is a common requirement before Medicare will cover health services, treatments, and equipment. The definition of what's medically necessary is not arbitrary but must conform to medical standards where you live.

Medicare Administrative Contractor (MAC)
Medicare hires companies as regional or national contractors to manage Original Medicare and its durable medical equipment program. There also are contractors who handle beneficiary appeals for Medicare Advantage and Part D drug plans.

Medicare Savings Programs
These are Medicare assistance programs for low-income persons that will help pay some or even all out-of-pocket Medicare expenses.

Medicare Special Needs Plan (SNP)
This is a type of MA plan that provides more focused and specialized health care for specific groups of people, including those who have both Medicare and Medicaid, live in a nursing home, or have certain chronic medical conditions.

Medicare Summary Notice (MSN)
A notice you get after your doctor or provider files a claim for Part A and Part B services in Original Medicare. It explains what the provider billed, the Medicare-approved amount, how much Medicare paid, and what you must pay. It also provides instructions to help you appeal deci-

sions you think are wrong.

Medicare Supplement Insurance
Another name for Medigap policies.

NCDs and LCDs
Medicare and its contractors around the country can issue national coverage determinations (NCDs) and local coverage determinations (LCDs) that govern coverage of medical services and devices. Sometimes, the same service is not covered the same way around the country due to LCDs.

Optional Supplemental Benefits
Some MA and Medigap plans cover health services not covered by Original Medicare, and usually will charge you additional amounts for such coverage. Examples include dental and vision insurance, and health coverage during foreign travel.

Out-of-Network Benefit
An out-of-network benefit provides a beneficiary with the option to access plan services outside of a Medicare plan's contracted network of providers. In some cases, a beneficiary's out-of-pocket costs may be higher for an out-of-network benefit.

Preferred Pharmacies

Increasingly, Medicare drug plans use proprietary pharmacy networks that charge less money than out-of-network pharmacies.

Preferred Provider Organization (PPO) Plan

A type of MA plan in which you use doctors, hospitals, and providers that belong to that plan's network. You can use doctors, hospitals, and providers outside of the network for an additional cost.

Private Fee-for-Service Plan

A type of MA plan in which you may go to any Medicare-approved doctor or hospital that accepts the plan's payment. The insurance plan, rather than the Medicare program, decides how much it will pay and what you will pay for the services you get. You may pay more or less for Medicare-covered benefits. You may have extra benefits Original Medicare doesn't cover.

Prospective Payment System

A method of reimbursement in which Medicare payment is made based on a predetermined, fixed amount. The payment amount for a particular service is derived based on the classification system of that service (for example, diagnosis-related groups, or DRGs, for inpatient hospital services). CMS usually sets new prospective payment levels each year for different providers. Different types of care facilities have their own PPS reimbursement rules.

Qualified Independent Contractor (QIC)
An entity that has a contract with CMS to review appeals following a redetermination by a Medicare Administrative Contractor and reconsiderations issued by Quality Improvement Organizations. QICs issue reconsiderations and represent level two within the five-level Medicare appeals process.

Quality Improvement Organization (QIO)
An entity that has a contract with CMS to monitor the appropriateness, effectiveness, and quality of care furnished to Medicare beneficiaries. QIO makes determinations as to whether the services provided were medically necessary and respond to beneficiary complaints about the quality of care provided.

Reconsideration

The decision made in the second level of the Medicare appeals process. A reconsideration consists of an independent on-the-record review of an initial determination, including the redetermination and all issues related to payment of the claim. A reconsideration is conducted by a QIC under Medicare Parts A and B and an Independent Review Entity under Parts C and D.

Respite Care

Medicare will cover certain temporary or periodic care provided by family members so that the usual caregiver can take some time off.

Step Therapy

Some Part D drug plans will require you to take a less expensive drug and demonstrate that it's not effective before approving coverage for a more expensive medication. Again, file an Exception Request if you and your doctor think step therapy could threaten your health.

Supplementary Medical Insurance

This is the formal name for Part B of Medicare, which pays a share of covered expenses involving doctors, outpatient services, and durable medical equipment. Do not confuse it with Supplemental Medicare Insurance (Medigap).

TRICARE and TRICARE for Life
Medical coverage for current and retired uniformed service members and their families.

APPENDIX
MEDICARE MANUALS

The Internet has become the primary and, on occasion, the only distribution source for health care information that you need to know to take the best care of yourself while minimizing medical expenses.

I have listed key Web addresses in endnotes throughout the book. These are the sources I kept coming back to time and time again. These addresses have been checked for accuracy but please accept my apologies for links to nowhere. They happen. If you encounter bad links, please email me with the details at medicarephil@gmail.com, and I'll post fixes on the *Get What's Yours for Medicare* website.

Beyond these citations, however, I wanted to provide a separate listing of key consumer Medicare documents provided by the Centers for Medicare & Medicaid Services (CMS). While I wish the agency was more consumer-friendly and, in my case, author-friendly, the fact remains that it puts out a digital mountain of content. It also deserves credit for continuing to push for the transparency of medical information, releasing data files that are helping empower consumers, directly and through the efforts of many pro-consumer think tanks and websites that have taken CMS information and turned it into powerful decision-making tools. The interpretation of CMS data is often a hotly contested process in its own right, but the agency's steady movement toward helping consumers and holding health providers accountable deserves appreciation and support.

Here are major CMS Medicare guides that can be downloaded or ordered in print by calling 1-800-MEDICARE. These guides are regularly updated and usually keep the same five-digit identification number, which you will find at the end of these Web addresses. This list roughly tracks the different parts of Medicare, beginning with general Medicare overviews, moving on to reports about Parts A, B, C (Medicare Advantage), D (prescription drugs), and then to items about consumer rights and appeals.

GENERAL

Medicare & You: http://www.medicare.gov/Pubs/pdf/10050.pdf

Medicare & the Health Insurance Marketplace: https://www.medicare.gov/Pubs/pdf/11694.pdf

Your Medicare Benefits: https://www.medicare.gov/Pubs/pdf/10116.pdf

ORIGINAL MEDICARE (A AND B)

Enrolling in Medicare Part A & Part B: https://www.medicare.gov/Pubs/pdf/11036.pdf

Choosing a Medigap Policy: A Guide to Health Insurance for People with Medicare: https://www.medicare.gov/Pubs/pdf/02110.pdf

Guide to Choosing a Hospital: https://www.medicare.gov/Pubs/pdf/10181.pdf

Are You a Hospital Inpatient or Outpatient: https://www.medicare.gov/Pubs/pdf/11435.pdf

Medicare Coverage of Skilled Nursing Facility Care: https://www.medicare.gov/Pubs/pdf/10153.pdf

Your Guide to Choosing a Nursing Home or Other Long-Term Care: https://www.medicare.gov/Pubs/pdf/02174.pdf

Your Discharge Planning Checklist: https://www.medicare.gov/Pubs/pdf/11376.pdf

Medicare Limits on Therapy Services: https://www.medicare.gov/Pubs/pdf/10988.pdf

Medicare and Home Health Care: https://www.medicare.gov/Pubs/pdf/10969.pdf

Medicare Hospice Benefits: https://www.medicare.gov/Pubs/pdf/02154.pdf

Your Guide to Medicare's Preventive Services: https://www.medicare.gov/Pubs/pdf/10110.pdf

Quick Facts About Payment for Outpatient Services for People with Medicare Part B: https://www.medicare.gov/Pubs/pdf/02118.pdf

Medicare Coverage of Kidney Dialysis & Kidney Transplant Services: https://www.medicare.gov/Pubs/pdf/10128.pdf

Medicare's Coverage of Diabetes Supplies & Services: https://www.medicare.gov/Pubs/pdf/11022.pdf

Medicare Coverage of Ambulance Services: https://www.medicare.gov/Pubs/pdf/11021.pdf

Medicare Coverage of Durable Medical Equipment and Other Devices: https://www.medicare.gov/Pubs/pdf/11045.pdf

Your Guide to Medicare's Durable Medical Equipment, Prosthetics, Orthotics, & Supplies (DMEPOS) Competitive Bidding Program: https://www.medicare.gov/Pubs/pdf/11461.pdf

Medicare's Wheelchair & Scooter Benefit: https://www.medicare.gov/Pubs/pdf/11046.pdf

PARTS C AND D

Understanding Medicare Part C & D Enrollment Periods: https://www.medicare.gov/Pubs/pdf/11219.pdf

What's a Medicare Advantage Plan: https://www.medicare.gov/Pubs/pdf/11474.pdf

Your Guide to Medicare Prescription Drug Coverage: https://www.medicare.gov/Pubs/pdf/11109.pdf

How Income Affects Your Medicare Prescription Drug Coverage Premiums: https://www.medicare.gov/Pubs/pdf/11469.pdf

How Medicare Prescription Drug Plans and Medicare Advantage Plans with Prescription Drug Coverage (MA-PDs) Use Pharmacies, Formularies, & Common Coverage Rules: https://www.medicare.gov/Pubs/pdf/11136.pdf

OTHERS

Medicare & Other Health Benefits: Your
Guide to Who Pays First: https://www
.medicare.gov/Pubs/pdf/02179.pdf
Medicare Rights & Protections: https://
www.medicare.gov/Pubs/pdf/11534.pdf
Medicare Appeals: https://www.medicare
.gov/Pubs/pdf/11525.pdf

NOTES

Chapter 2: Living Longer Is Great; Paying for It Isn't

1. Mortality in the United States, 2012. U.S. Department of Health and Human Services, Centers for Disease Control and Prevention, National Center for Health Statistics, http://www.cdc.gov/nchs/data/databriefs/db168.pdf.
2. "No, Giving More People Health Insurance Doesn't Save Money," *New York Times,* August 5, 2015, http://www.nytimes.com/2015/08/06/upshot/no-giving-more-people-health-insurance-doesn't-save-money.html.
3. Wells Fargo Middle Class Retirement survey, October 2014, https://www.wellsfargo.com/about/press/2014/middle-class-retirement-saving_1022.
4. "Medigap: Spotlight on Enrollment, Premiums and Recent Trends," April 1,

2013, Kaiser Family Foundation, http://kff
.org/medicare/report/medigap-enrollment
-premiums-and-recent-trends/.

Chapter 3: Leaving the Health Insurance Herd: You're on Your Own Now

1. "Aflac WorkForces Report," https://www
.aflac.com/business/resources/aflac-work
forces-report/.
2. Sheena Iyengar, *The Art of Choosing*
(New York: Twelve, 2010).
3. Barry Schwartz, *The Paradox of Choice:
Why More Is Less* (New York: Ecco, 2003).
4. If more actually is less, as these behavior-
alists maintain, then the reverse can also
be true: less is more. In this instance, this
would mean that providing a smaller
number of easily understood Medicare
options will lead to better outcomes for
consumers. Health insurance is certainly
not the same as retirement investing. But
at least in this case, default choices for
care are comparable to standardized
401(k) investments and rules for participa-
tion that force consumers to "opt in" to
solid investment choices unless they con-
sciously choose other alternatives.
5. Saurabh Bhargava, George Loewenstein,
and Justin Sydnor, "Do Individuals Make

Sensible Health Insurance Decisions? Evidence from a Menu with Dominated Options," NBER Working Paper No. 21160, May 2015, http://www.nber.org/papers/w21160.

Chapter 4: Get It Right the First Time

1. Enrolling in Medicare Part A & Part B, https://www.medicare.gov/Pubs/pdf/11036.pdf.
2. Here are major Medicare Web pages and publications explaining the agency's different enrollment periods:

When can I sign up for Part A & Part B?: https://www.medicare.gov/sign-up-change-plans/get-parts-a-and-b/when-sign-up-parts-a-and-b/when-sign-up-parts-a-and-b.html.

Understanding Medicare Part C & D Enrollment Periods: https://www.medicare.gov/Pubs/pdf/11219.pdf.

Special Circumstances (Special Enrollment Periods): https://www.medicare.gov/sign-up-change-plans/when-can-i-join-a-health-or-drug-plan/special-circumstances/join-plan-special-circumstances.html.

5-star special enrollment period: https://www.medicare.gov/sign-up-change-plans/

when-can-i-join-a-health-or-drug-plan/five
-star-enrollment/5-star-enrollment-period
.html.

3. Medicare Part B Enrollment: Pitfalls,
Problems and Penalties, http://www
.medicarerights.org/pdf/PartB-Enrollment
-Pitfalls-Problems-and-Penalties.pdf.

4. https://www.dmdc.osd.mil/milconnect/
faces/index.jspx?_afrLoop=55134347
74530848&_afrWindowMode=0&_adf
.ctrl-state=1cwgsqggc2_4.

5. http://www.tricare.mil/DEERS.

6. https://www.hnfs.com/content/hnfs/home/
tn/common/contact_us/tfl.html/pp/
content/hnfs/home/tn/bene/res.

7. Publication 969: Health Savings Accounts and Other Tax-Favored Health
Plans, http://www.irs.gov/pub/irs-pdf/
p969.pdf.

Chapter 5: What Medicare Covers and What It Doesn't

1. http://files.kff.org/attachment/fact-sheet
-the-medicare-part-d-prescription-drug
-benefit. See Figure 5.

2. Here are several references to Medicare's
explanation of its hearing, dental, and vision coverage: https://www.medicare.gov/
coverage/prosthetic-devices.html; https://

www.medicare.gov/coverage/hearing
-and-balance-exam-and-hearing-aids
.html; https://www.medicare.gov/coverage/
dental-services.html; https://www
.medicare.gov/coverage/eyeglasses-contact
-lenses.html.

3. http://www.medicare.gov/coverage/your
-medicare-coverage.html.

4. http://www.medicarerights.org/resources/
medicare-interactive.

5. https://www.shiptacenter.org/.

6. Medicare & Other Health Benefits: Your
Guide to Who Pays First, Centers for
Medicare & Medicaid Services, August
2015, https://www.medicare.gov/Pubs/pdf/
02179.pdf.

7. Medicare Rights Center, http://www
.medicareinteractive.org/page2.php
?topic=counselor&page=script&script
_id=621.

8. https://www.medicare.gov/Pubs/pdf/
11694.pdf.

9. http://www.medicare.gov/your-medicare
-costs/costs-at-a-glance/costs-at-glance
.html/.

10. "Medicare and Home Health Care,"
Centers for Medicare & Medicaid Services, May 2010, https://www.medicare
.gov/Pubs/pdf/10969.pdf.

11. https://www.medicare.gov/homehealth

compare/search.html.

12. Medicare contracts with private companies as recovery audit contractors (RACs). RACs audit a lot more than whether a patient's stay is observational or an admission. Their incomes are linked to how much money their audits can recover, and the observational-admission revenue differential has been seen as attractive low-hanging fruit for recovery efforts. If RACs could show that providers inappropriately billed a Medicare patient's hospital visit as an admission instead of an observational stay, it just might be cork-popping time.

One of the measures used to determine the appropriateness of these admission decisions is the patient's subsequent health status. This seems logical but the RACs don't have to make these decisions in real time, as doctors and hospitals do. Instead, they can select observation-admission decisions made as far back as three years, look at subsequent patient outcomes, and then initiate recovery procedures if certain patients with healthy post-hospital outcomes had been admitted rather than treated on an observational basis. Health care providers face the loss of not just their excess billings but all their billings for a patient.

To avoid these potentially costly RAC audits, hospitals and doctors began classifying more and more hospital visits as observational. Between 2006 and 2012, Medicare hospital visits were about flat but observational visits rose nearly 90 percent to 1.8 million, according to the Medicare Payment Advisory Commission (MedPAC), which advises Congress about Medicare.

To counter this trend, Medicare developed the Two-Midnight Rule in 2013. It says that if a patient's medical condition could reasonably be expected to require staying in the hospital more than two midnights, he or she should be formally admitted and care should be billed accordingly.

By giving the RACs a more precise time measure to use in their audits, however, the rule ran into stiff opposition from health care providers, and Medicare has prevented the RACs from auditing hospitals and doctors over its use. RACs say this has permitted some hospitals to abuse the system and boost their Medicare revenues. The hospitals deny this.

CMS continues to "improve" the Two-Midnight Rule but, for the most part, patient advocate groups say Medicare beneficiaries continue to be adversely affected by excessive hospital use of observational stays.

13. http://www.medicareadvocacy.org/self -help-packet-for-medicare-observation -status/.
14. https://www.medicare.gov/what-medi care-covers/part-b/what-medicare-part-b -covers.html.
15. https://www.medicare.gov/Pubs/pdf/ 10128.pdf.
16. https://secure.ssa.gov/poms.nsf/lnx/ 0601101020.
17. http://www.irs.gov/Businesses/Small -Businesses-&-Self-Employed/Passive -Activity-Loss-ATG-Exhibit-2-2-Modified -Adjusted-Gross-Income-Computation.
18. http://www.medicare.gov/coverage/ preventive-and-screening-services.html.
19. https://www.cms.gov/Medicare/Medi care-Fee-for-Service-Payment/SNFPPS/ Downloads/Jimmo-FactSheet.pdf.
20. https://www.medicare.gov/coverage/ manual-wheelchairs-and-power-mobility -devices.html.
21. https://www.opm.gov/healthcare -insurance/healthcare/plan-information/ important-facts-about-overseas-coverage/.
22. Medigap Enrollment Among New Med-

icare Beneficiaries, Kaiser Family Foundation, April 2015, http://files.kff.org/attachment/issue-brief-medigap-enrollment-among-new-medicare-beneficiaries.

Chapter 6: Medigap: The Glue That Holds Original Medicare Together

1. However, if you for any reason have not applied for a Medigap policy during the period when you have this guaranteed issue right, a Medigap insurer may be allowed to refuse to cover its share of your unmet Original Medicare expenses for a preexisting condition for up to six months after you buy the policy. This "preexisting condition waiting period" will then expire. However, this exclusion is permitted only if the condition was treated or diagnosed within a six-month "look-back period" before your coverage effective date. If Medigap coverage is replacing other creditable health insurance that covered your preexisting condition, your Medigap insurer might not be able to impose a waiting period. You cannot have had a break in your prior health insurance of more than 63 days or it won't count as creditable in this situation.
2. https://www.shiptacenter.org/.

3. http://www.medicarerights.org/.

4. http://www.naic.org/state_web_map.htm.

5. http://www.medicare.gov/pubs/pdf/02110.pdf.

6. http://www.medicare.gov/find-a-plan/questions/medigap-home.aspx.

7. Medigap: Spotlight on Enrollment, Premiums, and Recent Trends, Kaiser Family Foundation, April 2013, https://kaiserfamilyfoundation.files.wordpress.com/2013/04/8412-2.pdf.

Chapter 7: The Horse Insurers Want You to Ride: Medicare Advantage Plans

1. http://www.getwhatyours.org/medicare/MA_history.

2. https://www.cms.gov/medicare/medicare-contracting/medicare-administrative-contractors/medicareadministrative contractors.html.

3. http://kff.org/medicare/state-indicator/total-enrollment-by-plan-type/.

4. https://www.medicare.gov/find-a-plan/questions/home.aspx.

5. https://secure.ssa.gov/poms.nsf/lnx/0601101010.

6. https://www.medicare.gov/find-a-plan/staticpages/rating/planrating-help.aspx.

7. https://www.cahps.ahrq.gov/.

8. http://www.ncqa.org/HEDISQuality Measurement/WhatisHEDIS.aspx.

9. http://www.hosonline.org/.

10. https://www.medicare.gov/find-a-plan/ questions/home.aspx.

11. https://www.shiptacenter.org/.

12. http://www.medicarerights.org/.

Chapter 8: Mugged and Drugged: Part D Prescription Plans

1. http://kff.org/report-section/medicare -part-d-a-first-look-at-plan-offerings-in -2016-findings/.

2. http://kff.org/medicare/issue-brief/it-pays -to-shop-variation-in-out-of-pocket-costs -for-medicare-part-d-enrollees-in-2016/.

3. http://lab.express-scripts.com/insights/ behavioral-sciences/what-paul-revere -knew-about actionable-data.

4. Express Scripts also has the scale to pound away at the core efficiencies of the pharmacy fulfillment process. One of its five home-delivery drug shipment centers is near its home office. It ships out 100,000 prescriptions every day, a year's worth of business for a busy individual pharmacy. The center features a showplace computer-controlled prescription fulfill-ment unit. Visitors can literally walk

through its clear plastic and glass interior, watching as bins of specific drugs are automatically rotated into the proper position so they can dispense the proper dose of pills through plastic chutes into waiting containers that will be sent to consumers. Simultaneously, multiple bins dispatch their contents into their respective chutes, creating a cacophonous pharmaceutical symphony. A company representative says they're working to fashion chutes with softer linings — not to lessen the noise but to reduce pill breakage.

5. Here's a look at nonadherence for so-called specialty therapy medications:

Inflammation	40 percent
Multiple Sclerosis	23 percent
Oncology	38 percent
Hepatitis C	12 percent
HIV	23 percent
Growth Deficiency	38 percent
Pulmonary Arterial Hypertension	28 percent
Transplant	33 percent

6. http://www.aetnamedicare.com/help_and_resources/downloadable-forms-2016.jsp#formulary.

7. http://www.anthem.com/Shop/Find-Your-Covered-Drugs.

8. http://www.cigna.com/medicare/part-d/drug-list-formulary.

9. http://coventry-medicare.coventryhealthcare.com/prescription-drug-benefits/formulary/index.htm.

10. http://www.humana.com/pharmacy/medicare/tools/druglist/2016.

11. http://medicare.kaiserpermanente.org/medicare/pdfs/plans_current/comprehensive_formulary.pdf.

12. For PDP plans: http://www.uhcmedicaresolutions.com/health-plans/prescription-drug-plans/resources/prescription-drug-list.html.

13. For MA-PD plans: http://www.uhcmedicaresolutions.com/health-plans/medicare-advantage-plans/resources-plan-material/drug-list.html.

14. http://www.medicare.gov/find-a-plan/questions/home.aspx.

15. http://www.medicare.gov/find-a-plan/staticpages/rating/planrating-help.aspx?termId=2016SS1.

16. Executives at Express Scripts said the approval rate on patient requests to reconsider pharmacy rejections of prescription requests was high. According to executive Rebecca Rabbit, more than 70 percent of the people who call in and get a rejection at their pharmacy and ask for reconsidera-

tion wind up getting the drugs that they want. Most reconsiderations are for drugs not included in plan formularies.

17. https://www.cms.gov/Medicare/Appeals -and-Grievances/MedPrescriptDrugAppl Griev/downloads/ModelCoverageDeter minationRequestForm.pdf.

18. http://www.shiptacenter.org/.

19. http://www.medicare.gov/pharmaceu tical-assistance-program/state-programs .aspx.

20. http://www.medicare.gov/pharmaceuti cal-assistance-program/.

21. http://www.ssa.gov/medicare/prescrip tionhelp/.

22. http://www.medicare.gov/your-medicare -costs/help-paying-costs/medicare-savings -program/medicare-savings-programs .html.

Chapter 9: Medicare Moneyball: Financial Help and Pitfalls

1. "The Impact of Consumer Inattention on Insurer Pricing in the Medicare Part D Program," by Kate Ho, Joseph Hogan, and Fiona Scott Morton; March 2015, National Bureau of Economic Research, http://www.nber.org/papers/w21028.

2. http://graphics.wsj.com/medicare-billing.

3. http://www.healthcostinstitute.org/.

4. http://www.guroo.com/#!.

5. https://projects.propublica.org/docdol lars/.

6. https://projects.propublica.org/surgeons/.

7. http://www.consumerreports.org/cro/ health/california-health-cost-and-quality —consumer-reports/index.htm.

8. https://secure.ssa.gov/poms.nsf/lnx/ 0601101020.

9. http://www.hhs.gov/omha/Part%20B% 20Premium%20Appeals/partb_appeals .html.

10. http://www.getwhatsyours.org.

11. https://www.socialsecurity.gov/forms/ssa -561.pdf.

12. https://www.ahip.org/epub/OON-Report -2015.

13. https://www.medicare.gov/your-medi care-costs/help-paying-costs/extra-help/ level-of-extra-help.html.

14. https://www.shiptacenter.org/.

15. http://www.medicarerights.org/.

16. https://www.ssa.gov/pubs/EN-05-10508 .pdf.

17. Here's the FPL table for 2015 for the 48 other states and the District of Colum-bia:

Family Size	100%	135%	140%	145%	150%
1	$11,770.00	$15,889.50	$16,478.00	$17,066.50	$17,655.00
2	$15,930.00	$21,505.50	$22,302.00	$23,098.50	$23,895.00
3	$20,090.00	$27,121.50	$28,126.00	$29,130.50	$30,135.00
4	$24,250.00	$32,737.50	$33,950.00	$35,162.50	$36,375.00
5	$28,410.00	$38,353.50	$39,774.00	$41,194.50	$42,615.00
6	$32,570.00	$43,969.50	$45,598.00	$47,226.50	$48,855.00
7	$36,730.00	$49,585.50	$51,422.00	$53,258.50	$55,095.00
8	$40,890.00	$55,201.50	$57,246.00	$59,290.50	$61,335.00
9	$45,050.00	$60,817.50	$63,070.00	$65,322.50	$67,575.00
10	$49,210.00	$66,433.50	$68,894.00	$71,354.50	$73,815.00
Additional	$4,160.00	$5,616.00	$5,824.00	$6,032.00	$6,240.00

18. https://secure.ssa.gov/poms.nsf/lnx/0603030025.

19. https://secure.ssa.gov/poms.nsf/lnx/0603030025.

20. These examples are drawn from Social Security illustrations provided at https://secure.ssa.gov/poms.nsf/lnx/0603020055.

Example one, for an unmarried person: Mr. Smith lives alone and applies for the subsidy. He receives $1001.25 per month in Social Security benefits before the Medicare Part B premium deduction and a private pension of $375 per month before taxes. Assume that his countable resources are below the limit. His countable income is:

Social Security	$12,015 (12 × $1001.25)
Private pension	4,500 (12 × $375)
Total income	16,515
	−240 (12 × the $20 general income exclusion)
Countable income	$16,275

Assuming that the applicable FPL for a one-person family is $11,770, his subsidy income limits are as follows:

$11,770 × 135 percent = $15,889.50
$11,770 × 140 percent = $16,478.00
$11,770 × 145 percent = $17,066.50
$11,770 × 150 percent = $17,655.00

Analysis: Mr. Smith's countable income is greater than 135 percent of the poverty guideline, but it is less than 140 percent of the poverty guideline. Therefore, Mr. Smith is eligible for a 75 percent premium subsidy. Assuming that Mr. Smith's Part D premium is $35 per month, his subsidy covers $26.25 (75 percent) of his monthly premium. He is required to pay $8.75 per month for the 25 percent of the premium not covered by the subsidy, assuming there are no late enrollment fees.

Example two, for a married couple: John and Dorothy White are married and living together, and live in Kansas. Mr. White is age 70, receives Title II benefits of $925 and a private pension of $400 per month. He enrolls in Part D Medicare and applies for the premium subsidy. Mrs. White is not old enough for Medicare and is still working. She expects annual gross earnings of $13,230. Assume that the Whites' resources are within the limits for eligibility.

Mr. White's Social Security	$11,100	(12 × $925)
Mr. White's pension	+4,800	(12 × $400)
	−240	(12 × the $20 exclusion)
Countable unearned income	$15,660	
Mrs. White's Wages	$13,230	
	−780	(12 × $65 exclusion)
	$12,450	
$12,450 × .5 =	$6,225	(one-half exclusion)

Countable earned income	$6,225
Countable unearned income	<u>$15,660</u>
Total countable income	$21,885

Assuming that the FPL for a two-person family is $15,930, the subsidy income limits are as follows:

$15,930 × 135 percent = $21,505.50
$15,930 × 140 percent = $22,302.00
$15,930 × 145 percent = $23,098.50
$15,930 × 150 percent = $23,895.00

Analysis: The couple's countable income ($21,885) is greater than 135 percent of the FPL and less than 140 percent. Therefore, Mr. White is eligible for a 75 percent subsidy. Further information about Extra Help is contained in "Understanding the Extra Help with Your Medicare Prescription Drug Plan," Social Security Administration, https://www.ssa.gov/pubs/EN-05-10508.pdf.

21. https://secure.ssa.gov/i1020/start.

22. https://www.cms.gov/Medicare/Eligibility-and-Enrollment/LowIncSubMedicarePresCov/MedicareLimitedIncomeNET.html.

23. Color: Purple

Name: Deemed Status Notice

When: You automatically qualify for Extra Help because you receive both Medicare and Medicaid (known as being a "dual eligible"), or you're in a Medicare Savings Program (MSP) (see the next section of this chapter), or you receive Supplemental Security Income (SSI) from Social Security.

Color: Yellow

Name: Auto-Enrollment Notice

When: You automatically qualify for Extra Help because you're a dual eligible and use Original Medicare.

Color: Orange

Name: Change in Extra Help Copayment Notice

When: You automatically qualify for Extra Help but your copayment will change next year.

Color: Green

Name: Facilitated Enrollment Notice

When: You qualify for Extra Help because you're in an MSP, get SSI and applied for Extra Help.

Color: Tan
Name: LIS Choosers Notice
When: You already get Extra Help, you joined a Part D drug plan on your own (Medicare often assigns low-income beneficiaries to a Part D plan) and your plan premium is changing. (LIS stands for Low Income Subsidy.)

Color: Blue
Name: Reassign Formulary Notice
When: You already get Extra Help and Medicare has reassigned you to a new Part D plan next year.

Color: Gray
Name: Loss of Deemed Status Notice
When: No automatic qualification for Extra Help next year.

24. https://www.medicare.gov/your-medi care-costs/help-paying-costs/medicare -savings-program/medicare-savings -programs.html.

25. https://www.medicare.gov/your-medi care-costs/help-paying-costs/medicare -savings-program/medicare-savings -programs.html#collapse-2625.

Chapter 10: When You're Mad as Hell: Medicare Rights and Appeals

1. There are a dozen MACs around the country for Original Medicare, four MACs for Durable Medical Equipment (DME), and four for Home Health and Hospice administration. There also are other MACs that handle Medicare appeals involving Original Medicare, DME vendors (of which there are thousands and thousands), Medicare Advantage plans, and Part D drug plans. Here is the major link to the Medicare website that keeps track of MACs and their performance: https://www.cms.gov/medicare/medicare -contracting/medicare-administrative-con tractors/medicareadministrativecontract ors.html. From this page, you can find an interactive map at https://www.cms.gov/ Research-Statistics-Data-and-Systems/ Monitoring-Programs/Medicare-FFS -Compliance-Programs/Review-Contract or-Directory-Interactive-Map/ that will let you enter your state and see details on the MACs that would be involved with your Medicare insurance plans. You also can see CMS reviews of MAC performance and what amounts to a MAC scorecard at https://www.cms.gov/Medicare/Medicare

-Contracting/Medicare-Administrative
-Contractors/MACPerformanceCompli
ance.html.

2. http://www.medicarepartdappeals.com/.

3. medicarephil@gmail.com.

4. http://www.getwhatsyours.org.

5. https://www.cms.gov/Medicare/CMS
-Forms/CMS-Forms/downloads/cms1696
.pdf.

6. https://www.socialsecurity.gov/forms/ssa
-1696.pdf.

7. https://www.medicare.gov/Pubs/pdf/
10050.pdf.

8. http://www.vox.com/2015/9/30/9420047/
icd-10-transition-orcas.

9. http://www.nbcnews.com/health/health
-news/struck-turtle-theres-code-n437176.

10. http://www.medicare.gov/forms-help
-and-resources/mail-about-medicare/
medicare-summary-notice.html.

11.http://www.seniormedicarepatrol.org/
Training/CBT/story.html.

12. https://www.cms.gov/Medicare/Quality
-Initiatives-Patient-Assessment-Instru
ments/QualityImprovementOrgs/Down
loads/QIOPt Centered-.pdf.

13. https://www.cms.gov/Medicare/Appeals
-and-Grievances/MedPrescriptDrugAppl
Griev/downloads/ModelCoverageDeter
minationRequestForm.pdf.

14. https://www.cms.gov/Medicare/Medi
care-General-Information/BNI/index
.html.

15.https://www.cms.gov/apps/acronyms/
listall.asp?Letter=ALL.

16. https://www.medicare.gov/claims-and
-appeals/file-an-appeal/original-medicare/
original-medicare-appeals-level-2.html.

17. https://www.cms.gov/Medicare/Appeals
-and-Grievances/MMCAG/IRE.html.

18. http://www.hhs.gov/omha/.

19. http://www.medicareadvocacy.org/
advocacy-tips-how-to-prepare-for-medi
care-administrative-law-judge-alj-hearing/.

20. http://www.hhs.gov/omha/Data/index
.html.

21. http://www.pbs.org/newshour/making
-sense/medicare-rules-hospital-visits
-costly-adventure/.

22. To get a sense of the volume of claims,
appeals, and outcomes at the first two appeals levels, here are the detailed numbers
from Medicare for 2013:

At the first, or redetermination/
reconsideration appeals stage, MACs
denied about 15 million Part A claims out
of more than 208 million that were processed. Of these, fewer than 6 percent
were appealed, or about 830,000. Most
appeals were for inpatient fees (56 per-

cent), outpatient charges (22 percent), and home health care (12 percent). More than 80 percent of appeals were denied.

For Part B, MACs denied 101 million out of 934 million claims that were processed. Only about 3 percent of these denials — 3.2 million — were appealed. Appeals tended to be for physician (43 percent) or medical equipment (42 percent) charges. The likelihood of successful appeals for Part B charges was much higher — only 53.5 percent of appeals were denied.

At the second, or reconsideration stage, QICs processed about 1.4 million reconsiderations in 2013. In Part A, more than 70 percent were for acute inpatient hospital care and 18 percent were for home health care. More than 85 percent of these appeals were denied.

Part B appeals for reconsideration were spread across many categories, with ground transportation (aka ambulances) being the largest category at 14 percent, followed by imaging/radiology at 12 percent. Appeals for durable medical equipment were tracked separately, with oxygen (26 percent), surgical dressings, and glucose monitors (each at 17 percent) being the most common. Nearly 75 percent of non-equipment appeals were denied, while more than 90 percent of equipment claims were disallowed.

In Medicare Advantage and Part D prescription drug plans, the first level of appeal is handled by the plans' private insurers and Maximus handles second-level reviews in its role as an IRE. Roughly 10,000 Medicare Advantage appeals were filed with the IRE each month in 2013 and there was no processing backlog. In fact, three-quarters of the cases were processed in three or fewer days. The dollar amount of the average appeal was just shy of $3,000. Among about 32,000 appeals defined as substantive, an eighth of the level one denials were overturned. Fewer than 2,000 Part D appeals a month were received by Maximus in 2013. The dollar value of the average appeal was not disclosed in Medicare's report and about a third of the contested claims were overturned.

Chapter 11: So Many Stars in the Sky: Health Provider Quality Ratings

1. https://www.medicare.gov/find-a-plan/questions/home.aspx.
2. https://www.medicare.gov/find-a-plan/

staticpages/rating/planrating-help.aspx.

3. https://www.medicare.gov/physiciancompare/search.html.

4. https://www.medicare.gov/hospitalcompare/search.html.

5. http://health.usnews.com/best-hospitals.

6. www.consumerreports.org/.

7. http://www.healthgrades.com/.

8. http://www.leapfroggroup.org/.

9. https://projects.propublica.org/surgeons/.

10. https://www.medicare.gov/nursinghomecompare/search.html.

11. https://www.cms.gov/Medicare/Provider-Enrollment-and-Certification/CertificationandComplianc/Downloads/usersguide.pdf.

12. http://projects.propublica.org/nursing-homes/.

13. https://www.genworth.com/corporate/about-genworth/industry-expertise/cost-of-care.html.

14. https://www.shiptacenter.org/.

15. https://www.medicare.gov/homehealthcompare/search.html.

16. https://www.unos.org/.

17. https://www.medicare.gov/dialysisfacilitycompare/#search.

Chapter 12: Fuzzy Reception: How to See Health Care Providers and Networks Clearly

1. Medicare Managed Care Manual, Chapter 7 — Risk Adjustment, Centers for Medicare & Medicaid Services, revised September 19, 2014, https://www.cms.gov/Regulations-and-Guidance/Guidance/Manuals/downloads/mc86c07.pdf.
2. http://www.publicintegrity.org/health/medicare/medicare-advantage-money-grab.
3. http://www.hcup-us.ahrq.gov/reports/statbriefs/sb180-Hospitalizations-United-States-2012.pdf.
4. https://www.cms.gov/Research-Statistics-Data-and-Systems/Statistics-Trends-and-Reports/MedicareFeeforSvcPartsAB/downloads/DRGdesc08.pdf.
5. https://data.cms.gov/Medicare/Inpatient-Prospective-Payment-System-IPPS-Provider/kd35-nmmt?.
6. Yan S. Kim, Eric C. Kleerup, Patricia A. Ganz, Ninez A. Ponce, Karl A. Lorenz, and Jack Needleman, "Medicare Payment Policy Creates Incentives for Long-Term Care Hospitals to Time Discharges for Maximum Reimbursement," *Health Affairs,* June 2015, http://content.health

affairs.org/content/34/6/907.abstract.

7. Here are the pathways to MA plan provider networks from leading insurers:

Aetna, at http://www.aetna.com/dse/ search?site_id=medicare&langpref =en&tabKey=tab2&site_id=medicare &tabKey=tab2

Anthem, for doctors at https://www .anthem.com/Shop/Find-A-Doctor; for care facilities, at https://www.anthem .com/Shop/standalonefacilitysearch

Cigna, for doctors at http://www.cigna .com/medicare/medicare-advantage/ find-doctor; for other providers at https://providersearch.hsconnectonline .com/OnlineDirector

Coventry (owned by Aetna), at http:// coventry-medicare.coventryhealthcare .com/locate-a-provider/index.htm

Humana, at https://www.humana.com/ medicare/. Enter your ZIP and then click on "Add your doctors and hospi- tals" on the results page.

Kaiser Permanente, at https://healthy .kaiserpermanente.org/health/care/ consumer/locate-our-services/doctors -and-locations.

UnitedHealthcare, at https://www .uhcmedicaresolutions.com. Enter your ZIP, click on Your Plan Details, then scroll down (a long way) to the "Look up Provider" link under the phrase "Is my doctor covered?"

8. "Medicare Advantage: Actions Needed to Enhance CMS Oversight of Provider Network Adequacy," Government Accountability Office, Sept. 28, 2015, http://www.gao.gov/products/GAO-15-710.

9. Daniel R. Austin and Laurence C. Baker, "Less Physician Practice Competition Is Associated With Higher Prices Paid for Common Procedures," *Health Affairs,* October 2015, http://content.health affairs.org/content/34/10/1753.abstract; Laurence C. Baker, M. Kate Bundorf, and Daniel P. Kessler, "Vertical Integration: Hospital Ownership of Physician Practices Is Associated with Higher Prices and Spending," *Health Affairs,* May 2014, http://content.healthaffairs.org/content/33/5/756.abstract.

10. "Paying a Visit to the Doctor: Current Financial Protections for Medicare Patients When Receiving Physician Services," Kaiser Family Foundation, April 7, 2014, http://kff.org/medicare/issue-brief/paying-a-visit-to-the-doctor-current-financial-protections-for-medicare-patients-when-receiving-physician-services.

Chapter 13: Open Enrollment: How to Fix a Medicare Lemon

1. http://www.getwhatsyours.org.
2. https://www.medicare.gov/find-a-plan/ questions/home.aspx.
3. https://www.shiptacenter.org/.
4. Here are Web links to 2016 selected insurer formularies. You may need to find a specific plan in your area to access its formulary:

Aetna, at http://www.aetnamedicare .com/help_and_resources/download able-forms-2016.jsp#formulary

Anthem, at https://www.anthem.com/ Shop/Find-Your-Covered-Drugs

Cigna, at http://www.cigna.com/ medicare/part-d/drug-list-formulary

Coventry (part of Aetna), at http:// coventry-medicare.coventryhealthcare .com/prescription-drug-benefits/ formulary/index.htm

Humana, at https://www.humana.com/ pharmacy/medicare/tools/druglist/ 2016

Kaiser Permanente, at https://medicare .kaiserpermanente.org/medicare/pdfs/ plans_current/comprehensive_formu lary.pdf (this link is requires you to download the formulary file)

United HealthCare: PDP (stand-alone) plans, at https://www.uhcmedicaresolutions.com/health-plans/prescription-drug-plans/resources/prescription-drug-list.html; MA-PD plans, at https://www.uhcmedicaresolutions.com/health-plans/medicare-advantage-plans/resources-plan-material/drug-list.html

Chapter 14: What's Your Endgame? Getting Ready to Not Be Here

1. Tricia Neuman, Juliette Cubanski, Jennifer Huang, and Anthony Damico, "The Rising Cost of Living Longer," Kaiser Family Foundation, January 2015, http://files.kff.org/attachment/report-the-rising-cost-of-living-longer-analysis-of-medicare-spending-by-age-for-beneficiaries-in-traditional-medicare.
2. John A. E. Pottow, "The Rise in Elder Bankruptcy Filings and the Failure of U.S. Bankruptcy Law," University of Michigan Law School Scholarship Repository, August 31, 2010, http://repository.law.umich.edu/cgi/viewcontent.cgi?article=1127&context=law_econ_current.
3. Momotazur Rahman, Laura Keohane, Amal N. Trivedi, and Vincent Mor, "High-

Cost Patients Had Substantial Rates of Leaving Medicare Advantage and Joining Traditional Medicare," *Health Affairs,* October 2015, http://content.healthaffairs.org/content/34/10/1675.abstract.

4. https://www.genworth.com/corporate/about-genworth/industry-expertise/cost-of-care.html.
5. https://www.prepareforyourcare.org/.
6. http://theconversationproject.org/wp-content/uploads/2015/05/TCP_StarterKit_2015_Final_Writeable.pdf.
7. Atul Gawande, *Being Mortal* (New York: Henry Holt, 2014).
8. Active registries as of December 2015. Source: National Hospice and Palliative Care Organization, http://www.nhpco.org/.

Arizona: The registration form can be found at http://www.azsos.gov/sites/azsos.gov/files/bsd_ad_registration_agreement_20150618.pdf and the form along with an executed copy of the advance directive should be mailed to:

Secretary of State
Attn: Advance Directive Dept.
1700 W. Washington Street, Fl 7
Phoenix, AZ 85007

California: The registration form can

435

be found at http://ahcdr.cdn.sos.ca.gov/
forms/sfl-461.pdf and the form along
with an executed copy of the advance
directive should be mailed to:

Secretary of State
Special Filings Unit
PO Box 942870
Sacramento, CA 94277-2870

Idaho: The registration form can be
found at http://www.sos.idaho.gov/
GENERAL/FORMS/Registry_Form
.pdf and the form, along with an executed copy of the advance directive,
should be mailed to:

Idaho Secretary of State
Attn: Health Care Directive Registrar
700 W Jefferson St, Room E205
PO Box 83720
Boise ID 83720-0080

Louisiana: An executed copy of the
advance directive and a cover letter
should be mailed to:

Louisiana Secretary of State
Publications Division
PO Box 94125
Baton Rouge, LA 70804-9125

Montana: The registration agreement

can be found at https://media.dojmt.gov/
wp-content/uploads/H-Consumer
-Registration-Agreement.pdf and the
agreement, along with an executed copy
of the advance directive should be
mailed to:

Office of Consumer Protection
2225 11th Avenue
PO Box 201410
Helena, MT 59620-1410

Nevada: The registration agreement can
be found at https://media.dojmt.gov/wp
-content/uploads/H-Consumer
-Registration-Agreement.pdf and the
agreement and executed copy of the
advance directive should be mailed to:

The Living Will Lockbox
c/o Nevada Secretary of State
555 E. Washington Avenue, Suite 5200
Las Vegas, NV 89101

North Carolina: https://www.secretary
.state.nc.us/ahcdr/. Print out the forms
on www.sosnc.gov along with a $10 fee,
and mail to:

North Carolina Secretary of State
Advance Health Care Directive Registry
PO Box 29622
Raleigh, NC 27626-0622

Vermont: The registration agreement can be found at http://www .healthvermont.gov/vadr/documents/AD _registration_agreement.pdf and the agreement and executed copy of the advance directive should be mailed to:
Vermont Advance Directive Registry
(VADR)
PO Box 2789
Westfield, NJ 07091-2789

Virginia: Virginia advance directives may be stored electronically at https:// www.virginiaregistry.org/.

9. https://www.agingwithdignity.org/catalog/ product_info.php?products_id=28.
10. http://www.americanbar.org/groups/law _aging/MyHealthCareWishesApp.html.
11. http://www.polst.org/.
12. http://www.cancer.gov/about-cancer/ advanced-cancer/care-choices/palliative -care-fact-sheet#q1.

Acknowledgments

1. http://www.getwhatsyours.org.

Glossary

1. https://www.cms.gov/Newsroom/
MediaReleaseDatabase/Fact-sheets/2015
-Fact-sheets-items/2015-12-29.html.

ABOUT THE AUTHOR

Journalist **Philip Moeller** writes about retirement for *Money* and authors the *Ask Phil* Medicare column for PBS. He also is a Research Fellow at the Center on Aging & Work at Boston College and the founder of Insure.com, a leading site for insurance information.